MIDWIVES, SOCIETY AND CHILDBIRTH

'Readers will find much of interest in these articles, which add needed scholarly dispassion to a subject we should all care passionately about. A welcome volume!'

Judith Leavitt, *University of Wisconsin*

Midwives, Society and Childbirth is the first book to examine midwives' lives and work in the nineteenth and twentieth centuries on an international scale, comparing experiences from Sweden, Denmark, Italy, England, Spain and the United States. The approach is interdisciplinary with the studies written by a diverse team of social, medical and midwifery historians, sociologists, and those with experience of providing childbirth services.

Questioning many conventional historical assumptions for the first time, this book is fundamental to a better understanding of the effect on midwives of the unprecedented progress of science in general, and obstetric science in particular, from the late nineteenth century. The contributors challenge the traditional bleak picture of midwives' decline in the face of institutional obstetrics, medical technology, and the growing power of the medical profession. Was it really a uniform and unrelieved demise, as midwives lost their status, independence, and role?

Hilary Marland is Wellcome Lecturer at the Centre for Social History at Warwick University, has published on the history of midwives, and is an editor of *Social History of Medicine*. **Anne Marie Rafferty** is Director of the Centre for Policy in Nursing Research. She has written on nursing and midwifery history. Both editors are Research Associates at the Wellcome Unit for the History of Medicine in Oxford, UK.

STUDIES IN THE SOCIAL HISTORY OF MEDICINE

Series Editors: Jonathan Barry and Bernard Harris

In recent years, the social history of medicine has become recognized as a major field of historical enquiry. Aspects of health, disease, and medical care now attract the attention not only of social historians but also of researchers in a broad spectrum of historical and social science disciplines. The Society for the Social History of Medicine, founded in 1969, is an interdisciplinary body, based in Great Britain but international in membership. It exists to forward a wide-ranging view of the history of medicine, concerned equally with biological aspects of normal life, experience of and attitudes to illness, medical thought and treatment, and systems of medical care. Although frequently bearing on current issues, this interpretation of the subject makes primary reference to historical context and contemporary priorities. The intention is not to promote a sub-specialism but to conduct research according to the standards and intelligibility required of history in general. The Society publishes a journal, *Social History of Medicine*, and holds at least three conferences a year. Its series, Studies in the Social History of Medicine, does not represent publication of its proceedings, but comprises volumes on selected themes, often arising out of conferences but subsequently developed by the editors.

LIFE, DEATH AND THE ELDERLY
Edited by Margaret Pelling and Richard M. Smith

MEDICINE AND CHARITY BEFORE THE WELFARE STATE
Edited by Jonathan Barry and Colin Jones

IN THE NAME OF THE CHILD
Edited by Roger Cooter

REASSESSING FOUCAULT
POWER, MEDICINE AND THE BODY
Edited by Colin Jones and Roy Porter

MIGRANTS, MINORITIES AND HEALTH
HISTORICAL AND CONTEMPORARY STUDIES
Edited by Lara Marks and Michael Worboys

FROM IDIOCY TO MENTAL DEFICIENCY
Edited by David Wright and Anne Digby

NUTRITION IN BRITAIN
Edited by David F. Smith

HEALTH CARE AND POOR RELIEF IN
PROTESTANT EUROPE 1500–1700
Edited by Ole Peter Grell and Andrew Cunningham

MIDWIVES, SOCIETY AND CHILDBIRTH

Debates and controversies in the modern period

Edited by Hilary Marland and Anne Marie Rafferty

First published 1997
by Routledge
2 Park Square, Milton Park, Abingdon, Oxon, OX14 4RN

Simultaneously published in the USA and Canada
by Routledge
270 Madison Ave, New York NY 10016

Reprinted 1999, 2000

Transferred to Digital Printing 2005

Routledge is an imprint of the Taylor & Francis Group

Typeset in Baskerville by
Ponting–Green Publishing Services, Chesham, Buckinghamshire

British Library Cataloguing in Publication Data
A catalogue record for this book is available from
the British Library

Library of Congress Cataloguing in Publication Data
Midwives, society and childbirth: debates and controversies in
the modern period / edited by Hilary Marland and Anne
Marie Rafferty.
Includes bibliographical references and index.
1. Midwifery–Europe–History–19th century.
2. Midwifery–Europe–History–20th century.
3. Midwifery–Social aspects–Europe.
4. Midwifery–United States–History–19th century.
5. Midwifery–United States–History–20th century.
6. Midwifery–Social aspects–United States.
I. Marland, Hilary. II. Rafferty, Anne Marie.
RG950.M54 1997   96–41125
362.1'980233–dc20

ISBN 0–415–13328–9

CONTENTS

CONTENTS

FIGURES

TABLES

CONTRIBUTORS

Rebeca Barroso was a traditional midwife for twenty years, after which she completed her education as a Certified Nurse–Midwife at the Frontier School of Midwifery and Family Nursing. She received her MSN from Case Western Reserve University and is currently practising as a CNM in Minnesota.

Christoph Brezinka studied medicine at Innsbruck University, where he graduated as MD in 1984. Following training in obstetrics and gynaecology at Innsbruck University Hospital, between 1991 and 1993 he carried out research at Erasmus University Rotterdam, and in 1994 obtained a PhD for his research on the ultrasound of foetal heart vessels. He is now a lecturer at Innsbruck University Hospital. His special interest is in the history of obstetrics in the Alpine regions, and he is the author of several articles on the subject.

Raymond DeVries is Associate Professor of Sociology at St Olaf College in Northfield, Minnesota. He has a PhD in sociology (University of California, Davis). His publications include *Making Midwives Legal: Childbirth, Medicine and the Law* (1996). He recently spent a year in the Netherlands, at the Netherlands Institute for Health Care Research (NIVEL), studying the Dutch system of maternity care.

June Hannam is Head of History at the University of the West of England, Bristol, where she teaches women's history and labour history. She has published a biography of *Isabella Ford, 1855–1924* (1989) and articles on feminist and labour politics in the late nineteenth and early twentieth centuries. She is treasurer of the Women's History Network.

ix

Anne Løkke is research fellow and lecturer at the Department of History at the University of Copenhagen. Her published works include *Familieliv i Danmark 1600–1980'erne* ('Family life in Denmark 1600–1980') (1986, 4th edn 1997), co-authored with Anette Faye Jacobsen, and *Vildfarende børn – om forsømte og kriminelle børn mellem filantropi og stat 1880–1920* ('Erring children – neglected and criminal children between charity and state, 1880–1920') (1996). She is currently completing a monograph on infant mortality and infant welfare in Denmark 1835–1920.

Irvine Loudon qualified in medicine from Oxford University in 1951 and worked in general practice until 1981. He then obtained a Wellcome Research Fellowship in the History of Medicine in the University of Oxford and has worked full-time as a medical historian ever since. His publications include *Medical Care and the General Practitioner 1750–1850* (1986), *Death in Childbirth: An International Study of Maternal Care and Maternal Mortality 1800–1950* (1992), and *Childbed Fever: A Documentary History* (1996). He is currently editing the *Oxford Illustrated History of Western Medicine* and *General Practice under the National Health Service*, and is completing a monograph on puerperal fever from 1750 to 1950.

Hilary Marland is Wellcome Lecturer at the Centre for Social History, University of Warwick, Research Associate at the Wellcome Unit for the History of Medicine in Oxford, and is an editor of *Social History of Medicine*. She is author of *Medicine and Society in Wakefield and Huddersfield 1780–1870* (1987), and co-author of '*Mother and Child were Saved*': *The Memoirs (1693–1740) of the Frisian Midwife Catharina Schrader* (1987). She has edited several volumes: *Women and Children First: International Maternal and Infant Welfare c. 1870–1945* (1992, with Valerie Fildes and Lara Marks), *The Art of Midwifery: Early Modern Midwives in Europe* (1993), and *The Task of Healing: Medicine, Religion and Gender in England and the Netherlands 1450–1800* (1996, with Margaret Pelling). She is currently engaged in two projects: the study of puerperal insanity in nineteenth-century Britain, and Dutch midwives 1897–1941.

Joan Mottram is a research/administrative assistant at the Wellcome Unit for the History of Medicine, University of Manchester. She is currently preparing her MSc thesis for publication, a biography of John Roberton (1797–1876), the Manchester obstetrician and social reformer.

Teresa Ortiz, a graduate in medicine, received a PhD in the history of medicine from the University of Granada in 1987 with a dissertation on the medical profession in twentieth-century Andalucia, *Médicos en la Andalucía del siglo veinte: distribución, especialismo y participación de la mujer* (1987). Professor Ortiz teaches courses on the history of medicine and women in the health professions at the University of Granada, where she is Director of the Women's Studies Institute. She is currently working on 'Health professions in the eighteenth century' and 'Gender and Spanish medical discourse'.

Clara Martínez Padilla is qualified in medicine and works as a general practitioner in Granada. She is a post-graduate student in the history of science, and is working on a PhD thesis on the health professions in the city of Granada between 1874 and 1923.

Susan Pitt trained in medicine at the University of Oxford and then at Sheffield University. She practised as a doctor for two years before returning to study for a degree in history at the University of Wales, Lampeter. She has recently completed her PhD at Lampeter entitled, 'Midwifery and medicine: discourses in childbirth, c. 1945–1974'.

Anne Marie Rafferty is senior lecturer at and director of the Centre for Policy in Nursing Research, London School of Hygiene and Tropical Medicine, and Research Associate at the Wellcome Unit for the History of Medicine, University of Oxford. She is joint author of *An Introduction to the Social History of Nursing* (1988) and joint editor of *Nursing History and the Politics of Welfare* (1977), and was co-organizer of the Conferences 'Nursing, Women's History and the Politics of Welfare', held at the University of Nottingham in July 1993 and September 1996. She is consultant and contributor to the International Council of Nurses Centennial Project, directed from the University of Pennsylvania and conducted in collaboration with a team of historians from Canada and the USA. Her doctoral thesis was published as *The Politics of Nursing Knowledge* in 1996. She has contributed to textbooks on nursing history and written journal articles.

Christina Romlid is studying economic history at Uppsala University, Sweden. She is working on a thesis to be published in Swedish in 1997: 'Doctors' professionalization and the regulation of midwifery. A study of the Swedish midwife system c. 1663–1860'. In this study she shows how changes within Swedish maternity care during the eighteenth and nineteenth centuries were related to the struggle of dominant members of the medical profession to organize a national medical system.

Anne Thompson, currently working with the Maternal Health and Safe Motherhood Unit of the World Health Organization in Geneva, trained as a midwife at the British Hospital for Mothers and Babies, at Woolwich, London. She later practised in Cameroon, after studying at the Prince Leopold Institute of Tropical Medicine in Antwerp. A long career in midwifery concluded with her being part of a team which set up the first Masters Degree in Advanced Midwifery Practice, with the University of Surrey and the Royal College of Midwives. A long-standing interest in midwifery history, as well as its international perspectives, found an outlet in 1990, when she was elected Treasurer of the International Confederation of Midwives (ICM). She began doctoral studies in 1993 at the Wellcome Institute, London, focusing on the processes of professionalization which midwifery adopted during the first half of this century through the international organization for midwives, the ICM.

Jan Williams qualified as a general nurse specializing in critical care, before becoming a nurse teacher working with first pre- and then post-registration nurses. She became involved with the National Childbirth Trust when pregnant with her first child, trained as a teacher with the Trust and spent several years facilitating classes. During this time she completed an honours degree in Contemporary Cultural Studies at Middlesex University, her dissertation exploring the question of power in childbirth. A Masters Degree in psychology and health enabled her to study further the relationship between gender and health. She has just completed research examining how women are positioned as the 'invisible victims' of coronary heart disease. She currently lectures in Nursing and Health Studies at Middlesex University where she is programme leader for the BA and BSc degrees in nursing.

ACKNOWLEDGEMENTS

The initiative for this volume came out of the conference 'Nursing, Women's History and the Politics of Welfare', held in Nottingham in July 1993. This conference was set up by Jane Robinson and Anne Marie Rafferty, who were supported by Sarah Smith and the staff and student stewards of the Department of Nursing and Midwifery Studies at Nottingham. We are grateful to all those involved for creating such a stimulating and friendly meeting, which encouraged us to take six of the papers delivered in Nottingham on the subject of childbirth and midwifery and to build on them by commissioning six more. We would like to take this opportunity to thank the various bodies involved in funding the conference: the Wellcome Trust, London, the British Academy and in particular the NHS Women's Unit, who provided the finance to offer student bursaries. Hilary Marland would also like to thank the Wellcome Trust for supporting her work on Dutch midwifery through a Wellcome Fellowship. Both editors moved during the process of editing this volume, Anne Marie from Nottingham to the London School of Hygiene and Tropical Medicine, and Hilary from Erasmus University Rotterdam to the University of Warwick. We would like to thank the staff of all four institutions for their support of this venture.

Valuable comments on earlier drafts of the articles were provided by two anonymous referees, and Jonathan Barry and Bernard Harris, the series editors have been both patient and constructive in seeing this book through production.

INTRODUCTION

Midwives, society and childbirth: debates and controversies

Hilary Marland and Anne Marie Rafferty

In April 1938 an article was published in the Dutch Catholic midwives journal, the *Maandblad voor R.K. Vroedvrouwen*, which summed up the state of play regarding the competence of midwives in various European countries.[1] The preparations for the International Congress of Midwives in Paris in April had stimulated the writing of the article, which brought the question of midwives' competence to the fore. While the evidence given was patchy, the article is interesting in many ways. It revealed a deep interest in professional issues, status and roles, which went beyond national boundaries and local concerns. Discussing midwives' competence in Austria, Hungary, Czechoslovakia, Estonia, Switzerland, Germany, Belgium, France, England, Denmark, Sweden and Italy, it was far from parochial.

The article also clearly demonstrated that the tasks of midwives varied immensely between countries. In Austria, Hungary and Switzerland, midwives were firmly restricted to normal deliveries; at the first signs of complication the midwife was to call in a doctor. In Germany midwives were permitted in emergencies such as eclampsia and placenta praevia to hurry women to a clinic without first consulting a doctor. German midwives were also allowed to carry out vaginal and rectal examinations, but only with sterile rubber gloves and after disinfecting themselves; all such examinations were to be written up in a diary for presentation to the town doctor. Midwives could, under certain circumstances, deliver twins and breech births, but were not allowed to give medicines to stimulate contractions or relieve pain.[2] The English midwife was able to give pain relief in some cases, while in Belgium the midwife was allowed to give injections, of ergotine, caffeine and camphor, and to administer opium tincture. However, she was not allowed to

1

use instruments.[3] In Sweden she was, and Swedish midwives could repair ruptures too, as could French midwives who were also authorized to give vaccinations against smallpox and tuberculosis.[4]

The role of midwives varied, the article went on, not just in the actual carrying out of deliveries, but in the supervision of antenatal care, the right to intervene in cases of miscarriage, infant care, administering vaccinations, and treating sickness in women and their babies. The competence of midwives, the article stressed, depended not just on legal instructions, but practical circumstances, such as transport arrangements and the availability of doctors.[5] The article also indicated that what midwives were striving to achieve in terms of competence and standing varied enormously across the countries surveyed.

Above all, the article indicated the complexity of the issues surrounding midwives' competence and status as childbirth attendants, providers of health care and women workers in the 1930s. Historians have much more material at their disposal than the author of the 1938 article, and describing the details of regulations and definitions of competence in each country, subject to regional variations in some, is complex.[6] This book does not attempt this. Rather, it seeks to explore debates concerning the role of midwives from the nineteenth century through to the present day in various countries, debates which were to fundamentally affect their work, their relationships with other health care providers, and their social and economic standing. Discussions on midwives' potential and status had been ongoing for several decades in most of Europe and North America by the time the 1938 article was written, not just in relation to competition with doctors, but also linked to a growing awareness of the dangers of maternity, horror at high infant and maternal death rates, and the changing demands and expectations being made of preventive medicine.[7] What was the future of the midwife to be? Did she have one? Could it even be expanded? The debate ranged from the violent denunciations of the midwife in the United States,[8] through the struggles for midwife registration in Britain,[9] to the more measured but none the less significant discussions on the place of Dutch midwives in providing obstetric care.[10] No country in the Western world seems to have escaped such issues.

The article of 1938 appeared at a time when the debate on midwives' role had moved on considerably. In most countries – the great exception being the United States, where midwife numbers

2

had fallen dramatically and her place had been undermined – the debate had shifted by the 1930s. It had evolved from whether the midwife had a place in providing obstetric care and questions of competition with general practitioners and obstetricians, to what form that place should take, what the midwife's competence should consist of, and what her precise tasks should be. In a number of countries this resulted in legislative change and reformulations of midwives' duties, but, as several of the contributors to this volume suggest, the realities of practice could differ greatly from the legal requirements and regulations. Laws were subject to considerable reinterpretation and adaption.

Midwives have had a chequered career at the hands of historians, those who competed with them to provide midwifery care, legislators, organizers of maternity services, and the women with whom they have laboured. There is a sense in which midwifery has come to represent a metaphor for the broader struggles and debates about race, class and gender which have so energized the social history of medicine in recent years.[11] Within this context, the history of midwifery has often been represented as a moral fable in which midwives struggle towards, or from, the teleological goals of the increasing use of technology, the hospital and the professionalization of childbirth. As the chapters in this volume and revisionist histories show, more subtle forces are at work. What is so striking is that, in spite of the universality of childbirth, its cultural expression and professional and legal regulation vary enormously across time and space, even within the context of the Western world. Elaborating the factors that 'drive' – the regulation of midwifery teaching and practice, the organization of maternity care, the forces of competition around childbirth services, and the critical role that the midwife plays as a member of the communities she serves – provides the guiding rationale for this book. The chapters in this volume describe how the spatial, social and cognitive boundaries that define midwifery were contested; myths, learning and mortality were used as evidence to marginalize midwives from each other, or to distance them from groups portraying themselves as 'socially' or 'medically' superior.[12]

Inevitably, a study of midwives in the modern period is largely a survey of challenges to their role and bases for existence. The late nineteenth century and particularly the first three decades of the twentieth have been presented as a period of decline for the midwife in the face of the rising opposition of medical practitioners, the resolute increase in hospital births, and increased medical intervention in childbirth, particularly in the United States.[13] As childbirth came to be defined increasingly as abnormal, so was the midwife denied her role as attendant.[14]

Some seven countries are surveyed in this volume – Sweden, Denmark, Spain, Italy, the Netherlands, England and the United States, while Anne Thompson and Irvine Loudon provide international frameworks for reassessments of the midwife's role. The chronology stretches from the instrumental authorization of Swedish midwives in the early nineteenth century up to reflections on the position of midwives in American and Dutch maternity services in the late twentieth century.

The trio of competition from doctors, the rise of hospital deliveries, and the stepping-up of medical intervention – from forceps deliveries and caesarean section to pain relief and foetal monitoring – has fundamentally reshaped midwives' practices and standing in the medical hierarchy. This trio could be taken as a basis of a framework for elaborating the history of midwifery in the modern period. But there were numerous other challenges to the midwife, not all of them necessarily negative. More could be added to the list; Anne Thompson outlines the problem of the falling birth-rate, the challenge of the public health sector, and the economic crisis which rocked Europe in the 1930s in outlining the activities of the International Midwives' Union (IMU) and the problems midwives encountered in their national organizations and everyday practices.

The results of challenges were varied. Most groups of midwives participated to some extent in the introduction of technology, while in Sweden midwives' authorization to use forceps, while not fundamentally influencing their practices, did raise their public estimation. Change linked to 'medical progress' in childbirth brought mixed blessings. Similarly, the incursions of the new agents of public health, maternity nurses and health visitors, were seen as a direct and potentially damaging threat by some midwives, but other midwives sought to move into public health work themselves, and were actively encouraged in this by legislators and medical reformers, as in Sweden, Denmark and England.[15] None of the 'challenges' midwives faced can be seen as being totally divorced from each other; they interacted, with questions of practical competence becoming mixed with midwives' potential as agents of preventive medicine, improvements in their training impacting on realignments of their role *vis-à-vis* other health care personnel, and economic forces interlocking with patient demand.

While all of the countries appearing in this volume were actively questioning midwives' roles, specific concerns varied. The chapters demonstrate that the debates and their outcomes hinged on the long-term historical development of the obstetric professions, levels of institutional provision, systems of health care, particularly maternity services, economic forces, urbanization, changes in family life and the employment of women, religion, maternalist policies, the input and interests of various pressure groups – midwives and medical practitioners, public health reformers, politicians and governments, and mothers and their families – and on perceptions of particular national problems.[16] In the early twentieth century, the Spanish concentrated on midwife training partly in relation to changes in their education laws, Sweden on the need to authorize midwives to carry out instrumental procedures and involve themselves in public health work, Denmark on the midwife's use of antiseptic techniques, and the Netherlands on the problem of providing sufficient trained midwives to poor, deprived areas. Regional shortcomings, and the problems of placing obstetric attendants with sufficient training and authorization to carry out their work effectively, were often the key to discussions surrounding midwives' work.

A wide range of sources has been drawn upon by the contributors to this volume: archives of midwife organizations at the local, national and international level, midwifery and medical texts and journals, town archives, particularly public health records, government reports, and statistics of childbirth and mortality, coupled for the post-war chapters with interviews with midwives and other providers of obstetric care, and birthing women and their families. The chapters have been written by a broad cross-section of social, economic, medical, midwifery and nursing historians, sociologists, and those who have been or who are still active in delivering childbirth services; the chapters are not merely inter-disciplinary, but several of the authors themselves straddle several disciplines. This has resulted in interesting insights into the role of the midwife and changes in childbirth practice. Susan Pitt and Jan Williams provide challenging interpretations. Based on interviews with providers of obstetric care in South Wales between the 1950s and mid-1970s, Pitt outlines a complex argument to explain childbirth practices, suggesting that professional discourses do not split in a straightforward way along gender lines, but are affected by context. Williams, basing her findings largely on her own contact with women in National Childbirth Trust classes, also sees context, particularly that of the hospital, and the build-up of all-pervasive power structures as fundamentally affecting childbirth practices and women's birth experiences. Implicitly, taking issue with revisionist interpretations of the interplay between providers of obstetric services and birthing women and their families, in Williams' analysis 'power' remains the key to these relationships. Many may question this interpretation, but auto-histories of childbirth experiences, particularly in the hospital setting, will support Williams' findings.[17]

No single volume can present the complex issues involved in changes in the position of midwives across national boundaries, even when restricted to north-west Europe and the United States. What we have tried to present is a sample of the problems midwives encountered in their practices, how they negotiated around these issues, and interacted with the various parties involved at an international and national level, or, as in the studies of Granada midwives at the close of the nineteenth century, Manchester midwives between 1900 and 1914, midwives in the southern provinces of the Netherlands in the early twentieth century, and in the language islands of Northern Italy up until the 1970s, on a local basis.

It is regrettable that we have given no account of midwives during the Second World War and have little coverage of the post-war period, particularly the 1950s and 1960s, decades of persistent fall-off in the numbers of home births, changing conceptions on many aspects of fertility, pregnancy and childbirth, which were also marked by a stepping-up of maternity services.[18] Though questions related to class and gender are raised in several of the chapters, little attention has been given to ethnicity. The subtle professional and practical interchanges between midwives and nurses, and the 'myth of separation' of the two professions are in need of further analysis and have been barely touched on in this volume. There is also much more to be said on many of the subjects discussed herein, and our hope is that these will be combined with other studies and further developed by midwife historians.

Topics which recur predominantly in the chapters in different contexts and periods are those of competition, institutionalization, regionality, the public health challenge and the clash between 'traditional' and 'modern' midwives. One of the main aims of the volume was at the same time to build on but also to question the central theme of 'competition' between midwives and doctors; playing this theme out in a wide variety of settings resulted in a more nuanced account of competition and its effects. Competition between midwives and doctors was often a two-way process. Through vibrant local, national and international organizations, a striving for improved training and standards, midwives propelled themselves into situations where they could actively challenge the claims of doctors to practise midwifery. Anne Thompson demonstrates this at the international level through her analysis of the aims of the IMU in its early years, but in Sweden, Denmark, Spain, and Holland an organized profession with its own platforms gave midwives more opportunity to challenge efficiently and effectively. June Hannam's close study of the forging of the Midwives' Institute into an effective and important body, reflects the interests of its leadership in questions of citizenship and feminism tied in with the aims of bonding midwives together and furthering professional goals, and improving childbirth services. Prominent midwife figures emerged in all settings to stimulate change, most notably Hannam's Rosalind Paget, Thompson's leaders of the IMU, and Loudon's Mary Breckinridge, but also many less visible women, Ortiz and Padilla's midwife teachers and authors, Brezinka's local 'heroines', and Mottram's campaigning Manchester midwives.

The chapters demonstrate that we cannot simply talk of the challenge of 'the doctor'. In general terms, the midwife was much more likely to suffer from the competition of general practitioners, bent on gaining footholds into family practice or sometimes on pure economic survival, taking on normal deliveries in increasing numbers. But this too depended on the way maternity services were organized, on supply and need. The rapid rise in the number of general practitioners in the Netherlands was accompanied by a slow growth in the number of specialized obstetricians often supportive of midwives, by evolving perceptions of midwives' potential as health missionaries, and the problems of finding childbirth attendants in rural districts. In Sweden, too, shortage played a critical role, while doctors' increased involvement in obstetrics actually led to midwives' training being extended and to their authorization to use instruments. In Denmark economic and professional competition was balanced by the need to raise standards and to

7

're-educate' midwives. In Manchester debates on preventive medicine and issues such as the registration of births led to doctors lining themselves up for or against midwives, but many supported their reform, registration and improved training. In the language islands of Northern Italy, a subtle process was at work, in which midwives co-operated closely with doctors in a mutually supportive system of maternity care, but eventually at their own cost in terms of independence. Susan Pitt and Jan Williams discuss competition while drawing on other discourses, predominantly the roles of gender and power, which enveloped doctors and midwives, patients and their families.

Implicit in much of the debate early this century and part of the ammunition doctors employed in discrediting midwives was the notion that midwives had a negative influence on mortality rates, but, as Irvine Loudon shows, this was a misplaced belief. While accusations of adversely influencing the survival chances of women and their babies could badly affect midwives, they could also work in a positive way, provoking explosive responses and counter-challenges from midwives themselves, who accused doctors of infecting their patients. It could also result in a stepping-up of education and control, which in the end served to strengthen the midwife's influence, as Løkke convincingly demonstrates in the case of her 'antiseptic midwife' and Mottram for her Manchester midwives.

Nor can we assume that the rise of institutional birth was consistent and pervasive, although Irvine Loudon demonstrates that it could be a massive obstetric disaster in terms of maternal mortality.[19] Hospital birth was of little importance in Spain, the Netherlands, Sweden or Denmark in the early twentieth century. The delay in moving to the hospital was striking in some, especially isolated, regions. In more recent decades, the issues surrounding childbirth have been largely dominated by the place of birth, but the impact of gender, power, organization of services, professional authority and patients' demands, as outlined by Pitt, Williams, and DeVries and Barroso go far beyond the boundaries of the hospital maternity ward.

The importance of locality and regional influences is shown effectively in Christoph Brezinka's analysis of the language islands of Northern Italy; isolated, with a vibrant local culture, their own language, yet touched by many aspects of modernization, the system of home births by midwives survived longer here than in neighbouring regions. The need to make good regional short-comings in obstetric services and to recruit the midwife as the first line of attack in ridding childbirth of 'dangerous' practices is demonstrated by Marland's survey of the poor southern Catholic regions of Holland. In Sweden, problems faced by thinly populated and isolated regions in obtaining childbirth assistance give a rationale to the decision to equip midwives with instruments.

The midwife in defining her work sphere struggled not just with doctors, but also with the new public health nurses and health visitors, as many of them sought to carve out an extended role in maternity care.[20] The public health role was crucial in many settings to the development of the midwife profession: in the chapters of Loudon, Romlid, Løkke, Marland, and Mottram it emerges as one of *the* deciding influences. The midwife's position was often am-biguous: was she purely a birth attendant, a specialist in normal births, or did she have a broader role in providing antenatal care, supervision of the new-born, even vaccinating and providing health education? Would a broadening of her role secure her position or undermine it and her traditional image? Did excursions into public health work smack of a lack of fulfilment with her work as birth attendant, or was it simply a professional and economic imperative, or a new opportunity?

The qualified midwife also found it increasingly necessary to tussle with her traditional counterpart, the 'handywoman', to clean up her image, to build up a greater share of childbirth practice and to raise midwifery's professional credentials.[21] All countries had their granny midwives, their *bakers*, *hjälpkvinnor*, *parteras*, and bona fides, re-created in the traditional midwife of the USA in recent decades. Historically, handywomen were strongly associated, as Loudon shows, with maternal deaths. Many handywomen were popular and efficient, yet the lurid image of dirt and bad practice meant that the 'new midwife', 'Health Missioner', as depicted by June Hannam and Joan Mottram, needed to rid herself of this shadow of tradition.

Midwives strove to raise the level of their education and training in what could be seen as a two-pronged attack, to respond to the changing demands of those they assisted and to make clear the unsuitability of those who did not follow this path. At the same time, improving levels of training embroiled the midwife in questions of how she could match her knowledge to her competence and what she was allowed to do in practice. Ortiz and Padilla's chapter on Spain and case study of Granada provides a detailed insight into how changes in the education of midwives were wrought, and how this affected their practice, while several of the other chapters demonstrate how changing concerns with obstetric services and the increased input of medical men brought about the setting up of new training courses and facilities.

Despite the many challenges she faced, the midwife was still firmly stationed as the main provider of obstetric care at the close of the nineteenth century in most countries. Midwifery was a traditional means of female employment,[22] well established and rooted in society compared with the newer occupations of health visiting and district nursing. As nursing too developed a professional identity during the nineteenth and twentieth centuries, the two professions, one emerging, the other evolving, began to clash, particularly in the areas of maternity nursing and infant welfare. Maternalist policies related to anxiety about the decline in national populations and emerging welfare states also impacted on midwives and their relationship with nurses. Questions of status emerged between the two groups, and the situation became more complex in the twentieth century as midwifery, like nursing, came to be increasingly based in institutions.

The midwife's place of work was subject to great change, dictated by the shift to hospital births and the opportunity for medical interventions, and related to shrinking family sizes and women's changing expectations of childbirth practices and their needs. The impositions of an increasingly 'medicalized' culture need to be matched by the changing demands of women; some were demanding pain relief, many preferred doctors to attend them, while others sought the 'sanctuary' of a hospital to give birth, particularly poorer women who welcomed the break from household chores and child care that they could obtain in a well-run maternity ward.[23]

One of the most important shifts in midwife practice was from the private to the public sphere. In most countries of the Western world this process was slow and by no means all-embracing. The physical workspace of the midwife was more and more likely as the twentieth century progressed to be located in institutions, and her work came to be increasingly supervised, not just in terms of organization but also day-to-day practice. Yet at the same time the midwife also opted in many cases for a more public role, particularly to engage increasingly in public health work and maternity and child welfare, and in publicizing her campaign to protect her status and vision of childbirth practice. During this period, the midwife also loosened herself from ties of tradition to embrace formal training and 'antiseptic' practice. Few of the challenges the midwifes faced were purely adverse for her. The reverse was often true, as the midwife reassessed her ideas about her tasks, and in many cases extended them. Through her societies and journals she became stronger and better organized. What all the chapters in this volume show is the appearance of similar challenges to midwives across the Western world, though their timing, responses and implications differed substantially. The concluding chapter, which compares obstetric care in America with the Netherlands where one-third of babies are still delivered at home, illustrates how varied this shift could be. In a sense, the two countries mark the end result, or rather resting place, of diverging responses to the debate regarding the role of the midwife, the place of birth and the normality of childbirth. The constant series of challenges to midwives have been played out in varied ways in different national contexts.[24] The situation of the independent midwife in the Netherlands could not be more distant from the status of the American midwife, yet concerns overlap on retaining professional identity, the use of childbirth technology, meeting patients' expectations, and ensuring a viable working future. In finding solutions to these issues, the Netherlands, the United States and all other Western countries still share common ground, as the midwife time after time strives to re-create herself.

NOTES

1 'De bevoegdheden van de vroedvrouwen in de verschillende landen', *Maandblad voor R.K. Vroedvrouwen* ('Monthly Journal for R.C. Midwives'), April 1938, vol. 15:4, pp. 29–32. The article was reprinted from the January edition of the *Tijdschrift voor Verpleegkunde, Vroedkunde en Sociale Geneeskunde* ('Journal of Nursing, Midwifery and Social Medicine').

2 German midwives regrettably have received no coverage in this volume, but see E. Labouvrie, 'Selbstverwaltete Geburt. Landhebammen zwischen Macht und Reglementierung (17.-19. Jahrhundert)', *Geschichte und Gesellschaft*, 1992, vol. 18, pp. 477–506.

3 For Belgian midwives, see R. Schepers, *De Opkomst van het Medische Beroep in Belgie. De Evolutie van de Wetgeving en de Beroepsorganisaties in de 19e Eeuw*, Amsterdam, Rodopi, 1989; K. Velle, *De Nieuwe Biechtvaders. De Sociale Geschiedenis van de Arts in België*, Leuven, Kritak, 1991.

4 For French midwives, see R.G. Fuchs, *Poor and Pregnant in Paris:*

Strategies for Survival in the Nineteenth Century, New Brunswick, Rutgers University Press, 1992; F. Thébaud, *Quand Nos Grand-Mères Donnaient la Vie: la Maternité en France dans l'Entre-Deux-Guerres*, Lyons, Presses Universitaires de Lyon, 1986.

5 'De bevoegdheden van de vroedvrouwen', p. 29.

6 Irvine Loudon, however, provides us with an excellent overview of midwife practice in Britain, the USA and Europe in the first half of the twentieth century: I. Loudon, *Death in Childbirth: An International Study of Maternal Care and Maternal Mortality 1800–1950*, Oxford, Clarendon Press, 1992, especially chapters 13, 18, 24.

7 See, for example, the essays in G. Block and P. Thane (eds) *Maternity and Gender Policies: Women and the Rise of European Welfare States 1880–1950*, London and New York, Routledge, 1991; V. Fildes, L. Marks and H. Marland (eds) *Women and Children First: International Maternal and Infant Welfare, 1870–1945*, London and New York, Routledge, 1992; S. Koven and S. Michel (eds) *Mothers of a New World: Maternalist Politics and the Origins of Welfare States*, London and New York, Routledge, 1993.

8 F.E. Kobrin, 'The American midwife controversy: a crisis of professionalization', *Bulletin of the History of Medicine*, 1966, vol. 40, pp. 350–63; J.B. Litoff, *The American Midwife Debate: A Sourcebook on its Modern Origins*, Westport, CT and London, Greenwood Press, 1986; N. Devitt, 'The statistical case for the elimination of the midwife: fact versus prejudice, 1890–1935', *Women and Health*, 1979, vol. 4, pp. 81–96, 169–86.

9 J. Donnison, *Midwives and Medical Men: A History of Inter-Professional Rivalries and Women's Rights*, London, Heinemann, 1977; R. Dingwall, A.M. Rafferty and C. Webster, *An Introduction to the Social History of Nursing*, London, Routledge, 1988.

10 H. Marland, 'Questions of competence: the midwife debate in the Netherlands in the early twentieth century', *Medical History*, 1995, vol. 39, pp. 317–37.

11 See the excellent study by C.G. Borst, *Catching Babies: The Professionalization of Childbirth, 1870–1920*, Cambridge, Mass. and London, Harvard University Press, 1995, and also the survey articles by Borst, 'The professionalization of obstetrics: childbirth becomes a medical specialty', and J.B. Litoff, 'Midwives and history', in R.D. Apple (ed.) *Women, Health, and Medicine in America*, New York, Garland, 1990, pp. 197–216, 435–50.

12 See B. Heagerty, 'Class, gender and professionalisation: the struggle for British midwifery 1900–1936', PhD diss., University of Michigan, 1990.

13 W. Arney, *Power and the Profession of Obstetrics*, Chicago and London, University of Chicago Press, 1982; Kobrin, 'The American midwife controversy', Litoff, *The American Midwife Debate*; Devitt, 'The statistical case'; N. Devitt, 'The transition from home to hospital birth in the United states, 1930–1960', *Birth and the Family Journal*, 1977, vol. 4, pp. 47–58; J.W. Leavitt, *Brought to Bed: Childbearing in America, 1750–1950*, New York and Oxford, Oxford University Press, 1986.

14 A. Witz, *Professions and Patriarchy*, London and New York, Routledge,

1992, pp. 104–27; H. Marland, 'Smooth, speedy, painless and still midwife delivered? The Dutch midwife and childbirth technology in the early twentieth century', forthcoming, in L. Conrad and A. Hardy (eds) *Women in Modern Medicine*, Amsterdam, Rodopi, 1997.

15 See also E. Fox, 'An honourable calling or a despised occupation: licensed midwifery and its relationship to district nursing in England and Wales before 1948', *Social History of Medicine*, 1993, vol. 6, pp. 237–59, which explores the link between domiciliary midwifery and market forces.

16 Some groups of midwives, however, appear not to have been touched by the debate. Even in the USA black and immigrant midwives, working with predominantly poor rural populations, continued to practise and deliver large numbers of babies well into the mid-twentieth century: see Borst, *Catching Babies*; S.L. Smith, 'White nurses, black midwives, and public health in Mississippi, 1920–1950', *Nursing History Review*, 1994, vol. 2, pp. 29–49.

17 See, for example, the accounts in S. Kitzinger, *Giving Birth, How it Really Feels*, London, Victor Gollancz, 1987, and S. Kitzinger, *The Midwife Challenge*, London, Pandora Press, 1988.

18 But see J. Towler and J. Bramall, *Midwives in History and Society*, London and New York, Croom Helm, 1986, chapters 8–10; A. Oakley, *The Captured Womb: A History of the Medical Care of Pregnant Women*, Oxford, Basil Blackwell, 1984; A.S. Williams, *Women and Childbirth in the Twentieth Century: A History of the National Birthday Trust Fund, 1928–1993*, Stroud, Sutton, 1997.

19 See, in addition to Loudon's chapter in this volume, his study *Childbed Fever: A Documentary History*, New York, Garland Press, 1996.

20 See C. Davies, 'The health visitor as mother's friend: a woman's place in public health, 1900–14', *Social History of Medicine*, 1988, vol. 1, pp. 35–59.

21 See N. Leap and B. Hunter, *The Midwife's Tale: An Oral History from Handywoman to Professional Midwife*, London, Scarlet Press, 1993; A.S. Freedman, 'The granny midwife: an example of pariah medicine', *Research Studies*, 1974, vol. 42, pp. 131–7.

22 See the essays in H. Marland (ed.) *The Art of Midwifery: Early Modern Midwives in Europe*, London and New York, Routledge, 1993; A. Wilson, *The Making of Man-Midwifery: Childbirth in England, 1660–1770*, London, UCL Press, 1995.

23 See, for example, Leavitt, *Brought to Bed*; E. Ross, *Love and Toil: Motherhood in Outcast London, 1870–1918*, New York and Oxford, Oxford University Press, 1993; Wilson, *The Making of Man-Midwifery*, chapter 15.

24 See also R.G. DeVries, 'A cross-national view of the status of midwives', in E. Riska and K. Wegar (eds) *Gender, Work, and Medicine*, New York, Sage, 1993, pp. 131–46.

1

ESTABLISHING THE SCOPE OF PRACTICE

Organizing European midwifery in the inter-war years 1919–1938

Anne Thompson

'The midwives' story, like that of all women, is filtered through a distorted glass of words.'[1] Achterberg's generalization of early midwife practice is arguably even more pertinent to the events surrounding the emergence of midwifery as a profession in the early decades of this century than to the period she describes. Midwifery in many European countries (Britain excepted) had a long history of formal education, licensing, organization and control.[2] Despite all this, the decades leading up to the inter-war period saw midwives grappling with the problem of establishing a public image, a professional identity for themselves which would once and for all give the lie to the old stereotypes of handywomen and Sairey Gamps, to win them parity with other, newer, women's occupational groups.[3]

It has been claimed that the status of midwives reflects the status of women in society. This chapter does not permit any in-depth exploration of this assertion, but it is worth acknowledging from the outset that the midwives' struggle for recognition and status within various European countries took place against the backdrop of vigorous efforts to renegotiate the place and role of women in society as a whole.[4] The midwife's professional standing was uneven, just as the level of women's emancipation and occupational organization was uneven across the different countries of Europe. The last decades of the nineteenth century and the first decades of this saw irreversible social changes for women. Midwives had either actively to engage in this process of change, or, very probably, face extinction.

Within this context, the story of the birth of the International

Midwives' Union (IMU) is to a great extent the account of how a small and scattered body of women used the processes of professional organization to develop strategies to convert the threat of near-extinction into the opportunity for public recognition of midwifery's potential to make a unique contribution to the well-being of mothers and babies. A number of efforts had been made to organize midwives internationally before the First World War, notably the congress in Berlin in 1900 which brought together over 1,000 midwives from Denmark, Holland, Rumania, Russia, Switzerland, Sweden, Austria and Hungary.[5] Other meetings were held, in Scandinavia, Italy and again in Germany, but no lasting structure emerged. A congress planned for Vienna in 1914 had to be cancelled because of the outbreak of war.

Once the war was over it was possible for another, more durable attempt to be made. In Belgium, in 1919, a long-standing professional partnership between a midwife, Mlle Marie Perneel, the innovative matron of the maternity hospital at Bruges, and an obstetrician, Professor Franz Daels, from the University at Ghent, led to the first formal steps in the establishment of an organization for midwives, the IMU, which was to pass through many phases before it became what is now known world-wide as the International Confederation of Midwives (ICM).[6]

The records for the foundation years, 1919–32, are scanty in the extreme, and none are contemporaneous, since the proceedings of the IMU were not published in printed form until 1932. Even after that date little material survives, for the archives were lost in Belgium during the Second World War, and what remains has had to be gathered from member associations outside continental Europe. None the less, these sources, particularly the *Communications* of the IMU, published at two-yearly intervals from 1932 and complemented by contemporary accounts in French, Swedish, Dutch and English professional publications, offer evidence of the major preoccupations of the midwives at this time. The biennial congress took place in centres across Europe, including Antwerp, Prague, Vienna, Ghent, London, Berlin and Paris, and the *Communications* reported the proceedings of the meetings and the reports of the countries represented at the congresses. By 1939, in Paris at the last congress held before the outbreak of war, some eighteen European countries were represented (membership being corporate, not personal). Each issue of the *Communications* listed, together with the names of the member associations throughout

15

Europe, the professional journals published by them – an astonishing twenty or so – offering some measure of the vitality of the profession. The number of countries in membership varied but virtually all the European nations, except perhaps Spain and Portugal, belonged at some time or other, though not all were equally active. From representation by a handful of women at the first congress in 1919, around eight hundred participated in the Berlin congress in 1936; the Nazi Minister of Health's mother was a midwife and this, together with rampant pro-natalism in Germany, provided an extra stimulus.

During the early years of this century midwives throughout Europe were under threat of extinction. Midwifery had achieved very varied levels of professional organization, public recognition and state regulation in different countries.[7] Without a stepping-up of professional organization and increasing competence and sophistication in developing strategies to cope with the new challenges in the way health care was organized, midwifery could well have disappeared as a distinct occupational discipline. The early records of the IMU make it clear that midwives in Europe considered that common action across national, cultural and language barriers was essential to their survival.[8]

Midwives themselves, throughout the IMU debates of the inter-war years, identified five main factors which threatened the erosion and possibly the extinction of midwifery as a profession, namely, a falling birth-rate; a steady increase in the number of medical practitioners; a shift in the place of birth; the movement of other health care workers into the community, who focused on maternal and child welfare; and, throughout the 1920s and 1930s, the increasingly severe economic crisis.[9] Faced with such challenges, midwives were fighting for survival as a distinct professional group. A small group of women from a handful of countries embarked on setting up a permanent organization which had the authority to speak for the whole profession, despite the considerable differences in training, legal status and practice of the IMU's member associations. Only such an international mechanism had the capacity, they believed, to combat the challenges, raise the standards and the standing of the profession and breathe new life into midwifery.

This chapter will limit itself to a necessarily brief discussion of these five main challenges of the inter-war years as they constituted the stimulus for midwives to organize themselves for the first time, through the IMU, in a systematic manner across national boundaries, followed by an examination of the strategies adopted by the IMU to address the challenges.

THREATS TO SURVIVAL

The falling birth-rate

The first of the major threats to the survival of the midwife was the falling birth-rate. This was a Europe-wide phenomenon, which gave rise to acute anxiety among politicians in a period when war and the threat of war were rarely absent. Driven by these concerns, the pro-natalist movements in many countries used a variety of tactics to induce women to have more babies, but only Germany after 1935 succeeded in reversing the trend.[10] In France the birth-rate fell from 21.4 per thousand in 1920 to 14.6 in 1938. By 1938 the birth-rate had fallen below the death rate, with a population decline of 35,000 per annum. Politicians and doctors were swift to identify the culprits. Dr Doléris, a pro-natalist physician writing in 1918, exclaimed, 'What is woman's great duty? To have children, to go on having children, always to have children! If a woman refuses motherhood, if she limits or suppresses it, she forfeits her rights: she is good for nothing any more'.[11]

Looking back on those years, Professor Binet, a distinguished gynaecologist, wrote in 1946, 'In the modern society of the inter-war years feminine decadence found expression in the refusal of motherhood or its undue restriction'.[12] In 1920, France established an award for mothers – women with five children won a bronze medal, eight a silver one and ten a 'gold' medal. By the mid-1930s motherhood was honoured in public in a procession of 20,000 women from the Place de la Concorde to l'Étoile and a massive stone 'Monument aux Mères' was erected in the 13th *arrondissement*, copied from a similar sculpture in Berlin.[13]

Midwives, of course, were threatened in their very livelihood by the drop in the birth-rate and it is hardly surprising that their survival strategies included working very closely with the pro-natalist movement. Midwife associations also put their objections to birth limitation into a moral framework, and strongly resisted neo-Malthusianism. Many organizations concerned with maternal and child welfare during this period took a clear pro-natalist stance. Noting the fact that French feminists took the view that, in the name of republican solidarity, national and family interests should take priority over individual or personal needs, Klaus writes:

> Women who worked in organizations dedicated to protecting maternal and infant health [the IMU would seem to be a prime example] consistently defined their work in these terms. A few articulated a distinctive, women-centred approach to maternal and infant welfare, but they did not challenge the ideological basis of pro-natalism. Instead, they served goals defined by male politicians and physicians, often working under the direction and influence of men.[14]

Many authors, including Koven and Michel, Elizabeth Roberts and Angus McLaren, have explored the phenomenon of the falling birth-rate, particularly in relation to the changing position of women in society, their growing political awareness and economic independence, as well as the increasing acceptability of fertility control through the use of contraceptives and abortion.[15] The contemporary accounts of Pember Reeves and Llewelyn Davies make it painfully clear just why women were more and more reluctant to have large families.[16] The tension between women's desire for smaller families and official government pro-natalist policies impacted directly on the work and attitudes of midwives, yet there is very little overt acknowledgement of the issue in IMU records in terms other than the threat to midwives' livelihood posed by the falling birth-rate.

The pro-natalist movement was stimulated not just by the falling birth-rate but also by the fact that, despite some improvements, an unacceptably high number of babies continued to die in infancy. At a time of chronic political instability, the wealth and security of a nation were perceived as being largely assured by a growing, productive work-force – which could, if occasion demanded it, become the military defence of the country. Politicians and doctors had expressed increasing disquiet since well before the turn of the century about the general health of the population, and, more particularly, the high maternal and infant death rates. Table 1.1 shows the infant mortality rate in a number of European countries in 1934.[17]

Although these showed a notable improvement on the figures of the closing decades of the previous century, it was obvious that there was still enormous scope for improvement. The Netherlands had an infant mortality rate that was half of Italy's, demonstrating

Table 1.1 European infant mortality rates, 1934

	Number per thousand
France	69
United Kingdom	57
Germany	68
Italy	99
The Netherlands	40

Source: F. Thébaud, *Quand Nos Grand-Mères Donnaient la Vie: la Maternité en France dans l'Entre-Deux-Guerres*, Lyons, Presses Universitaires de Lyon, 1986, p. 51.

that there was little inevitability about such deaths and that vigorous preventive measures in the field of maternal and child welfare would give thousands more children throughout Europe the chance of survival into adult life.

In the early meetings of the IMU, in Vienna, Prague and Ghent, midwives recognized the implications of these figures and, after a certain amount of debate, agreed on the importance of strengthening their input with respect to the care of the new-born child and collaboration in what was known as 'mothercraft' activities. Previously, in many parts of Europe, the midwife's role had been largely limited to attendance at the birth and the immediate aftercare of the mother and her new baby. To meet the new challenges, midwives were pushed, frequently against their will, to move out beyond the 'private' domain where they had practised for centuries, into the increasingly sophisticated, multi-disciplinary world of public health care and the new social welfare provision for the protection of mothers and their babies. Both economic reality and political expediency seem implicated in the midwives' decision to focus more on the care of the new-born than on the still-barely-respectable domain of birth control.

The doctors' challenge

A second challenge to midwives was the steady increase in the number of doctors. Table 1.2 shows how the relative proportions of midwives and doctors shifted over a period of sixty years. Other European countries experienced similar increases in the number of medical practitioners.[18]

Much has been written in recent years about the problematic relationships between doctors and midwives.[19] The strategies used

ANNE THOMPSON

Table 1.2 Number of doctors and midwives licensed to practise in France, 1876–1936

Year	Doctors	Midwives
1876	10,743	12,847
1891	12,407	14,343
1906	18,211	13,011
1911	20,113	13,066
1921	20,361	10,574
1926	23,996	11,629
1931	25,410	11,011
1936	25,930	11,268

Source: F. Thébaud, *Quand Nos Grand-Mères Donnaient la Vie: la Maternité en France dans l'Entre-Deux-Guerres*, Lyons, Presses Universitaires de Lyon, 1986, p. 173.

by medical practitioners at the turn of the century to define and control the boundaries between the two groups have been described in terms of the concepts of deskilling and incorporation.[20] Part of the tactics used by the medical profession involved constructing ever more elaborate distinctions between 'normal' and 'abnormal' childbirth, which, when accepted, resulted in a progressive deskilling of the midwife, as responsibility shifted from her domain to that of the doctor. In many places, substantial parts of the midwife's role became incorporated into the recently 'invented' field of obstetrics, the preserve of qualified medical practitioners.[21]

Oakley and Houd suggest four reasons for the medical profession's claim to take over childbirth: the need for doctors to recruit new patients (the growing families of parturient women provided potential future clients); the fact that deliveries were seen as a valuable source of income; the need to provide 'teaching material' for medical students in hospital, and the redefining of childbirth as a pathological state, hence no longer the domain of midwives.[22] This tendency had already taken formal shape in France as long ago as 1893 with the passing of legislation, which, with the intention of justifying the steep increase in institutional provision for the thousands of women who came from the provinces each year in search of an anonymous delivery in Paris, defined childbirth as an illness.[23]

At the biennial congress of the IMU, which took place in Ghent in 1932, the Dutch midwives complained that 'in the Netherlands the midwives can hardly stand firm against the number of young physicians who are looking [for] practice. In consequence of this

20

the number of midwives diminishes'.[24] The situation was compounded by the fact that in many parts of Europe, midwifery services remained fee-based rather than salaried. Midwives were dependent on a sufficiently large case-load to earn a decent livelihood, and were therefore in direct competition with the doctors for maternity cases. It was not until 1936, for instance, that a comprehensive salaried service was established in England and Wales, with the passing of the new Midwives Act.

A list of proposed remedies for this situation, discussed at the IMU congress at Ghent in 1932, included the reduction in the number of training places made available for midwives. The '*numerus clausus*' debate which recurred throughout this period involved the imposition of an upper limit on the number of pregnant women who could be cared for by any midwife or doctor, as well as the extension of the midwife's responsibilities in pregnancy and the care of the new-born. A final suggestion gives an insight into how desperate midwives were to eliminate damaging competition with the medical profession – one delegate proposed 'compulsory high rates of salary for the physicians'. Presumably the rationale behind the suggestion was that well-paid doctors would have little incentive to invest energy in the care of child-bearing women of modest or reduced means, so leaving more of this group of clients for the midwives.[25]

The rise of institutional delivery

The third major challenge for midwives during these years was the move towards institutional delivery. 'Institutions' took many forms, from the great lying-in hospitals of the metropolitan centres of Vienna and Paris to tiny maternity clinics run by local doctors. For centuries, the woman's home had been the midwife's chief workplace. By the end of the First World War this situation was changing rapidly, and midwives were becoming alarmed at the erosion of the practice of home birth. The question of control was at issue here; in the woman's home the midwife was in a unique position of power, albeit still an invited guest. Unless complications set in, she would normally conduct her work single-handedly, and, significantly, collect her fee at the completion of her work. Conditions varied throughout Europe, and there were several different levels of midwife in some countries like Hungary. But, on the whole, the midwife enjoyed almost total autonomy, even when practising as a municipal midwife, so long as she maintained her licence to practise and respected local reporting and supervisory prescriptions.[26]

Faced with evidence of a significant move towards institutionalized delivery, the 1936 congress of the IMU, held in Berlin, took the place of birth as its main theme for debate (Table 1.3). Estonia and Lithuania recorded that most women entered hospital for confinement. Hungary, while claiming an 80 per cent home delivery rate, noted that in the capital, Budapest, 95 per cent of all births took place in hospital.[27] The move to birth within institutions had complex origins and proceeded at very different rates across Europe. While recognizing that institutions could offer facilities which were attractive to many women, such as respite from domestic responsibilities and more readily available pain relief, midwives were hesitant about the long-term wisdom of universal, systematized institutional birth. The tone of some sections of the debate at the 1938 Paris congress is almost evangelical in its defence of home birth. One delegate's paper put forward an impassioned plea to retain normal confinements in the home, in order to 'preserve the fundamental value of a family environment'.

Table 1.3 The place of delivery in Paris during the inter-war years

Year	Total births	Home %	Public hospital %	Midwife's house %
1920	69,670	42.4	33.6	23.2
1925	61,363	26.2	46.1	27.5
1929	60,212	16.7	51.9	31.3
1934	52,302	12.4	62.3	25.3

Source: F. Théband, *Quand Nos Grand-Mères Donnaient la Vie: la Maternité en France dans l'Entre-Deux-Guerres*, Lyons, Presses Universitaires de Lyon, 1986, p. 154.

It is worth noting (Table 1.3) the continued growth in the 1920s in popularity of birth in the midwife's own 'home', or small private clinics, up until the early 1930s, when the public maternity hospitals' ascendancy became permanently established.[28] By this time the maternity hospitals had doubled their capacity, and, with their modern new design, had lost much of the stigma previously associated with the public hospital. This, together with favourable insurance arrangements, meant that women, particularly in large cities like Paris, where accommodation was difficult to obtain and frequently lacking in privacy, readily chose the new institutions for delivery.

The debate over the place of birth had a double focus in the accounts of the IMU congresses during the inter-war years. Very real concern about the implications for midwives in terms of employment was compounded by the mounting evidence from many quarters that maternity hospitals were experiencing an increased incidence of puerperal fever. The consequent difference in maternal mortality rates between cases delivered at home by midwives and institutional births appeared dramatic in a number of countries where evidence was made available (Table 1.4). The congress participants were the first to recognize the doubtful validity of the data which were produced, largely for want of agreement on definitions of puerperal fever, and limited themselves to commenting cautiously that 'hospital confinements cannot be considered entirely as a form of progress'.[29]

Table 1.4 Maternal mortality rates per 1,000 births

Country/City	Hospital	Midwives	Overall
USA/New York	6.2–8.0	1.9	—
England	4.5	2.0	—
Hungary	9.6	1.2	3.0
Germany	7.07	2.1–2.3	2.9–3.0

Source: Communications of the International Midwives' Union 9, 1937, p. 24.

The tone of the debates in the IMU congresses during the last years before the war leaves no real doubt that the midwives continued to champion the home as the appropriate place for birth in most instances. The arguments put forward for retaining home birth ranged from the increased moral well-being which supposedly accrued to the family by keeping the event '*chez eux*' to the apparently reduced risk of puerperal fever. Though times were changing rapidly in terms of provision for 'institutional' birth, midwives well understood the strength that came from the fact that for centuries women had had access to 'their' midwife, often from 'their' village or *quartier,* a known and trusted figure, as much a part of the community as the parish priest or local pastor. Such a position was one of unique privilege, if frequently of poor financial reward, and the midwives were not yet convinced that a definitive change in the usual place of birth was in either their best interests or those of their clients. This feeling found formal expression in

Resolution II (a) of the last international congress to be held before the war, in Paris. It reads:

> The VIIIth International Congress of Midwives believes that, for the sake of the preservation of family life, the home is the best place for the infant to be born, where conditions are suitable and the pregnancy normal. The midwife is thus able to carry out her duties as adviser and friend in the moral as well as in the physical sphere, putting the mother in touch with all the various agencies for any help she may require.[30]

Just to make sure, though, that midwifery services were to be universally available, whatever the place of birth, the Resolution concludes with the firm statement (b):

> No birth should be allowed to take place without the assistance of a midwife, whether the doctor is present or not. Where the mother is unable to pay for this assistance it should be provided by the state.[31]

The challenge of public health personnel

The fourth challenge facing midwives came from the growing number of nurses, including district nurses or maternity nurses, who were taking on a 'social' or 'welfare' role in the community, in contrast to their traditional place of practice, the hospital. Their growing presence as sources of professional rivalry figure in the earliest accounts of the IMU.[32] The threat from these newly emergent groups is formally spelt out in the report of the second international meeting, held in Antwerp in 1923: 'The function of the midwife has lost his [sic] influence because it was insufficiently protected and because it was pushed back by the new-coming function of visiting nurse'.[33]

The challenge came from the multiplication of health care workers, '*visiteuses*', 'visiting attendants', health visitors, and '*puéricultrices*', whose practice base was the community and whose clients were also mothers and their children.[34] Midwives sensed that these new 'professionals' were encroaching on a field which was traditionally theirs, and in some countries strove to increase their public health role.[35] Yet, in many countries, midwives' poor social status combined with their very limited training (in some instances as little as three months), left them seriously disadvantaged when faced with specially trained, carefully selected personnel who, as one delegate claimed in 1928, seemed particularly to find favour with the middle class and aristocracy.[36] The German midwives, especially, were unimpressed by the new breed of salaried nurses employed by the municipalities and the sick funds, judging them 'too young' and with 'too little experience of practical life'. Similar concern was voiced about 'too young midwives' who were alleged to undermine the profession and were unable either to inspire public confidence or to solve the many social problems which they met.[37]

Numerically, midwives have always been a significantly smaller professional body than nurses, and there has been a persistent tendency for the larger body to rationalize absorption of the smaller. Not surprisingly, midwives (while sometimes sensitive to the point of paranoia on the issue) have continued to claim their uniqueness and their very different function and philosophy. The fear of a 'takeover bid' by nurses, particularly those who were creating a new type of nursing service in the community, was very real in the minds of midwives and was frequently debated in IMU's assemblies.

The relationship with the nursing profession was frequently ambivalent. Midwives themselves were divided at times on the degree of involvement they wanted with a profession which, at least in some parts of Europe, was better educated, better organized and commanded a higher level of public respect, even if its scope of practice was less readily identifiable than that of midwives, and its level of independence in practice notably less, at least in the community setting.

Economic crisis

The fifth and final challenge faced by the midwives, the economic crisis of the inter-war years, was a hardship shared by everyone. The long, severe period of economic depression resulted in many women employing unqualified help for their confinements, for the 'handywoman' or lay midwife was frequently content with payment in kind, and was less expensive than the professional.[38] There is insufficient scope here to explore in detail the impact of the Depression on midwifery in the different countries of the Union, but the records' constant preoccupation with midwives' capacity to earn their living by the practice of a profession under threat is clear.

The economic challenge was frequently just as acute in urban areas as in the villages. Although there was a more concentrated number of births in the towns, there was a correspondingly high proportion of health care personnel and the competition between doctors and midwives was potentially much greater.

In the countryside, sheer lack of cases frequently drove midwives to other occupations to make ends meet – in one case as a 'hauler of coals'. At the London congress in 1934 midwives were told of the difficulties of midwives in rural Austria:

> where the distances between towns were so great that even on the plains it was difficult to get a doctor; while in the mountains a midwife had frequently to climb through the snow for three hours on skis with her equipment in a rucksack on her back. The people were often very poor and might not be able to pay her fee.[39]

A relatively new phenomenon was beginning to complicate the already precarious economic balance of midwives, particularly in the towns. An increasing number of women in many countries were covered for childbirth by some form of insurance provision, whether through 'sick club' contributions or state mechanisms. In an eloquent paper in defence of home birth given at the 1938 Paris congress, a laywoman told the delegates just how strongly such provision militated both against personal midwifery care and against home birth.[40] Talking of the way in which in times of economic difficulty insurance cover offered great advantages to all groups of women she went on, 'as far as the working classes are concerned, arrangements made by social insurance amount to a real premium in favour of hospitalisation'. Such a system offered women 'healthy conditions, security, comfort, rapidity of care, tranquillity, simplification and sometimes even economy'. Given the living conditions of many women, particularly in overcrowded cities, it was not surprising that the option of institutional birth was accepted so swiftly.[41]

This particular congress gave more attention than had its predecessors to the problems of unemployment, sickness and old age and their impact on midwives' ability to earn a decent living and remain in the profession. A special study had been commissioned by the IMU for the congress on legal measures taken in the countries of the member organizations. Three categories of provision were identified. First, countries in which the midwife was relatively well protected since she was a government servant; second, countries with new organizations, 'where something, admittedly imperfect as yet, has been done by the Government', and, third, countries in which the government granted no allowances whatsoever to the profession. The report is incomplete and sometimes even contradictory in its listings, but its interest lies in the range of mechanisms which had been either put in place or suggested to resolve what the IMU describes as the 'tragic circumstances of midwives'. These included the setting up of a Rural Assistance Scheme and additional fees from public funds for such duties as vaccination and antenatal clinics, part of the fee to be paid into a pension fund. Not all was gloom. The Estonian midwives reported a rise in salary since the previous congress, although they went on to note that virtually all births took place in hospital, that the number of independent midwives was being reduced, and that a state service was being created to serve rural areas. The congress concluded with resolutions requiring the remuneration of midwives to be sufficient to ensure a pension on retirement and payment of premiums sufficient to protect them in case of illness and accident. Where the state was not responsible for midwives, the IMU called for state intervention to contribute to insurance schemes for midwives.[42]

REDEFINING MIDWIFERY

Emerging quite rapidly from its obscure post-war beginnings in Bruges, the IMU gradually developed a range of tactics to deal with these challenges. Midwives from most European countries met at the biennial congresses of the inter-war years. There the debate was focused on ways in which midwives could restructure their education, practice and employment conditions so that they could remain viable as a profession in the face of odds which, on the North American continent at least, effectively wiped out the legal practice of midwifery for the first half of this century.[43]

There was a degree of consensus among member organizations of the IMU during the 1920s and 1930s on the strategies necessary for professional organization and survival. This is somewhat surprising, given the very different backgrounds of midwifery in the many European countries involved. While Swedish, Finnish and Norwegian midwives were authorized under certain conditions to use obstetric forceps,[44] in some countries midwives were forbidden

27

to perform an episiotomy or repair the perineum, or even to administer pain-relieving drugs. Dutch midwives had a level of education and a degree of autonomy in practice which were the envy of many of their colleagues – though they too had many complaints about restrictions on their work – but for midwives from a number of other countries such status and freedom remained a dream which they hoped the IMU would be able to assist in realizing.[45] Women's expectations of care in childbirth were changing, and midwives had to adapt their practice to meet these expectations, as well as to consolidate their position as 'guardians of normal childbirth'.

The records show that midwives focused on a redefinition of their role and consequent broadening of the curriculum as central to their survival strategy. From its very first meetings the IMU capitalized on the fact that maternal and child welfare was high on the political agenda, in attempts to expand midwives' role and to incorporate 'social' elements of care. Improving educational standards, strengthening legislation and increasing their competence, winning the right to use a number of vital drugs such as oxytocics and analgesics, and broadening the practice base to include the care of the new-born as well as administration of the developing vaccination programmes, were key tactics designed to improve public perception of the midwife's relevance and effectiveness as well as to stem the tide of the medicalization of childbirth.[46]

The ambiguity inherent in pressing for an expansion of their role was not lost on the midwives. 'Creeping medicalization' remained a risk for them, as well as for their clients, and occasional firm statements which emerged from the debates of the IMU bear witness to the midwives' anxiety: 'the control of a physiological act by a doctor of medicine, surgery and midwifery, is a luxury which ought to be regarded as such by the medical associations, by administrative authorities and by the governing powers'.[47]

One key strategy which was developed in response to the various challenges of the period was to attempt to expand the scope of midwifery practice by incorporating aspects of social welfare and the care of the new-born; socio-medical activities 'to be done by no-one but the midwife', as Franz Daels, the IMU's 'founding father', put it at one of the earliest meetings.[48] A year later he returned to the theme with the comment, 'it is an indisputable fact that the profession of a midwife has been discredited, because her task as a missionary of hygiene among the people was not understood and still less encouraged'.[49]

Politicians and doctors had expressed increasing disquiet since well before the turn of the century about the general health of the population, and, more particularly, the high maternal and infant death rates prevalent during this period. Growing awareness of the 'social' components of ill-health, bad housing, poverty, poor nutrition and ignorance, was translated into a maternal and child welfare movement which reached its peak during the early years of the IMU's development.[50] One aspect of this movement which both threatened midwives by undermining their special role, and offered them a professional opportunity tailored to their particular gifts, was the burgeoning of community-focused care for mothers and their families. Small wonder, then, that every congress from 1922 until 1939, in addition to underlining the profession's commitment to the protection of mothers and their babies, demanded a three-year training programme for midwives with a significantly increased 'social' component to the curriculum. Dutch midwives set the standard in this, and were much envied by those countries in the IMU who saw a long hard battle ahead of them to achieve similar goals. In 1921 Holland's midwifery training was extended from two to three years, with special emphasis on the care of the new-born, the needs of pregnant women and maternity nursing, though the discussion on the role of midwives versus doctors and nurses in the postnatal care of infants continued well beyond this date.[51] Most countries continued to insist on a clear demarcation between the work of the nurse, whose task was 'to nurse her medical patients and the midwife to look after her patients in confinement and her nurslings'.[52]

By the end of the inter-war period midwives were much more overt about the formal adoption of a social welfare aspect to their work. In Paris, in 1938, the delegate from Estonia remarked that:

> Adequate remuneration for their social work would promote the appointment of midwives in places where the exercise of midwifery alone would not afford them a livelihood. In this way the problem of redistribution of midwives in rural districts could be solved.[53]

It is apparent that by now the midwives' strategies had at least as much to do with the economics of survival as with the identity and status of the profession. In a more authoritarian vein the delegate from Latvia reported,

> in addition to their midwifery work, their social work is of great importance. They deal with the education of the public in matters of moral and physical hygiene. If need arises, they may force a mother to feed her Child.[54]

German legislation of December 1938 made it obligatory for pregnant women to ask for the help of the midwife, and doctors were required to see that a midwife was present at every birth. In defining midwifery as a liberal profession rather than a trade 'the profession is at once placed on a higher plane, at the same time losing the right to an eight hour day'.[55] The same law formally incorporated the social work element into the midwife's role in the following terms, 'Midwives may, in so far as their work allows them, do social work in maternal and infant welfare, for which they receive special remuneration'. Since Germany was the only member country of the IMU with a rising birth-rate, it was not surprising that the writer felt able to comment that, 'These new laws have been particularly successful in solving the problems of the profession of midwifery in Germany'.[56]

The content of this new 'social' element in the midwifery curriculum is rarely defined in contemporary records, although the subject recurs constantly throughout the years and from all the member countries. In some instances it seems to mean little more than extending the role of the midwife to incorporate the care of 'nurslings' – although artificial feeding remains firmly the domain of the doctor when it is mentioned.[57] By the end of the 1930s the midwives' care of the new-born extended to child welfare clinics and vaccination programmes. The 1934 congress was probably the most explicit with regard to defining the nature of the 'social' component of the curriculum. In the last year of training, pre-ventative medicine and social laws were to be studied (though not learned by rote). Actual experience was to be gained in clinics for children, the infant welfare service, antenatal consultations, and the school medical service. Medical and social instruction was to include visits to institutions for backward children, dispensaries for tuberculosis, venereal diseases and tumours, as well as convalescent homes and labour exchanges.[58]

In its early years it seems that the IMU more or less consciously chose to ignore some of the major social issues which faced the women they cared for. Although 'social evils' are mentioned from time to time in congress debates as a source of concern, they remain discreetly undefined and go unreported in the official records, but they included two contemporary preoccupations: sexually transmitted diseases, particularly syphilis and gonorrhoea, and abortion. A French text, quoting one of the professional journals, records the Secretary General, Marie Godillon, as saying

> The midwife has an undeniable moral influence on her clients . . . she can take part in the fight against the scourge of abortion. If she realises that one of her clients is inclined to bad thoughts the midwife will succeed eventually in recalling her to her duty. Often being a surrogate mother for her client the midwife will quite naturally find the right words to show the shame and the danger of abortion and contrast them with the joys of motherhood.[59]

Midwives, particularly the French who were very sensitive to their old reputation as 'angel makers', '*faiseuses d'anges*', took very great care to distance themselves from the issue of abortion. It would be impossible to gauge from the published proceedings of the IMU during these years the extent to which contraception and abortion figured in the discussions on women's health and fertility during this period. Leap and Hunter's recently published oral history of midwives in England in the first half of the century comments on the reticence of the midwives: 'We got the impression that midwives felt they had to keep themselves ignorant of abortion to ensure they weren't accused of being involved in an illegal activity'.[60]

Since the IMU aspired to be an influential instrument for the establishment of midwifery as an organized, state-regulated, respected profession in many countries, it is perhaps understandable that the official record is silent on abortion. Thébaud's work makes it clear that during the years under discussion midwifery's political strength lay in its potential as an agent for the pro-natalist movement.[61] Brooke Heagerty's penetrating study of the processes of professionalization put in place by English legislation in 1902 underlines the great importance placed on the 'moral' qualities of the new breed of uniformed, certified midwife, an emphasis designed, she maintains, to distance them from the handywomen or lay midwives who were all too frequently perceived as abortionists.[62]

As for birth-limitation, the reasons given by McLaren to explain the medical profession's opposition to birth-control during the late

nineteenth century, namely a lack of interest in preventive measures, the belief that contraception was not an 'appropriate' subject
for 'respectable physicians' to study, and simple ignorance of its
effects, seem tacitly to have been adopted by midwives a couple of
decades on and were compounded by official anxiety about the
almost universally falling birth-rate.[63] Simple economics and professional self-interest must also have determined policy, for to
positively encourage birth-control in societies where the falling
birth-rate was already causing alarm and thereby creating a surplus
of unemployable midwives would surely constitute an incomprehensible 'own goal'. Better to keep silent, to work at reducing
the number of babies abandoned in Paris, or preventing the
occurrence of rickets in Germany, or notifying communicable
diseases in Czechoslovakia.[64]

By the end of the 1930s, though still giving abortion and
contraception a wide berth, IMU midwives were being more
explicit about their responsibilities with regard to other 'social
skills' in relation to issues such as the abandonment of new-born
babies and the spread of venereal disease, particularly syphilis. They
had a precedent. In 1938, Mme Brault, from the French Ministry
of Health, reported to congress the role played by midwives,
particularly those of the *Assistance Publique*, in reducing over the
decades the numbers of abandoned babies in Paris. The problem
had been enormous, with some 19,000 cases in 1860 in a population
of one million inhabitants. By 1938 there were only 1,100 cases for
a population of 7,000,000. Her concluding remark that 'we owe this
to the midwives of the state services who understand their duty',
however flattering, has to be ranked as quite outrageous over-
simplification, if not pure hyperbole, with its implication that
midwives were the unique factor in the massive drop in the
numbers of babies abandoned over the past eighty years![65]

CONCLUSION

This overview of the major challenges facing midwifery in Europe
during the inter-war years serves both to introduce and to explain
in part the direction taken by the IMU. The falling birth-rate, the
growing number of doctors, the increase in institutional births, the
rise in the number of maternal and child welfare workers, and the
long-drawn-out recession of the inter-war years presented a formidable package of obstacles to a group of women who, with a few

notable exceptions, had previously not been held in very high regard as a profession, and whose educational background was frequently, on their own admission, a very inadequate basis on which to build a strong professional body.

In the face of such challenges midwives were not passive. In developing a response they fought on two fronts. On one hand, from all over Europe they came together to form a small but tenacious organization which worked to retain and strengthen a midwifery profession with a clearly delimited field of competence, complementary to, but independent of obstetric practice. On the other hand, midwives used similar demarcationary strategies in relation to other groups of health care workers, particularly nurses and the emergent specialist groupings associated with maternity and child welfare provision. Their aim was to make sure that no one but a qualified midwife undertook the practice of midwifery. The expansion of their traditional role into newer domains of 'social work' – however ambiguously defined – constituted an essential part of their strategy for equipping themselves with the educational background essential for adapting their ancient craft to the needs of women in a fast changing world and establishing the practice of midwifery within the mainstream of women's professional development in the early part of this century.

Without a growing level of professional organization and an increasing competence and sophistication in developing strategies to cope with the new challenges, midwifery could well have suffered extinction as a distinct occupational discipline. It is significant that the organization which they set up to strengthen the profession's identity and to promote its advancement was not an association of individuals. Each country had its own midwifery organizations, sometimes several, well practised in dealing with professional issues in the national arena. The record of these years makes it clear that midwives in Europe considered that only the concerted voice of those organizations would have sufficient authority to ensure common action across national, cultural and language barriers which was essential to their survival and the IMU was the tool which they used for that purpose.

NOTES

1 J. Achterberg, *Woman as Healer*, Boston, Shambala, 1990, p. 120.
2 I. Loudon, *Death in Childbirth: An International Study of Maternal Care and*

Maternal Mortality 1800–1950, Oxford, Clarendon Press, 1992, pp. 398–444; J. Donnison, *Midwives and Medical Men: A History of Inter-Professional Rivalries and Women's Rights*, London, Heinemann, 1977; J. Towler and J. Bramall, *Midwives in History and Society*, London, Croom Helm, 1986. A detailed account of Dutch midwives' earlier efforts (they were in the vanguard then as they are today in the protection and development of midwifery) to consolidate their professional status and role *vis-à-vis* their medical counterparts, general practitioners and obstetricians, is found in M.J. van Lieburg and H. Marland, 'Midwife regulation, education, and practice in the Netherlands during the nineteenth century', *Medical History*, 1989, vol. 33, pp. 296–317. A contemporary account of the state of affairs in England towards the turn of the century is found in 'The amelioration of the present condition of midwives', report of meeting, *Nursing Notes*, no. 2 (new series), 1 Feb. 1888.

3 B. Heagerty, 'Class, gender and professionalisation: the struggle for British midwifery 1900–1936', PhD diss., University of Michigan, 1990.

4 S. Rowbotham, *Women in Movement: Feminism and Social Action*, London and New York, Routledge, 1992; M. Vicinus, *Independent Women: Work and Community for Single Women 1850–1920*, London, Virago, 1985.

5 'History of the International Confederation of Midwives and other meetings', *Conference Programme, ICM Congress*, London, 1954.

6 Ibid. This programme contains a list of all the pre-war presidents of the IMU. A much earlier account of the origins of the IMU is given by the co-founder Franz Daels. (Marie Perneel, the midwife founder, seems to have died during the year following the inauguration of the IMU in 1919.) Prof. Daels writes some thirteen years after the events of which he speaks, with the result that there are some minor inconsistencies of dating. None the less, his record is doubly precious, since he was not only General Secretary of the IMU during the time he writes of, but his paper is the only reasonably full account of the events of the first ten years of the IMU's life, when *Communications* was simply a roneod (now lost) document: 'History of the International Congresses of Midwives', *Communications of the International Midwives' Union* (hereafter referred to as *Comm.*) 6, Ghent, 1932, pp. 14–21.

7 Loudon, *Death in Childbirth*, chapter 24, on midwives in France, Sweden, Norway, England, Denmark and Germany. See also H. Marland, 'Questions of competence: the midwife debate in the Netherlands in the early twentieth century', *Medical History*, 1995, vol. 39, pp. 317–37, and the chapters by Romlid, Ortiz, Løkke and Loudon in this volume.

8 *Comm. 6–10*, 1932–39, *passim*.

9 Ibid.

10 E. Roberts, *A Woman's Place: An Oral History of Working-Class Women 1890–1940*, Oxford, Basil Blackwell, 1984, p. 85; F. Thébaud, *Quand Nos Grand-Mères Donnaient la Vie: la Maternité en France dans l'Entre-Deux-Guerres*, Lyons, Presses Universitaires de Lyon, 1986, pp. 11–23; *Comm. 9*, 1937, pp. 28–31, speech of Dr Frick, Minister of the Interior, to the Berlin Congress, followed by national reports on falling birth-rate. See also A. Mitchell, *The Divided Path: The German Influence on Social Reform*

in France after 1870, Chapel Hill and London, University of North Carolina Press, 1991.

11 Thébaud, *Quand Nos Grand-Mères Donnaient la Vie*, p. 11. I wish to acknowledge a considerable debt to this author, whose work filled many gaps and started many new trains of thought about the motivation behind the professional organization of midwives in Europe during this period.

12 Ibid., p. 9.

13 Ibid., p. 22.

14 A. Klaus, 'Depopulation and race suicide: maternalism and pronatalist ideologies in France and the United states', in S. Koven and S. Michel (eds) *Mothers of a New World: Maternalist Politics and the Origins of Welfare States*, London and New York, Routledge, 1993.

15 Koven and Michel, *Mothers of a New World*; Roberts, *A Woman's Place*; A. McLaren, *A History of Contraception from Antiquity to the Present Day*, Oxford, Basil Blackwell, 1990.

16 M.L. Davies (ed.) *Maternity: Letters from Working Women Collected by the Women's Cooperative Guild*, first published 1915 by G. Bell & Sons, London, Virago, 1978; M. Pember Reeves, *Round about a Pound a Week*, first published 1913 by G. Bell & Sons, London, Virago, 1979. Pember Reeves' book was first published in 1913, the result of a four-year study of working-class families in Lambeth undertaken by the Fabian Women's Group.

17 A.S. Wohl, *Endangered Lives: Public Health in Victorian Britain*, London, Methuen, 1983, pp. 10–42: R.G. Fuchs, *Poor and Pregnant in Paris: Strategies for Survival in the Nineteenth Century*, New Brunswick, Rutgers University Press, 1992, *passim*; Thébaud, *Quand Nos Grand-Mères Donnaient la Vie*.

18 Ibid.

19 Donnison, *Midwives and Medical Men*, *passim*; W.R. Arney, *Power and the Profession of Obstetrics*, Chicago, University of Chicago Press, 1982; J. Gélis, *L'Arbre et la fruit: la naissance dans l'Occident moderne*, Paris, Fayard, 1984.

20 A. Witz, *Professions and Patriarchy*, London and New York, Routledge, 1992, pp. 109–27.

21 A. Oakley and S. Houd, *Helpers in Childbirth: Midwifery Today*, New York, Hemisphere Publishers, for WHO Regional Office for Europe, 1990. See also for an extensive account of the shift in definitions of the profession of obstetrics: Arney, *Power and the Profession of Obstetrics*.

22 Oakley and Houd, *Helpers in Childbirth*, pp. 24–35.

23 Fuchs, *Poor and Pregnant in Paris*.

24 *Comm. 6*, 1932, p. 45. I am grateful to Hilary Marland for drawing my attention to the fact that Dutch midwives may indeed have grumbled about their dwindling numbers, but, in reality, they held their own numerically during the 1920s and 1930s: 1910 – 924 1920 – 920, 1930 – 933, 1940 – 1, 139: J.J. Klinkert, *Verloskundigen en Artsen. Verleden en Heden van enkele Professionele Beroepen in de Gezondheidszorg*, Alphen a/d Rijn and Brussels, Stafleu, 1980, p. 72.

25 *Comm. 6*, 1932, pp. 45–6, 75.

26 *Comm. 6–10*, 1932–39, *passim*. For confirmation of this tradition of a high level of autonomy in practice throughout the early modern period, see H. Marland (ed.) *The Art of Midwifery: Early Modern Midwives in Europe*, London and New York, Routledge, 1993.

27 *Comm. 9*, 1937, p. 24.

28 See also the chapter by Ortiz in this volume for births in the midwife's home, p. 74.

29 *Comm. 9*, 1937, p. 25.

30 *Comm. 10*, 1939, p. 74.

31 Ibid.

32 Ibid., p. 56; *Comm. 6*, 1932, pp. 14, 107 on the competition of 'visiting nurses'. See also E. Fox, 'An honourable calling or a despised occupation: licensed midwifery and its relationship to district nursing in England and Wales before 1948', *Social History of Medicine*, 1993, vol. 6, pp. 237–59.

33 *Comm. 6*, 1932, p. 15.

34 Y. Knibiehler, V. Leroux-Hugon, O. Dupont-Hess and Y. Tastayre, *Cornettes et Blouses Blanches, les infirmières dans la société française (1880–1980)*, Paris, Hachette, 1984, especially the discussion 'L'infirmière visiteuse, apôtre de l'hygiène', pp. 140–65. See also the revue *Puéricultrice*, Paris, fragments on the inter-war years in the ICM archive. The expansion of other forms of home visiting is addressed in a number of studies, including C. Davies, 'The health visitor as mother's friend: a woman's place in public health, 1900–14', *Social History of Medicine*, 1988, vol. 1, pp. 39–59; L. Marks, 'Mothers, babies and hospitals: "The London" and the provision of maternity care in East London, 1870–1939', in V. Fildes, L. Marks and H. Marland (eds) *Women and Children First: International Maternal and Infant Welfare, 1870–1945*, London and New York, Routledge, 1992, pp. 48–73.

35 See the chapters by Romlid, Løkke, Mottram and Marland in this volume.

36 *Comm. 6*, 1932, p. 107.

37 Ibid., p. 90.

38 N. Leap and B. Hunter, *The Midwife's Tale: An Oral History from Handywoman to Professional Midwife*, London, Scarlet Press, 1993, pp. 22, 36.

39 'The Sixth Congress of the International Midwives Union. Conference Report', *Nursing Notes*, July 1934, p. 108.

40 'Domiciliary midwifery – an address given at the Paris Congress by a lay person', *Nursing Notes*, Aug. 1938, pp. 125–6.

41 See also A. Wilson, *The Making of Man-Midwifery: Childbirth in England, 1660–1770*, London, UCL Press, 1995, pp. 204–6 for the displacement of home by hospital births.

42 'VIIIth International Congress of Midwives, Conference Report', *Nursing Notes*, June 1938, p. 85; *Comm. 10*, 1939, p. 63.

43 J.B. Litoff, *The American Midwife Debate: A Sourcebook on its Modern Origins*, Westport, CT and London, Greenwood Press, 1986.

44 See the chapter by Romlid in this volume for the use of forceps by Scandinavian midwives.

45 *Comm. 9*, 1937, pp. 21–8. See also Marland, 'Questions of competence'.
46 *Comm. 8*, 1936, p. 60.
47 Ibid., p. 55.
48 Daels, 'History of the International Congresses of Midwives', *Comm. 6*, 1932, pp. 14–21.
49 M.O. Haydon, 'The International League of Midwives', *Nursing Notes*, Sept. 1923, p. 109.
50 J. Lewis, *The Politics of Motherhood: Child and Maternal Welfare in England, 1900–1939*, London, Croom Helm, 1980. See also the two contemporary studies of working-class, childbearing women in England which, through their first-hand accounts, paint a vivid picture of the situations of social deprivation which the welfare movement attempted to address: Pember Reeves, *Round about a Pound a Week*; Davies (ed.) *Maternity*. A European perspective on the maternal and child welfare movement is provided by H. Marland, 'The medicalization of motherhood: doctors and infant welfare in the Netherlands, 1901–1930', in Fildes, Marks and Marland (eds) *Women and Children First*, pp. 74–96.
51 Marland, 'Questions of competence', p. 332.
52 *Comm. 6*, 1932, p. 71.
53 *Comm. 10*, 1939, p. 58.
54 Ibid., p. 58.
55 Ibid., p. 110.
56 Ibid., p. 111.
57 Ibid., p. 80.
58 *Comm. 8*, 1936, pp. 57–8.
59 Thébaud, *Quand Nos Grand-Mères Donnaient la Vie*, p. 168.
60 Leap and Hunter, *The Midwife's Tale*, p.101. For further discussion, see M. Chamberlain, *Old Wives' Tales: Their History, Remedies and Spells*, London, Virago, 1981, p. 119; E. Shorter, *Women's Bodies: A Social History of Women's Encounter with Health, Ill-health and Medicine*, New Brunswick, Transaction Publishers, 1991; C. Usborne, *The Politics of the Body in Weimar Germany*, London, Macmillan, 1992.
61 Thébaud, *Quand Nos Grand-Mères Donnaient la Vie*.
62 Heagerty, 'Class, gender and professionalisation'.
63 A. McLaren, *Birth Control in Nineteenth-Century England*, London, Croom Helm, 1978, pp. 116–40.
64 *Comm. 9*, 1937, p. 32.
65 *Comm. 10*, 1939, p. 63. See also Fuchs, *Poor and Pregnant in Paris*.

2

SWEDISH MIDWIVES AND THEIR INSTRUMENTS IN THE EIGHTEENTH AND NINETEENTH CENTURIES

Christina Romlid

The predominance of relatively independent midwives is a characteristic of contemporary Swedish maternity care. It is they who are wholly in charge of all uncomplicated deliveries as well as of prenatal care, with the exception of the routine medical examinations that a doctor always carries out on a pregnant woman.[1] Midwives are able to prescribe contraceptives, insert IUDs, and to undertake obstetrical operations using their hands, forceps or a vacuum extractor when permitted by an obstetrician, and also when such permission cannot be obtained, as in an emergency situation.[2]

The relatively strong position of Swedish midwives today is often accounted for by reference to their authorization to use obstetrical instruments, including sharp tools, in 1829. By the end of the nineteenth century, a group comprising 72 per cent of all Swedish midwives was authorized to use instruments; this figure exceeded 90 per cent in eighteen of Sweden's twenty-four counties.[3] This creation of a class of autonomous midwives during the nineteenth century did of course influence the modern division of labour between midwives and obstetricians which emerged in the twentieth century. But what were the reasons underlying the decision made in the nineteenth century to give midwives the power to use instruments? To answer this question, it is necessary to turn to Swedish midwives' early history.[4]

THE MAKING OF THE SWEDISH MIDWIFE

The formal training of Swedish midwives commenced at the beginning of the eighteenth century when a physician, Johan von

Hoorn, versed in obstetrics in Holland and France, was appointed as Stockholm's city doctor (1708). Following the requirements of ordinances issued in the 1680s he began to train the city's midwives. Besides instituting the first training course for midwives and writing the first Swedish obstetrical textbooks, he also introduced a midwife statute for Stockholm. By this statute, issued in 1711, the municipal authorities were obliged to ensure that other cities obtained the services of midwives who had sat an examination in the capital. Midwives called from Stockholm to other towns and cities became obliged in turn to train women there. These regulations were revised in 1723, when von Hoorn became the first paid, state-employed teacher of midwives, and the midwife school in Stockholm was turned into a national institution to serve the whole of Sweden. The *Collegium Medicum*, a professional and supervisory corporation, established with the support of the Crown in 1663, and made up of the leading medical men of Stockholm, was from then on obliged to ensure that midwives, trained and examined in Stockholm, were distributed throughout the country. Cities and parishes outside of Stockholm also became obliged either to send women to Stockholm for training, or to appeal to the *Collegium Medicum* to persuade trained midwives to move to the places where they were needed. Furthermore, the provincial governors and the municipal authorities were made responsible for ensuring that rules concerning midwives were followed in their respective spheres of influence.[5]

Up until the second half of the eighteenth century supervision of the new provisions for maternity care was mainly attended to by the *Collegium Medicum*; the changes made at the beginning of the eighteenth century had largely been a result of von Hoorn's interest in this subject. In the second half of the eighteenth century, however, the situation changed drastically. What had hitherto been a matter promoted by a few doctors turned into an affair of state. This change had its roots in the mercantilistic ideas that had started to heavily dominate the Swedish political scene from around the middle of the eighteenth century.[6]

Since the aim of mercantilism was to create a powerful state by bringing about an increase in national wealth and national military power, a large, healthy population came to be viewed as a national asset. Production needed labour power and the army needed soldiers. This meant that the demographic situation began to attract attention and to be considered as a state responsibility. In addition to the importance assigned to the medical training of clergymen, and the need for more midwives and district medical officers, the training of midwives came to be viewed as being of great national value, especially since statisticians, economists, and doctors argued that trained and licensed midwives would reduce the unnecessary high level of infant mortality, saving infants' lives and thereby stimulating population growth.[7] Three tactics were discussed in connection with boosting population growth: the need to stimulate the birth-rate, encouragement of immigration, and ways of offering a better health service, but the focus came to be on the latter tactic. As a result of the new emphasis given to population issues, and the promises made ensuring its increase by statisticians, economists, and doctors,[8] the state began to invest money in maternity care. This resulted in the appointment of the first Swedish Professor of Obstetrics in Stockholm in 1761, and the opening of the first public maternity hospital and training school for midwives and doctors, also in the capital, in 1775.[9]

The number of deliveries taking place at the maternity hospital was, however, very small up until the turn of the century. Between 1775 and 1785, when there were a total of approximately 70,000 births in Sweden per annum, only about 200 of these were delivered at the maternity hospital. The numbers did increase around 1800, to about 500 deliveries a year, but stayed at this low level up until the 1880s when the bacteriological 'revolution' made institutional births safer.[10]

As the number of patients at the maternity hospital in Stockholm, mainly unmarried and poor women, was too small in the eighteenth century to satisfy the training requirements of either doctors or midwives, the midwife pupils continued to accompany trained and examined midwives in their work around Stockholm, while the Professor of Obstetrics attended to the theoretical part of their education.[11] In order to ensure that the southern part of Sweden, Scania, also developed a formal system of midwife training, the Parliament (*Riksdag*) appointed a midwife teacher to be stationed in Lund in 1772, and established a chair of obstetrics associated with Lund University in 1783. The *Collegium Medicum*, which wished to see midwife training centralized in Stockholm, refused, however, to acknowledge these appointments until 1792.[12]

The first national midwife statute was also introduced during this period, in 1777. It was a strict ruling that forbade all midwife training outside of Stockholm or by any person other than the midwife teacher who also held the chair of obstetrics. This had been proclaimed before, as, for instance, in a royal missive of 18 October 1757, when parishes and towns were charged to closely follow the decree of 1723 and acquire a midwife trained in Stockholm; yet the position assumed by officialdom, on the question of whether the local training of midwives should be permitted, had been ambiguous. In a royal missive of 30 October 1752 the Crown, for instance, gave the district medical officers and the midwives who had already been examined in Stockholm the right to train women locally.

The statute of 1777 was, in contrast, clear in its ruling on this question: the training of midwives was to be limited to Stockholm and strictly enforced. The statute also included what has come to be known in Swedish midwifery history as the 'quackery paragraph'. In this section it was laid down that it was – with the exception of situations of great emergency – unlawful to summon an unlicensed woman to a birth, and illegal to practise as a midwife without a licence. Those ignoring this rule would be fined or imprisoned for fourteen days, the penalty being more severe if the woman or the child died. The peasantry protested in Parliament at the proclamation of this paragraph, arguing that it would deprive women of help during labour. As a result of the protests, the Crown withdrew the 'quackery paragraph' from the regulation in 1780, and also reinstated the right of the district medical officers and the examined midwives to train women locally.[13]

Even though trained midwives were considered of great importance in the second half of the eighteenth century, according to the statute of 1777, they were forbidden the use of instruments. Deliveries that required the use of forceps or sharp instruments should, according to the statute, be left to the doctors. The implicit intention of this statute was to create a gendered division of work: midwives were to take care of the so-called 'normal' or 'natural' deliveries, while doctors were to manage the 'unnatural', 'complicated' cases. This division of maternity care was further justified along gender lines in a speech written by the surgeon and obstetrician Herman Schützercrants and delivered at a meeting of the Swedish Royal Academy in 1777. Of the two sexes, it was, according to Schützercrants, only the male sex which possessed the qualities of rationality and strength, and, therefore, men, not women, should take care of complicated deliveries.[14]

The Swedish state's interest in population issues increased

41

dramatically after the defeats of the Finnish–Russian War of 1808–09 when Sweden lost its supremacy over Finland, and thereby more than one-third of the country and over one-fourth of the population to Russia. The war, particularly the epidemics that had ravaged the military camps and that had been spread by the home-coming soldiers throughout Sweden, exacerbated a tense situation. Between the years 1808 and 1809 mortality exceeded natality. The loss of Finland was considered a national disaster and a tremendous setback for the self-image of Sweden as a great power.[15] It was at this time, when Sweden was shaken to its very foundations by political as well as demographic and epidemiological crises, that Stockholm's leading medical men launched a massive campaign to bring about political changes in health care. The campaigners, who wanted to spread medical science across the country and exterminate the quacks, defined the situation and put forward solutions in a way that successfully coincided with the state's needs. It was argued in the ensuing debate that the population had to be increased and its health had to be improved if Finland was to be recaptured and the country rebuilt.[16]

As a result of the campaign, a number of medical reforms and changes were implemented, the health care budget was increased in Parliament, and the *Collegium Medicum* was given more power and converted into a National Board of Health, a civil service department, in 1813. In 1812 the parliamentary medical committee, set up in 1810 to give suggestions on how to improve public health care and medical services,[17] presented its report outlining how the shortage of trained midwives could be ameliorated. This report resulted in turn in the drawing up of a new national midwife statute that came into force in 1819.[18] In this statute the 'quackery paragraph' was reinstated, and it became unlawful to summon an unlicensed woman to a delivery and illegal to practise as a midwife without a licence. The 1819 statute was, however, milder than the version that the *Collegium Medicum* had tried to introduce in 1777. In 1777 the only exception to the ruling was a situation of great emergency, while the statute of 1819 included an addendum that made it legal to practise as a midwife without a licence in places lacking a licensed midwife. The statute of 1819 also differed from that of 1777, in that it made provision for midwife training to be extended from three to six months, imposed a number of public health duties besides maternity care on the midwife, authorized midwives to give medicines in accordance with the textbook in use at the midwife schools, and ruled that the training of midwives outside of Stockholm was to be forbidden, with the exceptions of Scania and Gotland.[19] The special stipulation for Gotland was revoked in 1822.[20]

THE INSTRUMENTAL AUTHORIZATION OF MIDWIVES

The first proposal to give midwives legal authority to use instruments during delivery was put forward in 1824 by Stockholm's midwife teacher and Professor of Obstetrics, Pehr Gustaf Cederschjöld, who was also a Member of Parliament. This request did not receive any support from the National Board of Health, but Professor Cederschjöld came back with a new petition in 1828 which the Board as well as the Crown supported. The reason for the change of policy, given by Professor Cederschjöld and which the National Board of Health as well as the Crown agreed upon, was concern for the safety of the mother and the child. It was said that the remoteness of many localities made it impossible to reach a doctor in time. In other words, according to the authorities, in a critical situation there was, for the majority of the population, no medical help available, especially since trained midwives were not allowed to use obstetrical instruments. According to the accounts given by the National Board of Health this not only meant that the public's confidence in trained and licensed midwives was seriously diminished, it also disrupted the principal purpose behind their training, that is the saving of mothers' and infants' lives. Only if the statute of 1819 were changed and midwives were authorized to use instruments would it be possible for them to practise their art effectively.

In 1829 it became possible for women who had attended the basic six-month midwife course, passed the examination, distinguished themselves as moral and decent persons, skilful in their work, in possession of the necessary physical strength, and thereby judged by the midwife teacher as suitable to qualify, to attend an additional three-month training programme given by the midwife teacher in the use of obstetrical instruments. If the midwife passed the examination that concluded this special course, she became authorized to undertake instrumental deliveries. However, she was only allowed to do so when it was impossible to summon a doctor, and then in the presence of a witness. She was also required to write a report whenever she performed an instrumental procedure, to be signed by the district medical officer or the town physician and thereafter sent to the National Board of Health for further scrutiny.[21] Up until 1858 the additional course in the use of instruments was only taught at the midwife school in Stockholm. Thereafter the public midwife school in Gothenburg (opened in 1856) was also given the right to train midwives in the use of instruments. The midwife school in Lund was never accorded this right.[22]

It is important to stress the background to this legislation; it connects war and soldiers with maternal care and midwives, and thus points towards the importance of population politics in midwife history. As mentioned above, it was Pehr Gustaf Cederschjöld who took the lead in pushing for legislation to authorize midwives to use instruments. He did this at a time when maternal and infant welfare was a prominent national issue. This was largely due to the alarming reports which were circulating regarding the inferior quality of the recruits to the compulsory national military service (established in 1812), which the National Board of Health presented to the Crown at the end of the 1810s and beginning of the 1820s. The reports, based on doctors' annual inspections of enrolled conscripts, undertaken on every man aged 21, stated that far too many young men were being excluded on grounds of ill health. In these reports the National Board of Health stressed the importance of improved infant welfare, as well as the need to change the population's way of life and living conditions, in any attempt to raise the general condition of army recruits.[23] The increased attention on infant welfare meant that the number of midwives, as well as the quality of their training, came to be of central importance. In 1822 it was decided, in an attempt to improve the situation and increase the number of midwife pupils, that twelve young women from the rural areas would be supported annually through training in Stockholm at the public expense.[24]

The decision to give midwives the right to use instruments was a radical measure that strongly diverged from usual practice. It also received comment from abroad: in 1847 the German Professor of Medicine and author of several books on gynaecology, Dr Hermann Kilian, condemned the late Professor of Obstetrics, P.G. Cederschjöld, the driving force behind the initiative, for wanting to give midwives the same rights as doctors and trying to make midwives into obstetricians. This was a grave accusation, with wider political repercussions, being made at a time when women were being excluded from the medical profession.[25] In spite of this and similar accusations made towards the end of the nineteenth century, Swedish policy remained intact. It was only in 1919 that the midwives' privileges to use sharp instruments and the blunt hook were withdrawn. Henceforth midwives' right to use obstetrical instruments would be restricted to forceps.[26] The midwives' use of forceps has remained a skill and a right considered necessary to her ability to perform her work efficiently; the midwife needs to know at what point to call in an obstetrician, and midwives are still able to apply forceps in emergencies.

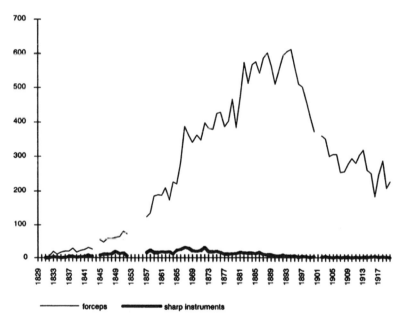

Figure 2.1 The number of instrumental interventions undertaken by Swedish midwives, 1829–1920 (various years)

Sources: See the Swedish Medical Society's journal *Hygiea*, 1844–45, 1847–51; *Sundhets-Collegii Underdåniga Berättelse*, 1851–60; *BiSOS, K. Helso- och sjukvården*, 1861–1910, and *Allmän hälso- och sjukvård 1911–20*. For the number of births, see *Historisk statistisk för Sverige. Del. 1. Befolkning 1720–1967*, Stockholm, K.L. Beckmans Tryckeri, 1969, Table 37, p. 108.

Note: Data are missing for 1830, 1842, 1844 and 1901. For the years 1853, 1855 and 1856 only the total number of operations is known. As the average number of births per annum was roughly 108,000 (1831–60), 136,000 (1861–90), and 135,000 (1891–1920), the number of operations undertaken by midwives never even reached the figure of 0.5 per cent.

The number of forceps operations carried out by midwives did, of course, decline, as the number of doctors increased and took over such procedures as the regulations specified them to do (see Figures 2.1 and 2.2). The radical reduction in the number of operations undertaken by midwives in the 1890s, which is shown distinctly in Figure 2.1, coincided, for example, with the large increase in the number of district medical officers that took place during this decade.[27] One interesting question is whether midwives, when empowered to do so, were as aggressive and interventive in their use of instruments as some accusations levelled at doctors claim. As Figure 2.1 shows, midwives undertook relatively few operations. Sharp instruments were seldom utilized. Most common were operations with the help of forceps. There were of course great variations in the number of operations per midwife as well as great disparities in the total number of deliveries that a midwife undertook. In 1891 one midwife was recorded as attending 193 deliveries, while the average number was only 41.[28] Instrumental deliveries were rare, and many of the midwives who were authorized to use instruments can never have performed an instrumental delivery during their entire working life. The greatest number of instrumental interventions by midwives was, as can be seen in Figure 2.1, carried out in 1894, when they performed a total of 616 procedures (612 with forceps and four with sharp instruments). This figure was still very low, accounting for only 0.46 per cent of the total number of births, which in this particular year totalled 134,866.[29]

It is not known, as no data were collected on the subject in the nineteenth century, just how much doctors intervened with instruments during the same period. The figures are, however, known for the period 1913 to 1920, when the number of operations undertaken by doctors far exceeded the number of midwife operations in the nineteenth century, varying from 1,458 in 1916 to 1,980 in 1920.[30] The total number of births amounted to 124,766 in 1916 and 141,979 in 1920. The number of instrumental interventions performed by doctors was, therefore, also relatively low, less than 1.5 per cent of the total births.[31] As the number of instrumental interventions carried out by doctors in the nineteenth century is unknown, it is impossible to assess whether overall instrumental rates declined, remained stable, or increased with the growing participation of doctors in midwifery work.

Another interesting question is why the original policy on

46

midwives' authorization to use instruments was preserved for such a long period. Why were Swedish midwives during the greater part of the nineteenth century and well into the twentieth century allowed to use the tools that in other European countries were regarded as deeply controversial[32] and which some Swedish doctors also opposed?[33] The low number and slow increase of doctors help explain why this policy was retained for such a long period, even

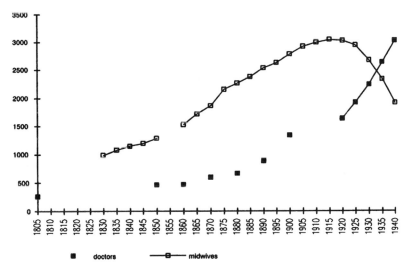

■ doctors   ———□——— midwives

Figure 2.2 The total number of midwives and doctors in Sweden, 1830–1940
(various years)

Sources: Riksarkivet: Sundhetskollegiets arkiv, Inkomna handlingar, E16B Uppgifter om barnmorskor, vols 1–17; Sundhetskollegiets arkiv, Koncept B1A, vol. 30, no. 203; vol. 31, no. 432; vol. 32, no. 401; vol. 33, no. 978; vol. 34, no. 115; vol. 35, no. 1374; vol. 36, no. 1822; vol. 37, no. 1727; vol. 38, no. 2223; vol. 39, no. 1886; Sundhetskollegiets arkiv, E14B Uppgifter om barnmorskor, vols 1–8; Sundhets-kollegiets skrivelser till Kungl. Maj:t, vol. 68, no. 6; vol. 69, no. 5; vol. 71, no. 6. See also *Sundhets-Collegii Underdåniga Berättelse om Medicinalverket i Riket*, 1851–60; BiSOS, K. *Helso- och sjukvården*, 1861–1910; *Sveriges officiella statistik (SOS)*, Allmän hälso- och sjukvård 1911–44; G. Kearns, R.W. Lee and J. Rogers, 'The interaction of political and economic factors in the management of urban public health', in M.C. Nelson and J. Rogers (eds) 'Urbanisation and the Epidemiologic Transition', (*Meddelanden från Familjehistoriska projektet*, Department of History, Uppsala University), Uppsala, 1989, Table 39, p. 66 and S. Vallgårda, *Sygehus og sygehuspolitik i Danmark. Et bidrag til det specialiserede sygehusvæsens historie 1930–1987*, København, Jurist- og ökonomforbundets Forlag, 1992, p. 323.

Note: The reduction in the number of midwives from around 1920 onwards was due to the extension of hospitalized maternity care, accelerated during the 1930s and 1940s. Thus in 1940, for instance, 65 per cent of all births took place in hospital, in 1950 94 per cent.

though it was considered an emergency measure. As can be seen in Figures 2.2 and 2.3, the number of midwives far outnumbered the number of doctors in the nineteenth century. In the second half of the nineteenth century there were at least three times as many midwives as doctors in Sweden. The total number of midwives was, for instance, 1,527 in 1860, while the total number of doctors in the same year only amounted to 472. In 1880 the figures were 2,264 and 663 respectively.[34]

The number of doctors did not rise in any significant way for many decades, and it was only well into the twentieth century (between 1930 and 1940) that the ratio between doctors and the population reached the same figure as the ratio of midwives to the population (see Figure 2.3). Midwives also, to a greater extent than doctors, lived in the rural areas which contained the overwhelming majority of Sweden's population. In 1869, for example, about 87 per cent of the population lived in rural areas; approximately 75 per cent of midwives resided in the countryside, compared with 52 per cent of doctors.[35]

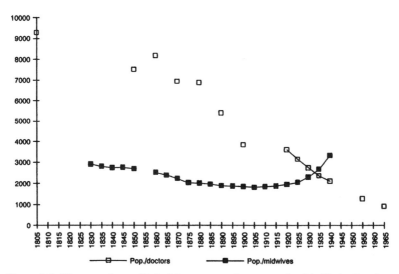

Figure 2.3 The number of inhabitants per doctor and midwife in Sweden 1805–1965 (various years)

Sources: See sources for Figure 2.2 in addition to *Historisk statistik för Sverige*, Table 2, pp. 44–5 and Table 4, pp. 46–8.

RESISTANCE TO MIDWIVES: THE
INSTRUMENTAL SOLUTION

According to the annual reports concerning maternity care that the provincial governors were obliged to send to the National Board of Health after 1830, and which included a massive collection of letters from the district medical officers and the clergy, in general country people strongly resisted the employment of midwives.[36] They were said to prefer the traditional birth attendant, the so-called 'hjälpkvinnor' (help-women), whose knowledge was acquired by experience.[37] The diffusion of trained midwives into rural areas was therefore slow. By 1886 only 61.4 per cent of parishes employed a midwife.[38] There were, of course, great regional differences in the employment of midwives as well as between urban and rural areas. Cities and provinces close to midwife training schools, for instance, had a large proportion of trained midwives per inhabitant by the mid-nineteenth century.

The employment of midwives was decided by the *sockenstämman*, a parish institution which served as a local direct self-government under the chairmanship of the parish clergyman. At the *sockenstämman*'s meetings parishioners were entitled to vote according to their land assessment. This voting power was extended in 1843, when tax-payers were also allowed to vote. Voting power finally came to be based on personal wealth and income in 1862. According to the reports, the usual explanation given at these meetings for not hiring a midwife was that it was too expensive and also unnecessary as *hjälpkvinnor* were considered just as good. If the need should arise, and complications occured, it was claimed to be possible to summon a doctor or a midwife from a nearby town or city. There was also a reluctance amongst the village women to employ a midwife. For instance in the province of Blekinge, according to the district medical officer's report of 1901, at least half of the deliveries were carried out by *hjälpkvinnor*.[39] It was usual, moreover, according to the reports, to summon midwives only when a complication arose or when a situation occurred which *hjälpkvinnor* could not handle. Midwives' reports on instrumental interventions also reveal that the summoning of a midwife was often done as a last resort. In 1857 141 instrumental interventions were undertaken by midwives. In 104 cases at least 24 hours, and as many as five days and nights, had passed before a midwife was summoned and requested to assist.[40]

Up until 1908 parishes were not obliged to employ a midwife, only strongly recommended to do so. The authorities considered the acceptance of the midwives to be a question of confidence, and as such not enforceable by legal means, which explains why the employment of midwives did not become compulsory earlier.[41] Many district medical officers also refrained from using the law to prosecute *hjälpkvinnor* who fell foul of the 'quackery paragraph' on the grounds that it would not increase confidence in midwives. Rather, it only exacerbated the rural population's reluctance to employ them.

There was also a strong belief that the authorization of midwives to use instruments would have a positive influence and raise public confidence in their abilities; according to the reports this was true amongst the country people.[42] The parishes also preferred to hire a midwife who was able to use instruments rather than one without authorization. According to the National Board of Health's report of 1861, between 1851 and 1860 the municipalities paid special attention when hiring a midwife to her authorization to use instruments.[43] In the 1880s it was said to be almost impossible for midwives without this qualification to find employment outside the towns.[44] Midwives authorized to use instruments seem, in other words, to have met a demand that existed in the countryside. It is likely that this demand, in combination with the large number of midwives compared with doctors, prolonged the time-span during which midwives were allowed to use all obstetrical instruments. It seems that not only supply from above, but also demand from below, determined the development of Swedish maternity care.

THE MIDWIVES' ROLE IN PUBLIC HEALTH

Swedish midwives' role was not limited to delivering babies. They were also assigned an important role within the public health sector, that the authorities built up in the early and mid-nineteenth century. In a letter to the government in 1840, the National Board of Health claimed that midwives had a beneficial influence on overall health care, and that they were extremely important for the enlightenment of the rural population.[45]

In all three of the midwife statutes that were enacted during the nineteenth century (1819, 1840, and 1856), it was prescribed that midwives should, besides midwifery, be taught how to vaccinate and inoculate and be trained in the art of applying leeches and blood-letting. The statute of 1856 – which remained in force until 1907 – also dictated that midwives were to be trained in infant welfare. The statute of 1840 – in which basic midwife training was extended from three to nine months – also included a detailed specification of the midwife's compensation for services other than deliveries. This list included blood-letting, applying leeches, giving enemas, catheterizing, remedying a prolapsed or altered uterus, putting in or taking out a pessary, the treatment of haemorrhage, and other complaints requiring lengthy medical care. According to this statute it was also possible to fine a midwife who, having been given due notice, neglected to attend a sick person. It seems as if the statute was describing a different set of clients than women in childbirth. Midwives were also seen as being able to play a major role in influencing attitudes, traditions and habits, and were also obliged in the statutes to see to it that every baby they delivered was vaccinated against smallpox within a year. They were expected to promote the country people's faith in inoculation in general, and give sensible advice in the field of infant care, such as recommending baths and domestic cleanliness.[46]

According to the district medical officers' reports, the midwives also performed a good deal of medical work apart from deliveries, and, once they had come to enjoy public confidence, were used by the rural population when illnesses and diseases occurred.[47] The textbook in use at the midwife schools from the 1820s up to 1873 also included special sections concerning women's and children's diseases. It was in these sections that the midwife learned how to recognize diseases and illnesses such as prolapsed or altered uterus, uterine-polyp, cancer and venereal diseases, as well as how to treat infant sickness, such as rachitis and whooping cough.[48] The Professor of Obstetrics and midwife teacher in Gothenburg, Gustaf Fredrik Hjort, also suggested in the 1860s that clinical midwife training should, in accordance with the textbook, be extended to include gynaecology and children's diseases. If the midwife was trained to recognize different types of women's and children's diseases she would, according to Professor Hjort, be able to make the correct judgement as to whether she ought to direct the sick person to a doctor or treat the case herself. Professor Hjort also argued that this was a necessary step since the midwife was in most cases the first person to be consulted for gynaecological complaints and diseases, and in many places was the only person available to consult.[49]

51

Hjort's suggestion to bring midwife training into line with prevailing conditions and perceived health needs was not well received.[50] The main opponent to this proposal, Fredrik A. Cederschjöld – Professor of Obstetrics and midwife teacher in Stockholm, and the son of the late Professor P.G. Cederschjöld – revised the textbook and deleted the sections that dealt with gynaecology and children's diseases, as he considered that these fields were the province of the doctor.[51] This action was later criticized in an article published in 1884 in the *Tidskrift för hemmet*, one of Sweden's first widely read women's magazines.[52]

A COMPARISON WITH NEIGHBOURING COUNTRIES

As has been indicated, during the nineteenth century Swedish midwives were enabled to play a major role within maternity care and the public health sector. This situation seems to have been facilitated by the large number of midwives in relation to doctors. Compared with its neighbouring countries – Denmark, Norway, and Finland – Sweden had an extremely large number of midwives in relation to the number of doctors. In 1870 the ratio for Sweden was 3.11 midwives for every doctor. In the same year the figure was 1.63 in Finland, 1.42 in Norway, and 1.4 in Denmark in 1871. There seem to have been yet higher ratios of midwives earlier in the nineteenth century in contrast to Norway, Finland, and Denmark.[53]

If one considers the differences between these countries regarding the midwife's right to use obstetrical instruments and compares this with factors such as wealth, the degree of urbanization, and the density of doctors, a pattern emerges that indicates that the midwife's role could be extended under certain circumstances. Thus, in conclusion, at least amongst the Scandinavian countries, it seems to hold true that midwives could be given greater freedom of action in a poor and only partially urbanized country, which accordingly had a low effective demand for and low density of doctors. In Denmark, the wealthiest and the most urbanized of the Scandinavian countries in the second half of the nineteenth century, midwives never seem to have been allowed to use any instruments whatsoever. Denmark also had the highest density of doctors and midwives, at least in the 1870s (see Figure 2.4). Next to Denmark, in the second half of the nineteenth century, in terms of wealth, urbanization, and the density of doctors, was Norway,

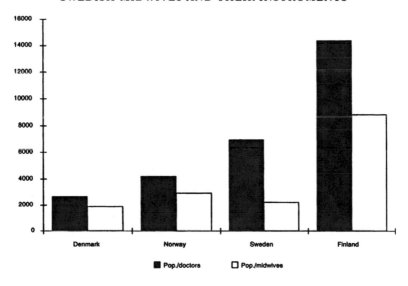

Figure 2.4 The number of inhabitants per midwife and per doctor in Norway, Sweden, Finland (1870) and Denmark (1871)
Sources: BiSOS, K. Helso- och sjukvården, 1870, pp. 66–7; *Historisk statistik för Sverige,* Table 4, pp. 46–8; G. Kearns, R.W. Lee and J. Rogers, 'The interaction of political and economic factors in the management of urban public health', in M.C. Nelson and J. Rogers (eds) 'Urbanisation and the Epidemiologic Transition', *(Meddelanden från Familjehistoriska projektet,* Department of History, Uppsala University)), Uppsala, 1989, Table 39, p. 66; B. von Bonsdorff, *The History of Learning and Science in Finland 1828–1918. Vol. III: The History of Medicine in Finland 1828–1918,* Helsinki, The Finnish Society of Sciences, 1975, p. 22; K. Lundström-Björk, '"Ett himmelrike för barnaföderskor". En etnologisk undersökning kring anstaltsförlossningens genombrott i Jakobstad', *Jakobstads museums publikationer,* Jakobstad, 1990, p. 22; *Norges Offisielle Statistik. Historisk Statistik,* Oslo, Statistisk Sentralbyrå, 1969, Table 34, p. 58; V. Falbe-Hansen and W. Scharling, *Danmarks Statistik,* vol. 5. Kjøbenhavn, 1881, pp. 80–1, 82, and *Statistiske undersögelser Nr 19. Befolkningsudvikling og sundhetsforhold 1901–60,* Köpenhamn, Det statistiske Departement, 1966, Table II.

where instrumental authorization was given on a half-permitted/half-forbidden basis, but never institutionalized.[54] It was, for instance, not illegal to teach a midwife how to use forceps; neither was it especially encouraged. Midwives never received a thorough training in the use of forceps, and it never became possible for them to become licensed or authorized for the task of applying them.

After Denmark and Norway, in terms of the same criteria – wealth, urbanization, and the density of doctors – was Sweden, with Finland coming last.[55] The latter two countries were poor, rural, and had low densities of doctors. The instrumental authorization of midwives was also implemented in both of these countries, with Finland giving midwives the right to use instruments in 1879.[56] Sweden's density of midwives was, however, much higher than in Finland; it was also higher than in Norway and almost as high as in Denmark. The number of midwives authorized to use instruments also seems to have been very small in Finland at least in comparison with Sweden. According to information that the Swedish doctor E.W. Wretlind received from the Finnish Professor of Obstetrics, Josef Pippingsköld, in 1883 only a small fraction of midwives in Finland received a training in the use of instruments.[57] The number of operations undertaken by Finnish midwives was also very low, especially in comparison with the number in Sweden. In 1890 510 forceps operations were carried out by Swedish midwives and only 49 by Finnish midwives; the Swedish midwives, also allowing for demographic differences, performed more than five times as many forceps procedures as their contemporaries in Finland.[58]

STATE, POVERTY AND MILITARY NEEDS

As the comparison with neighbouring countries has shown, the character of the Swedish midwife created during the nineteenth century was governed by harsh economic circumstances. Sweden was a poor, rural country with a small population spread over a large area. These factors, in combination with the state's need for a large and healthy population and the leading medical men's struggle to organize a nationwide medical system, created a situation in which it was necessary to allow midwives to take a major role. Not only were midwives trained in large numbers, but their responsibilities within maternity care and public health were extended during the nineteenth century. This course of events has indisputably been important in determining the relatively strong position that Swedish midwives hold today. It is, in other words, a position that came about as an effect of poverty.

Military needs have also played an important role in Swedish midwives' history. The importance of trained midwives was from the very beginning linked to the nation's need for strong and healthy soldiers. In the first Swedish obstetrical textbook, published by Johan von Hoorn in 1697, it was stated that trained midwives would not only save babies' and mothers' lives but would also provide the country with soldiers and make it possible for the nation to live in peace.[59] The midwife's position was also greatly strengthened in the 1820s when the poor quality of the military recruits was pinpointed as a national problem. Alarming reports regarding ill health amongst recruits also led to improved maternal and child welfare provision in other countries, but at a much later stage. In England, for instance, it took until the turn of the century and the Boer War before this problem attained national importance and triggered off improvements in the area of maternal and child welfare.[60]

Swedish midwives were also brought in again in the 1930s as agents to improve maternity services. In this decade, and fitting into a European pattern, the falling Swedish birth-rate again became a question of political importance.[61] It was declared that the Swedes were a dying race and that the nation was seriously threatened as the falling birth-rate, amongst other factors, increased the risk of war. In the concluding report of the Population Committee, set up in 1935 to deal with this question, it was declared furthermore that it was necessary to strengthen the health of the coming generations in order to prevent invasion by undesirable races.[62] A number of social reforms were enforced and military needs opened up a new field of action for midwives.

It is apparent that these needs have played an important part, and in combination with other factors, determined the role of midwives within the Swedish health system. The midwives have simply been brought in to act time and again, not only as deliverers of babies, but also as deliverers of the nation. Poverty and military needs seem, in other words, to have been prerequisites for the attainment of the Swedish midwives' relatively strong position.

ACKNOWLEDGEMENTS

I would like to thank Lynn Karlsson and the editors for thoughtful comments and careful reading.

NOTES

1 For midwives' work in the health service, see L. Milton, 'Barnmorskan i välfärdsstaten. En yrkeskårs förändring mellan 1930 och 1960', unpublished paper, Department of History, Uppsala University, 1994, p. 7. Routine medical examinations have traditionally been carried out by a doctor, either a general practitioner or an obstetrician/ gynaecologist. Also, it is considered advisable that every pregnant woman arranges a check-up with a doctor. The necessity for these

examinations is, however, under discussion, and it seems possible that in the future they will not be carried out to the same extent.

2 Midwives' rights and duties were regulated by specific midwife statutes up until 1994, when the regulations were replaced by a new law, which gave overall responsibility to all health care personnel. The law of 1994 includes more general principles as to how health professionals should act and contains only eighteen paragraphs. As a result of the new law, a new description of midwives' competence is being prepared. The rights stated in the old regulation are expected to be included in the revised description. For midwife regulation prior to 1994, see B. Sjölenius, *Hälso- och sjukvårdsrätt. Del I: Personalen i hälso- och sjukvården*, Lund, Lund Studentlitteratur, 1989, pp. 425–7, and, for the new law, see *Svensk författningssamling*, Stockholm, Norstedt, 1995, no. 953, pp. 1932–5. The decision as to whether a complicated delivery should be undertaken by a midwife or a doctor varies from clinic to clinic. There are no general instructions, and the conduct of individual deliveries seems to depend very much on the obstetrician in charge.

3 *Bidrag till Sveriges officiella statistik (BiSOS), K. Helso- och sjukvården*, Stockholm, Norstedt, 1900, Table 29.

4 This chapter is based on research in progress to be presented as a thesis, published in Swedish, in 1997: 'Doctors' professionalization and the regulation of midwifery. A study of the Swedish Midwife-system c. 1663–1860'.

5 V. Djurberg, *Läkaren Johan von Hoorn. Förlossningskonstens grundläggare i Sverige*, Uppsala, Almqvist and Wicksell, 1942, pp. 12–24, 30–1, 39–40, 58–71, 76–83, 276.

6 For mercantilism, see E.F. Heckscher, *Sveriges ekonomiska historia från Gustav Vasa. Del II: Det moderna Sveriges grundläggning*, part 2, Stockholm, Albert Bonniers, 1949, pp. 812–90; L. Magnusson, 'Korruption och borgerlig ordning. Naturrätt och ekonomisk diskurs i Sverige under Frihetstiden', in *Uppsala Papers in Economic History*, Research report no. 20, Department of Economic History, Uppsala University, 1989. For an English translation of E.F. Heckscher's work on mercantilism, see *Mercantilism* (with a new introduction by L. Magnusson), London and New York, Routledge, 1994.

7 See the Health Commission's annual report of 1755, the Statistical Bureau's report of 1761, and the *Collegium Medicum*'s parliamentary report of 1765. See also the economist Johan Fredrik Kryger's booklet presented by the Swedish Academy of Science in 1763, and the textbook that Sweden's first Professor in Economics, Anders Berch, published in 1747. Berch's book was in use at Swedish universities well into the nineteenth century. For these works, see O.E.A. Hjelt, *Svenska och finska medicinalverkets historia 1663–1812*, vol. 2, Helsingfors, Central-Tryckeriet, 1892, pp. 481–2; H. Sandblad, *Världens nordligaste läkare. Medicinalväsendets första insteg i Nordskandinavien 1750–1810*, Stockholm, Almqvist–Wicksell, 1979, pp. 7–9, 11; J. Pontén, *Gudar, präster och läkekonst*, Södertälje, Fingraf, 1980, p. 21, and S. Lindroth, *Svensk lärdomshistoria. Frihetstiden*, Södertälje, Fingraf, 1989, 2nd edn, pp. 98–101.

8 See, for instance, the estimates and comments on the mortality figures

of 1749 given by the *Collegium Medicum* at the request of Parliament. See also the Statistical Bureau's report of 1755: K. Johannisson, *Det mätbara samhället*. *Statistik och samhällsdröm i 1700-talets Europa*, Stockholm, Norstedt, 1988, p. 172, and Sandblad, *Världens nordligaste läkare*, p. 8. For a shorter English presentation, see K. Johannisson, 'The people's health: public health policies in Sweden', in D. Porter (ed.) *The History of Public Health and the Modern State*, Amsterdam, Rodopi, 1994, pp. 166–9.

 9 Hjelt, *Svenska och finska medicinalverkets historia*, pp. 486, 521.

10 For the number of births at the maternity hospital, see L. Lindgren, 'Från barnbördshus till modern kvinnoklinik', in Allmänna Barnbördshuset direktion (eds) *Allmänna Barnbördshuset 200 år 1775 23/6 1975*, Stockholm, LiberTryck, 1975, p. 17. For the total number of births in Sweden, see BiSOS, A. *Befolkningsstatistik*, 1861, p. LIV.

11 Hjelt, *Svenska och finska medicinalverkets historia*, p. 482.

12 For Scania, see E. Essen-Möller, 'Bidrag till förlossningskonstens och den obstetriska undervisningens historia i Skåne. Ett bidrag till Lunds universitets historia', in *Lunds universitets årsskrift*, Lund and Leipzig, C.W.K. Gleerup and Otto Harrassowitz, 1943, vol. 39, pp. 38–47.

13 B. Lundqvist, 'Det svenska barnmorskeväsendets historia', in B. Lundqvist (ed.), *Svenska barnmorskor*, Stockholm, Svenska Barnmorskeförbundet, 1940, pp. 62, 73–9, and Hjelt, *Svenska och finska medicinalverkets historia*, pp. 498, 504–5, 509–10.

14 H. Schützercrants, *Tal, om Den tilväxt och de hinder, som Barn-Förlossnings-Vetenskapen haft i flere åldrar til närvarande tid*, Stockholm, Johan Georg Lange, 1777.

15 H. Nicander, 'Utdrag af Tabell- Verket angående Födde och Döde i Sverige Åren 1806–1810', *Kongl. Vetenskaps Akademiens Handlingar*, 1813, pp. 66–8; S. Carlsson – J. Rosén, *Svensk historia*, vol. 2, Stockholm, Alb. Bonniers, 1970, 3rd edn, pp. 229, 255–6.

16 For the keen debate regarding health care improvements, see the medical journal *Vettenskaps-Journal för Läkare och Fältskärer*, 1810, vol. 1, nos 3 and 4, where articles from newspapers and magazines as well as parliamentary protocol, etc. were reprinted.

17 'Kongl. Maj:ts Nådiga Förordnande af en Committé för allmänna Läkarevården den 24 Maji 1810', in *Handlingar angående Medicinska kunskapers inhämtande af blifvande Prester, för att dermed kunna gå Församlingarnes innevånare tillhanda*, Stockholm, J.P. Lindh, 1818, p. 1.

18 Riksarkivet: Kommittéarkiv intill 1900 (ÄK 681), Kommitté ang. läkarevården, no. 55, dated 18 Jan. 1812, and *Collegium Medicums* arkiv, E1A Kungliga brev, vol. 15, no. 192, dated 16 Dec. 1812.

19 Lundqvist, 'Det svenska barnmorskeväsendets historia', pp. 91–7.

20 Riksarkivet: Sundhetskollegiets skrivelser till Kungl. Maj:t, vol. 42, no. 576, dated 7 July 1823.

21 For Cederschjöld's letter to the National Board of Health in 1824, the Board's letter to the Crown in 1828, and the Crown's response to the Board's letter in 1829, see Riksarkivet: Sundhetskollegiet, E2 Inkomna handlingar, allmän serie, vol. 21, no. 1126, dated 24 May 1824;

Sundhetskollegiets skrivelser till Kungl. Maj:t, vol. 54, no. 12, dated 29 Dec. 1828; E1A Kungliga brev, vol. 7 no. 3, dated 21 Feb. 1829.

22 For the royal letter, see Riksarkivet: Sundhetskollegiet, E1A Kungliga brev, vol. 34, no. 42, dated 4 April 1858. See also Lundqvist, 'Det svenska barnmorskeväsendets historia', p. 114.

23 See, for instance, the following reports at Riksarkivet: Sundhetskollegiets skrivelser till Kungl. Maj:t, vol. 35, no. 68, dated 20 Dec. 1819 and Sundhetskollegiet, BlA Koncept, vol. 9, no. 141, dated 26 Feb. 1821.

24 Riksarkivet: Sundhetskollegiets arkiv, E1A Kungliga brev, vol. 4, no. 66, dated 8 Aug. 1822.

25 Kilian's judgement was discussed at several meetings of the Swedish Medical Society in 1849–50: E. Nachmansson, 'Bidrag till kännedom om Pehr Gustaf Cederschjölds liv och verksamhet', Svenska Läkaresällskapets Handlingar, 1926, vol. 52, pp. 231–3.

26 Svensk Författningssamling för år 1919, Stockholm, Norstedt, 1920, p. 2295, paragraph 14; O. Gröné, 'Något om barnmorskorna och barnbördshusen. Bidrag till förlossningskonstens historia under 1900-talets första deccennier', Svenska läkartidningen, 1949, vol. 46, p. 2568.

27 A. Hollberg, Medicinalstyrelsens förslag till nya barnmorskeförfattningar, Stockholm, Isaac Marcus, 1906, pp. 46–7.

28 E.W. Wretlind, 'Barnmorskeyrkets sociala ställning och betydelse förr och nu', Jordemodern, 1893, vol. 6, p. 166.

29 BiSOS, A. Befolkningsstatistik, 1894, Table 13, pp. 32–3.

30 Allmän hälso- och sjukvård 1916, Stockholm, Norstedt, 1919, Table L, p. 30 and Allmän hälso- och sjukvård 1920, Stockholm, Norstedt, 1922, Table I, p. 28.

31 Statistisk Årsbok för Sverige 1921, Stockholm, Norstedt, 1921, Table 40, p. 44 and Statistisk Årsbok för Sverige 1927, Table 48, p. 59.

32 Statement based upon an assertion made by the Swedish midwife teacher and Professor of Obstetrics Gustaf Fredrik Hjort which he, in turn, based on the discussions he had with medical colleagues in Europe during a study trip in 1854–55. See G.F. Hjort, 'Barnmorskornas i Sverige utöfning af den operativa förlossningskonsten', Forhandlinger ved de Skandinaviske Naturforskeres Ottende Møde, i Kiøbenhavn fra den 8de til den 14de juli 1860, Kiøbenhavn, Thieles Bogtrykkeri, 1861, p. 860.

33 Ibid., p. 873.

34 Sundhets-Collegii Underdåniga Berättelse om Medicinalverket i Riket, Stockholm, Norstedt, 1860, p. 196; BiSOS, K. Helso- och sjukvården, 1880, Table 27; G. Kearns, R.W. Lee and J. Rogers, 'The interaction of political and economic factors in the management of urban public health', in M.C. Nelson and J. Rogers (eds) 'Urbanisation and the Epidemiologic Transition' (Meddelanden från Familjehistoriska projektet, Department of History, Uppsala University), Uppsala, 1989, Table 39, p. 66.

35 Historisk statistik för Sverige. Del. 1. Befolkning 1720–1967, Stockholm, KL Beckmans Tryckeri, 1969, 2nd edn, Table 4, p. 46; BiSOS, K. Helso- och sjukvården, 1869, pp. 86–7, and G.F. Berggren, 'Bidrag till Sveriges provinsialläkarestatistik', Eira. Tidskrift för Helso- och Sjukvård, 1877, vol. 1, pp. 668–9.

36 It is not possible to provide a full list of footnotes for this section, as it is based upon an extensive examination of the reports concerning maternity care, that the provincial governors were obliged to send to the National Board of Health every year. For a full list, see my forthcoming thesis. For the reports that have been used, see Riksarkivet: Sundhetskollegiets arkiv, Inkomna handlingar, E16B Uppgifter om barnmorskor, vols 1–17. See also printed excerpts concerning maternity care from the district medical officer's report in *Sundhets-Collegii Underdåniga Berättelse.*

37 For the continuing role of 'unqualified' midwives and opposition to this, see the chapters by Løkke, Loudon, Marland, Mottram and Thompson in this volume.

38 Lundqvist, 'Det svenska barnmorskeväsendets historia', p. 124.

39 Ibid., p. 126.

40 *Sundhets-Collegii Underdåniga Berättelse,* 1857, p. 287.

41 For the National Board of Health as well as the Crown's view of this matter, see Riksarkivet: Sundhetskollegiet, B1A, Koncept, vol. 22, no. 783, dated 3 April 1834 and Sundhetskollegiets arkiv, E1A, Kungliga brev, vol. 10, no. 36, dated 26 April 1834.

42 Riksarkivet: Sundhetskollegiets skrivelser till Kung. Maj:t, vol. 57, no. 426, dated 25 Aug. 1831.

43 *BiSOS, K. Helso- och sjukvården,* 1861, p. 55.

44 E.W. Wretlind, 'Böra läkare åtaga sig vården af normala förlossningar?', *Eira. Tidskrift för Helso- och Sjukvård,* 1884, vol. 8, p. 323.

45 For the National Board of Health's letter to the Crown (1 Jan. 1840), see Riksarkivet: Sundhetskollegiets skrivelser till Kungl. Maj:t, vol. 71, no. 6, dated 1 Jan. 1840. For the public health role of midwives, see also the chapters by Løkke, Marland, and Mottram in this volume.

46 For midwife statutes, see Lundqvist, 'Det svenska barnmorskeväsendets historia', pp. 91–7, 106–12, 115–22.

47 See, for instance, the printed excerpts concerning maternity care in the district medical officers' reports, in *Sundhets-Collegii Underdåniga Berättelse.* See especially the excerpts concerning the province of Kristianstad (1855, p. 269); the province of Malmöhus, Höganäs district (1857, p. 285); the province of Skaraborg, Mariestad's district (1855, p. 266), and the province of Södermanland, Nyköpings district (1852, p. 228 and 1858, p. 230).

48 See, for instance, P.G. Cederschjöld, *Handbok för barnmorskor,* Stockholm, Carl Deleen, 2nd edn, 1829, pp. 292–305, and the 7th edn of the same book, Stockholm, Adolf Bonnier, 1868, pp. 306–31 and 352–61.

49 Hjort, 'Barnmorskornas i Sverige utöfning af den operativa förlossningskonsten', pp. 875–7 and G.F. Hjort *Om utsträckning af Barnmorskeundervisningen. Föredrag vid Skandinaviska Naturforskare-mötet i Stockholm 1863,* Götborg, A. Lindgren, 1866, pp. 21–3.

50 G.F. Hjort, *Om qvinnans utöfning af läkarevården, samt om hennes utbildande härför,* Göteborg, Handelstidningens Bolags tryckeri, 1869, p. 4.

51 F.A. Cederschjöld, *Lärobok för barnmorskor*, Stockholm, P.A. Norstedt & Söner, 1873.

52 'Svenska qvinnors verksamhet inom olika grenar af läkarekonstens område', *Tidskrift för hemmet*, *Tillegnad Nordens qvinnor*, 1884, vol. 26, pp. 261–4.

53 See sources for Figure 2.4.

54 I. Blom, '*Den haarde Dyst*'. *Fødsler og fødselshjelp gjennom 150 år*, Oslo, J.W. Cappelens, 1988, pp. 68–72.

55 According to calculations on the GDP-ratio for the year 1873, Denmark's national product per capita was 10 per cent higher than Norway's, while the Swedish national product per capita was a little more than half of Denmark's. Finland had the lowest national product per capita. In 1860 (and respectively in 1880) the degree of urbanization in each of the Nordic countries was the following: Denmark 23 per cent (28 per cent), Norway 15 per cent (20 per cent), Sweden 11 per cent (15 per cent), Finland 6 per cent (8 per cent). See O. Krantz and C-A. Nilsson, 'Relative income levels in the Scandinavian countries', *Economy and History*, 1974, vol. XVII, pp. 59–60, and L. Jörberg, 'Den ekonomiska utvecklingen i de nordiska länderna 1850–1914', unpublished paper, Department of Economic History, Lund University, 1980, p. 2 and Table 4, p. 11.

56 Information kindly given by Lea Henriksson with reference to S-L. Hänninen's book *Kätilötyön vaiheita*, Helsinki, Kustannusosakeyhtiö Otava, 1965, page reference unknown. See also G. Heinricius, *Obstetrikens och gynäkologiens historia i Finland under 18de och 19de århundradet*, Helsingfors, Frenckellska Tryckeri-Aktiebolag, 1903, p. 429.

57 Wretlind, 'Böra läkare', p. 323.

58 *Bidrag till Finlands officiela statistik. XI. Medicinalverket 1890*, Helsingfors, 1892, p. 94, and *BiSOS, K. Helso- och sjukvården*, 1890, Table 30. As is specified in *Statistiske undersögelser Nr 19*, Table I, p. 10 the Finnish population, during this period, was half that of Sweden's.

59 L. Milton, 'Från jordgumma till edsvuren barnmorska. staten och baranafödandet under svensk stormaktstid', unpublished paper, Department of History, Uppsala University, 1992, p. 15.

60 J. Lewis, *The Politics of Motherhood: Child and Maternal Welfare in England, 1900–1939*, London, Croom Helm, 1980, pp. 12, 15.

61 Milton, 'Barnmorskan i välfärdsstaten', pp. 17, 19.

62 E. Eglán, *Genus och politik. En jämförelse mellan svensk och fransk abort- och preventivmedelspolitik från sekelskiftet till andra världskriget*, Uppsala, Acta Universitatis Upsaliensis, 1994, pp. 240–1.

3

HOW TO BE A MIDWIFE IN LATE NINETEENTH-CENTURY SPAIN

Teresa Ortiz and Clara Martínez Padilla

Since the mid-eighteenth century Spanish midwifery has been shaped along gender lines, differentiating between male theory, obstetric surgical science, and mostly female practice, in one of the few professions carried out by women. After the mid-eighteenth century surgeons controlled access to midwifery, directing midwife training through the *Colegios de Cirugía* (Colleges of Surgery), and the surgeons, the physicians, and the local authorities governed the profession between them.[1] In this chapter we shall analyse the changes that took place with respect to access to the profession throughout the nineteenth century, and the practice of midwifery in the city of Granada at the beginning of the twentieth century.

In the first half of the nineteenth century, surgery and medicine were combined into one occupational category, and teaching was imparted in the faculties of medicine and their clinics. This process was accompanied by one of the worst periods of regulatory chaos in the history of the Spanish health professions, and a multitude of degrees and diplomas came and went.[2] In the midst of this confusion of rules, terminology and prerogatives, the situation of the *matronas* or *parteras* (midwives) remained unchanged, with scarcely any challenge or modification taking place until 1861, when new regulations were imposed. These were based on the 1857 *Ley Moyano*, a law regulating public education, which laid down rules for the training of midwives without, however, modifying their sphere of responsibility, which had been formally limited to attendance at normal deliveries since the mid-eighteenth century.

TERESA ORTIZ AND CLARA MARTÍNEZ PADILLA

ACCESS TO THE PROFESSION OF MIDWIFERY

The new 1861 regulations increased the number of places in Spain where would-be midwives could acquire a qualification. To the ancient *Colegios de Cirugía* in Barcelona, Madrid and Cadiz, already converted into faculties of medicine and surgery, were added the faculties of Granada, Santiago, Valencia and Valladolid.[3] Students of midwifery were now obliged to gain practical experience in maternity homes or in hospitals with delivery wards, as well as to study theory over four semesters, each lasting for six months, in daily 1½ hour classes, for a total of 850 hours. These theory classes were given in hospitals by one of the physicians who, though not a member of the university, was authorized to teach by the university rector.[4] The curriculum included basic obstetric theory, practical midwifery, post-delivery nursing of the mother and baby, and the care and 'spiritual' support of the new-born, including instructions on how to conduct the baptism ceremony. At the end of the course, it was obligatory to undergo a final qualifying examination (*Reválida*) in the university itself, before a tribunal of three professors.[5]

The 1861 regulations, whose principles were preserved until the beginning of the twentieth century, broke with a hundred-year-old tradition of training midwives within academic precincts.[6] They also set out the training of *practicantes* (medical assistants), an occupational group created by the *Ley Moyano*. This group inherited the long and diverse tradition of the practitioners of minor surgery which had existed since the reform of surgical studies during the Spanish Enlightenment in the second half of the eighteenth century. *Practicantes* and midwives figured in the new law as doctors' assistants. The former were charged with 'the mechanical and auxiliary part of surgery', which included dressing the patients' wounds, administering remedies, giving vaccinations, blood-letting, and 'the arts of the dentist and the chiropodist'. Midwives were to perform normal deliveries, to attend women in their confinements, and to function as 'mere assistants' to the doctor in complicated cases.[7] Each occupational category involved a clear gender assignment. Midwifery was an explicitly female activity, and, although women were not expressly prohibited from access to the career of *practicante*, it remained a male preserve. The age requirements for admission to the course differed too, with a younger minimum age limit (16 years) for *practicante* entrants than for the midwives (20 years). It was also obligatory for the midwife pupils to be married or widowed, and to be of 'proven morality'.[8] Aspirant *practicantes* and midwives had to pass an elementary education examination, the contents differing according to the gender of the applicant. Geometry, physics and natural history were tested in the young men, while artistic drawing and domestic hygiene were exclusive to the young women.[9]

The application of the 1861 regulations seems to have had a negative effect on the total number of midwives qualifying; the figure fell by some 30 per cent over the next eight years and did not recover until the 1870s (Table 3.1). The increase in the number of universities where qualifications could be gained, and the increase, in theory, of centres of training, do not appear to have been sufficient to compensate, however, for the formidable demands of the *Moyano* law. The prerequisite level of education could still only be obtained by very few, and the requirement stipulating the necessity for hospital training was utopian. In fact, in 1865, the office of the Secretariat of the University of Madrid issued a warning in the medical press that there was still no maternity home in the area authorized to give the necessary practical training to midwives.[10] Two of the universities that had recently become involved in the training of midwives, Santiago and Valladolid, had scarcely begun to award diplomas.

Table 3.1 Number of midwives qualifying in Spanish universities, 1853–1912

Years	Total	B	M	S	Number by university V	G	Sa	Va	Z	Other
1853–60	170	81	15	14	53	6	0	0	0	1
1861–68*	121	61	16	12	25	5	1	1	0	0
1877–82	202	82	39	21	41	11	0	4	4	0
1883–88	264	157	19	27	19	17	2	1	20	2
1889–94	454	198	41	73	64	19	6	5	48	0
1895–90	505	189	55	80	62	17	6	11	82	3
1901–06	585	208	67	100	81	22	8	17	74	8
1907–12	454	153	69	91	59	21	0	17	37	7
Total	2,755	1,129	321	418	404	118	23	56	265	21

Source: AGA, Sección Educación, *Libros de registro de títulos*, numbers 91, 104–6.
Note: B: Barcelona; M: Madrid; S: Sevilla; V: Valencia; G: Granada; Sa: Salamanca; Va: Valladolid; Z: Zaragoza.
* There are no data for the years 1869 to 1876, when the *Libertad de Enseñanza* law was in force.

The new training provisions for midwives and the creation of the title of *practicante* were highly contested amongst physicians, who perceived these developments as constituting a threat to their profession. Although the qualification did not give midwives one iota of autonomy, the simple fact that they had moved back into the public arena awoke abiding jealousies, sparking an age-old conflict of interests, from which the physicians would, nevertheless, continue to emerge the victors.

The criticisms made of the contents of the new law and the calls for its repeal led invariably to the denigration of midwives,[11] who were charged with lacking the interest or qualities necessary to benefit from any training plan whatsoever:

> however much the new plan for midwives wants to instruct them and to teach them morality, they will know no more . . . nor will they have any less envy and resentment towards the physicians who have occasion to judge their conduct.[12]

The liberal revolution of 1868 to 1874 applied its principles of extending individual rights and of political decentralization to education, and freedom of learning and teaching at all levels was decreed.[13] The *Libertad de Enseñanza* law established the right of all Spaniards, whatever their academic qualifications, to open educational centres and to run them according to their own criteria.[14] In the heat of this reform, *enseñanzas libres* (liberalized education courses) of all kinds sprang up both within and beyond the universities. Schools of *practicantes* and midwives run by university lecturers opened in Cadiz and Cordoba. The private Cadiz school was directed by three young lecturers who would, years later, become professors in different faculties of medicine,[15] and offered as its principal novelty the possibility of acquiring a training without having to attend classes:

> the students may do their studies in the towns and villages where they reside, presenting themselves at set times for practical exercises and individual examinations on the materials that they have studied, which will serve as a test for the final examination (*Reválida*).[16]

At least twenty-eight students must have passed through the school, most of them from towns in the province or other cities.[17] In 1871, a new university founded in Cordoba by the provincial government (*Universidad Libre de Córdoba*) started a midwifery course offering theory classes and hospital-based practice, but with a worse response than in Cadiz. In three years only five students had completed their studies.[18]

The *Libertad de enseñanza* policy also opened up an opportunity unheard of in the history of the Spanish midwife profession: it allowed the midwives themselves to be teachers within regulated and recognized educational institutions. At least two schools making use of this provision were created in Madrid between 1868 and 1876. The first, founded between 1868 and 1870, was promoted as a 'special school of obstetrics for ladies or the teaching of midwives' and Francisca Iracheta, a midwife trained at Madrid University, was 'the teacher charged with the theoretical and practical training for deliveries', a task which she performed under the direction of her husband, a doctor of medicine and surgery, José López de Morelle.[19] The school admitted women over 18 years of age, although it warned that the under-twenties and unmarried women would be unable to take their examinations at the university. All entrants were required to have completed or to be engaged in a course of elementary studies, and were offered a training course that could be followed in four to six months.[20] Complementary to the teaching, students were to study a manual written for the purpose by Francisca Iracheta herself. Published in 1870, it was the first of its kind authored by a woman in Spain.[21] Its contents conformed to the national syllabus requirements, and were presented in the form of questions and answers, with the author signalling the points she considered essential for midwives to know. The book contained illustrations as learning aids, as well as 'a pattern for fashioning an artificial pelvis, with which to practise in the absence of a dummy'.[22]

Iracheta's book was one of the first childbirth manuals aimed at midwives to be written in the nineteenth century. It revived, in its format and objectives, a tradition begun in Spain in 1750 by Dr Antonio Medina,[23] whom Iracheta cites in the first few pages.[24] In 1866, the Professor of Obstetrics at the University of Madrid had written what was probably the first nineteenth-century obstetrical manual for midwives. It was 270 pages long, and focused on the female anatomy and the physiology of childbirth. It was written in a language replete with technical terms, which were printed in italics accompanied by a brief explanation. The book was commissioned by the government, probably in an attempt to solve the problem of the shortage and antiquity of Spanish textbooks, and

65

also to contribute to the teaching of midwives in accordance with the 1861 law.[25] Four years later Iracheta's book was published, with a very different perspective, opting for a more pedagogical and direct style, and including a glossary of obstetrical terminology which gave the correct pronunciation 'to avoid [the midwives] feeling foolish among persons of perfect learning'.[26] In 1871, another short manual written by the Professor of Obstetrics at the recently founded *Universidad Libre de Córdoba*[27] added to the range of textbooks on offer, several of which were written by teachers connected to the various midwife training establishments.

Iracheta says in the prologue of her book that she wrote it to contribute to the 'good of all of my kind, and particularly for those of my sex, unjustly disregarded by men'. She demonstrates a strong and decided character in her ideas about her profession, and does not shy away from polemic. She begins by analysing the distinct meanings of the words *matrona* and *partera*, which appear as synonyms in the legal texts and in the medical press, despite the second term's pejorative connotation. It is clear, she wrote, that a *matrona* is 'the practitioner of obstetrics, that is to say of deliveries', while 'any woman who, without training, performs deliveries as an "intruder" or healer, is known only by the name of *partera*'.[28] For Iracheta the profession of midwifery was 'decent, helpful and fitting for women',[29] and 'one of the few resources available to women for making a living for themselves, [and] if necessary for their families'.[30]

Iracheta entered the public arena and appeared in the press under her husband's auspices, something which was obligatory at the time. The new marriage legislation denied wives the possibility of signing contracts or publishing scientific or literary writings as author or translator without the express permission of their husbands.[31] The fact that her husband was a doctor added a useful note of professional authority, reinforced by his proclamation printed at the beginning of the book, which declared him to be 'in complete accord with her doctrines'.[32]

Several years later, in 1875, another midwife, Pilar Jáuregui de Lasbennes, followed Iracheta's path as a teacher in a similar school, and also wrote on professional matters, in the Madrid medical and general press. Jáuregui advertised in the medical press as:

> a practitioner of deliveries, qualified at the Madrid Faculty of Medicine, [who] offers herself to serve as an assistant in those

cases when, due to the duration of the delivery or some other reason, the physicians cannot remain for the necessary time at the side of the women in labour. She has been exercising her profession for a long time, and she has carried out hundreds of deliveries. For this purpose she offers her residence, Calle del Pez, 32.[33]

Months later, the same publication announced the foundation, on her initiative, of a school for midwives which she would herself direct in collaboration with Angel Pulido,[34] a young newly-qualified doctor who would become a 'prominent figure' in the medical profession.[35] The teaching was divided between them, with Jáuregui taking the practice and he the theory. The school was connected to the *Museo Antropológico* (anthropological museum), a scientific institution recently set up by the celebrated surgeon Pedro González de Velasco, proponent of science education reform and largely responsible for the introduction of various experimental disciplines into Spain.[36] Midwifery was taught in the museum school until at least 1878;[37] we have found no further details of its activities thereafter.

Pilar Jáuregui was also connected to the museum circle through her activities in promoting and defending her profession; she published several articles in the journal founded by Dr González de Velasco, *El Anfiteatro Médico Español* (1873–83). As in most of her writings, she argued time and again for a good and continuous theoretical and practical training for midwives, and for the admission to the profession of single women over 20 years old. She also called for the creation of posts funded by the local authorities, and for the prosecution of unauthorized practitioners, who were intruding into midwifery, as a way of promoting the dignity of the profession.[38] When writing on training, she defended the study both of normal and difficult obstetrics and of 'the afflictions of the womb', not to challenge the doctors' authority, but in order to be of assistance to them. This form of collaboration was based strictly on a patriarchal relationship between the sexes, and reflected a vision of the profession in which gender outweighed skill. In tune with the opinions of craniologists and physicians of the period,[39] she believed that her physiological system in general, her greater sensibility, the abnormal circumstances in which the needs of our sex are periodically placed, are further inescapable obstacles ... to achieving the performance of operations like the physician-surgeon.[40] This idea of the woman as a prisoner of her body was not shared by Francisca Iracheta, whose ideological positions were less deterministic and gender-based. Iracheta agreed with Jáuregui in the general objectives of improving and defending the profession, but, although she also agreed with the limitation of midwifery practice to normal deliveries, she declared that:

> nobody believes . . . as far I as know that there may be women as apt and worthy as men to be adorned, like them, with scientific titles, and if any entertain the opposite opinion, all could be resolved if they tested the fitness of both men and women . . ., with repeated and rigorous examinations.[41]

If any doubt should linger that she believed gender to be outweighed by skill, she asked that 'in the case that male midwives were permitted to exist, neither should they be conceded more authority than midwives', claiming that only 'a superior class of doctor' should act in complicated births.[42] In 1870, when Iracheta wrote the above, there were no female doctors in Spain and no woman had ever followed a degree course at university (or studied abroad). The first female students of medicine began their studies three years later, in the midst of a polemic that lasted for more than a decade, with one of the fiercest opponents of this development being Jáuregui's partner, Dr Angel Pulido, who found midwifery, together with nursing, the only fields of medical practice suitable for women.[43]

It is difficult to assess the impact that these Madrid schools had on the training of midwives, because of the scarce information available. At any rate their effect was not reflected at all in the University of Madrid's degree register, where the number qualifying remained obstinately small when compared, not only with a city of similar size like Barcelona, but also with smaller cities at lower levels of economic development, like Seville, Valencia and even Zaragoza (Table 3.1).

In 1876 the *Libertad de Enseñanza* was revoked, and, although private forms of education continued at several educational levels, we hear no more of any midwifery school until the end of the century, and then in a completely different educational and social context. In 1888 a new law was passed, which remained in force until 1904. Faithful to its predecessor in terms of curriculum content, the stipulation of practical sessions in hospital clinics and professional obligations, the law's main innovation was the total removal of any kind of official teaching, including the hospital-based theory classes. The midwives and *practicantes* were now simply expected to 'have previously learned' the knowledge required.[44] It also eliminated the age, marital and elementary education requirements for entrants, and seems to have had a positive effect on the number of graduates. Between 1877 and 1882 the number qualifying increased rapidly – representing the greatest increase of the sixty-year period examined – not only at the universities of Madrid, Seville, Valencia and Zaragoza, but also in the country as a whole (Table 3.1).

To acquire the precise training necessary to gain a qualification, schools like the Barcelona 'Academia de Matronas – run by reputable teachers of the faculty of medicine' must have been essential. It operated between 1893 and 1900 and advertised in *El eco de las matronas*, the first professional journal for midwives.[45] Unlike its Madrid predecessors, there were no outstanding midwife teachers; on the contrary, the instruction appears to have been dominated by anonymous male university teachers, whose names remain unidentified during eight years of advertisement. The academy's director, also editor of the journal, was the gynaecologist Juan Doménech. It is unknown whether he shared the teaching with his wife Concepción Pérez Tomás, a midwife and the editorial assistant of *El eco* between 1893 and 1895.[46] The academy seems to have been successful, and took students from all four Catalan provinces.[47]

The academy also provided training for *practicantes*, who, at the beginning of the century became a threat to midwives, as a result of their authorization to attend childbirths. In 1901 *practicantes* began to receive an elementary education in obstetrics,[48] and in 1902 the title of '*practicante* authorized for the performance of normal deliveries' was created.[49] This qualification was only valid for practice in towns with fewer than 10,000 inhabitants, and opened up a new market that was probably not fully served by trained midwives. Nevertheless it posed an undeniable threat to the monopoly that midwives had enjoyed for centuries, and added significantly to the credentials of a profession that was increasing in strength and organization.[50] The *practicantes* took full advantage of new opportunity, with 177 of them obtaining the qualification between 1901 and 1906, and 301 over the following six years.[51] This increase coincided with a reduction in the number of midwives qualifying over the same period (Table 3.1). Although nothing prevented women from studying to be *practicantes*, they did not choose this professional path and remained faithful to a career in which, paradoxically, they achieved neither autonomy nor even a leading role.[52]

PRACTISING MIDWIFERY IN GRANADA AT THE TURN OF THE CENTURY

Once midwives had completed their studies, they were able to exercise their profession either privately, or within a public institution, or both, for the two activities were not deemed incompatible. The cities offered the greatest opportunities for employment, but competition was also much stronger there. In 1900 the city of Granada had a population of almost 76,000 with an economy based on recently introduced sugar-refining industries and the service sector. It boasted some ten midwives and 105 physicians.[53] Only three or four of these midwives would have occupied paid public posts.

The most important public welfare institution was the *Beneficencia Provincial*, funded by the provincial government, which ran the city hospitals.[54] (From the mid-nineteenth century, the *Beneficencia Municipal* and *Beneficencia Provincial* had set up welfare provisions, including medical services, for the poor, though levels of services varied greatly.) In Granada, provisions for maternity cases were made at the maternity home, where all cases of full-term pregnancy that applied were attended, and the wards of the provincial hospital, San Juan de Dios, which dedicated itself to premature deliveries.[55] Care in the wards of the provincial hospital came under the jurisdiction of the Professor of Obstetrics of the faculty of medicine, and they were staffed by doctors and student interns. There are no reports of midwives being appointed there between 1873 and 1923, although it was probably in the wards that pupil midwives gained their practical experience in the first years of the century. In the maternity home, however, the staff consisted of a surgeon, a nurse, a porter, and a midwife, who had to be resident there.[56] This unique position for a midwife within the *Beneficencia Provincial* was in great demand, and several midwives held the post in succession. The first of these, Eloisa Vílchez, resided in the home between 1885 and 1894,[57] and received a salary which rose from 912 pesetas in 1886 to 1,250 in 1888.[58] This considerable increase over two years seems to have been in response to a demand

70

presented by Eloisa Vílchez herself, in which she protested about her increased workload and the abolition of her *ración*, ('allowance' or payment in kind) which she had hitherto enjoyed.[59] The salary and accommodation seem to have formed an attractive combination, to the point where the provincial government was requested to open her post to public competition, a petition that was eventually turned down.[60]

For its part, Granada City Council set up, as one aspect of its welfare provision, the *Beneficencia Municipal*, an organization to care for poor inhabitants requiring medical attention but not hospital admission. In 1893 it created a casualty service based in the city's *Casa de Socorro* (assistance house), where municipal doctors provided all kinds of health care, including attendance at deliveries.[61] For births, however, they counted on the 'assistance' of one of the two municipal midwives or their substitutes. These midwives, unlike the doctors, were not on permanent duty in the *Casa de Socorro* but were called when required, so they could continue to carry out their other private or public work, attending home deliveries in different parts of the city.[62] Within the *Casa de Socorro*, the function of the municipal matron was limited to that of assistant to the doctor, while outside in the mothers' homes or in her own house, she could perform her work with greater autonomy.[63]

Both normal and complicated deliveries took place in the *Casa de Socorro*, although, for the latter, the city also had special clinics at the San Juan de Dios hospital and at the maternity home. In any case, the 'complicated' deliveries assisted at the *Casa* could not have been too serious, as there were no beds for the hospitalization of patients. However, the number of complicated cases grew, from 28 in 1899[64] to 54 in 1904,[65] the only period for which we have data. This seems to indicate a growing interest and participation in deliveries on the part of the municipal doctors, although it is not known whether this was in collaboration with the municipal midwives or at their expense.

By 1895 the Granada *Beneficencia Municipal* had its first *matronas titulares* (official midwives), Pilar Ortiz Grimaud and Cristina Martín,[66] and at the beginning of 1896 another three were nominated as assistant midwives at the *Casa de Socorro*,[67] honorary posts for which there was no remuneration except when they had to substitute for one of the office holders for a period longer than fifteen days.[68] Pay does not appear in any case to have been the key reason for midwives' participation in the municipal health services. The

71

annual salary budgeted for the official midwives was 500 pesetas in 1893,[69] which fell to half that figure in 1896,[70] and disappeared altogether in 1899, because of 'the recent economies agreed'.[71] These economies do not seem to have affected the rest of the municipal health functionaries who continued to collect their salaries, all of which were higher, from the 1,250 pesetas paid to the veterinary surgeon to 2,000 for the chief physician. Apart from the midwives, the person in the *Casa de Socorro* with the smallest income was the porter, who earned 1,000 pesetas.[72] Outside the world of public functionaries, the city's unskilled labourers earned 540 pesetas in the mid-1880s, somewhat more than the midwives.[73] The inequality of salaries was not peculiar to Granada City Council, but was standard in industry too, which consigned women's work to the cheapest and most ancillary categories, thus helping to perpetuate the patriarchal social order.[74]

In 1904 a new system of payments was approved by the city council, giving five pesetas for every delivery attended.[75] This new form of remuneration, probably combined with the demand for midwives' services, must have encouraged a slow increase in the number of places, for by 1917 there were seven municipal midwives, assigned to different districts of the city.[76]

In any case, the low and at times non-existent pay of the midwives suggests the possibility that these posts were sought after as part of a professional strategy, to achieve qualifications and recognition for the purposes of obtaining work in the private sector. Angustias Sánchez Martín, who had been established in private practice in the city centre since 1889,[77] claimed as much when in 1896 she secured the post of assistant matron at the *Casa de Socorro*, with the sole aim of 'achieving the corresponding qualification'.[78] Most of her colleagues referred to their public positions in local press advertisements and on the doors of their houses, using their municipal work to guarantee their professional status.[79] Midwives normally engaged in private practice alone and associations between them were rare. Working with a physician was somewhat more common, and had already been tried out in the field of teaching. This collaboration must have provided a reciprocal warranty, with the doctor conferring his scientific authority and the midwife her moral authority, thus neutralizing the force of custom in questions of reproduction and sexuality without altering the gender structure of the organization of the professions. We do not know the terms of this collaboration, but we can suppose that it was largely subject to the principles of professional subordination that governed all the legislative norms. It is not surprising that broad sectors of the Spanish medical profession expressed great animosity and hostility at the arrival of the first medical women,[80] and to their interest in participating equally in the speciality of gynaecology, which was jealously guarded by the male gynaecologists, proponents of the most extreme gender-based medical ideas.[81]

The first midwife at the Granada *Casa de Socorro* shared a consulting room with one of its physicians, at least between 1895 and 1899, a period when the institution admitted a large number of difficult deliveries, as seen above. Advertisements appearing in the local press show the evolution of their professional relationship, as one in which there was a gradual loss of the midwife's importance. Her position shifted from being an autonomous professional, backed by her own curriculum and knowledge, as in:

> Doña Pilar Ortiz Grimaud, a practitioner honoured with a first-class mark in deliveries. Midwife to the *Casa de Socorro* and to *La Sociedad Humanitaria*. Specialist in diseases of the womb. Méndez Núñez, 17[82]

to being endorsed by the physician, although retaining her authority:

> Diseases of the womb. Gynaecological consulting room for the healing of diseases of the womb by the practitioner Doña Pilar Ortiz Grimaud, with a first-class qualification in deliveries, under the direction of Don Manuel Arenas Pérez, physician-surgeon. Méndez Núñez, 17[83]

She ended up, four years later, as the physician's assistant:

> Diseases of the womb. Don Manuel Arenas Pérez, graduated in Medicine and Surgery, is honoured to offer the public his new gynaecological consulting room, specialized in the examination and healing of diseases of the womb. Counting on the assistance of the qualified and intelligent practitioner of deliveries Doña Pilar Ortiz Grimaud, who will examine those patients who so desire. Jesús and María (Street), 3[84]

The inversion of roles was complete. While in the second advertisement appearing in 1895 the physician appeared as an inducement to attend Ortiz's clinic, by 1899 the reverse was the case.

On the other hand, it is clear from the earlier publicity that Ortiz promoted herself as a specialist not only in deliveries, but also in 'diseases of the womb', which raises a question as to the real prerogatives of the midwives, which often exceeded the legal limits of attending normal childbirths. In the same period, María Morales, qualified at the University of Madrid, announced her 'speciality in the healing of sterility'.[85] In 1878 Pilar Jáuregui argued for the instruction of midwives in 'the afflictions of the womb, as it is less distressing for a female to be examined by another woman than by the physician', with midwives having to refer to the physicians in severe cases.[86] Barcelona midwives at the end of the century and the beginning of the twentieth century were often advertised as '(female) surgeons' and even as '(female) physicians', something which caused irritation amongst some physicians, who took advantage of this situation to attack these and all midwives, accusing them of being intruders.[87]

Professional encounters between patient and midwife, for whatever purpose, could take place either in the woman's or the midwife's house. In cities like Granada some midwives established consulting hours for receiving patients,[88] and in the largest cities this was the norm, as in Barcelona, where 72 per cent of those practising in 1929 had consulting hours.[89] It was also common for them to offer bedrooms to those women needing them, as did several midwives in Granada and Barcelona between 1895 and 1929.[90] Rosalía de Queral, for example, maintained a flat near Barcelona's railway station where she offered

> board and lodging for pregnant women with attendance at delivery. Ladies in suffering are invited to come to this clinic, where they will find the solace they seek before and after childbirth.[91]

This custom was also practised outside of Spain. According to a report in the medical press, Parisian midwives working in the city's welfare service had to provide: 'two large rooms, well-aired, with bed, cradle, chairs, night table and dressing table; they must also offer . . . food, medicines, white clothing, swaddling clothes, and all the white bedclothing that the mother would need for 11 days'.[92]

In rural areas the presence of midwives, and doctors, must have been irregular. There were many calls for the creation of official midwife posts to be funded by local councils, as in the cities, to correspond with the positions which had existed for physicians since 1854.[93] The creation of such posts was seen as a way of protecting and reinforcing the midwifery profession and of preventing the intrusion of 'mercenaries' and 'healers' with their inadequate knowledge.[94] It was also claimed to be a way of improving health care, and ensuring adequate coverage of an area in which physicians did not normally become involved, due to the custom of delivering with a midwife or, in her absence, with another woman, and also to the physicians' scant training and interest in midwifery.[95]

Yet no order obliging local authorities to provide official midwives came into force until 1924.[96] In the meantime the *practicantes* saw their opportunity, extended their activities, and encroached on the work of midwives. The 1904 *Instrucción General de Sanidad Pública* (General public health order) compelled councils to employ one physician and one *practicante* for every 300 families.[97] In these posts the *practicantes* were authorized to perform deliveries, for which they had been receiving specific training since 1901. However, the general repercussions on the way deliveries were attended were negligible. The greatest impact was on the professional status of the two groups, and for midwives was much less favourable.

CONCLUSION

Throughout the nineteenth century, access to the profession was controlled by doctors within the universities, although to judge by their teaching practices, their interest was more centred on the exercise of power than on the real improvement of midwives' training. Some midwives took advantage of the few opportunities that opened up for them and became recognized teachers and public figures themselves. Many midwives probably exceeded the legal limits in their practice of obstetrics, and performed other activities related to women's health, although what happened behind the doors of their clinics remains a secret about which there is very little information. At the beginning of the twentieth century, Spanish midwives still had no power over their own training, and lacked the minimum professional organization necessary to reflect a collective identity or to declare the existence of any group interests. There were only minimal attempts to apply the models of collective organization that functioned for most health professionals, including the *practicantes*.[98]

Little changed until midwives' formal organization became obligatory in the late 1920s, when midwives had to become members of their professional body, the *Colegio de Matronas*, as was already the case for all other medical practitioners. From that moment onwards, national maternity insurance and then national health insurance schemes, the appearance of nursing as a new female health profession, the consolidation of medical specialities, and the growing presence of women in Spanish public life became elements which shaped the history of Spanish midwives that is still to be written.

ACKNOWLEDGEMENTS

The text was translated from the Spanish by Richard Davies. We would like to thank Hilary Marland and Anne Marie Rafferty for their helpful comments.

NOTES

1 T. Ortiz, 'From hegemony to subordination: midwives in early modern Spain', in H. Marland (ed.) *The Art of Midwifery: Early Modern Midwives in Europe*, London, Routledge, 1993, pp. 99–106.
2 A. Albarracín Teulón, 'La titulación médica en España durante el siglo XIX', *Cuadernos de Historia de la Medicina Española*, 1973, vol. 12, pp. 15–80.
3 'Reglamento para la enseñanza de practicantes y matronas', *Gaceta de Madrid*, 28 noviembre 1861.
4 Ibid., tít. I, cap. III.
5 Ibid., cap. IV, art. 38.
6 See Ortiz, 'From hegemony', pp. 100–2.
7 'Reglamento para la enseñanza', tít. III, cap. V.
8 Ibid., tít. III, cap. I.
9 'Ley General de Instrucción', *Gaceta de Madrid*, 9 septiembre 1857, tít. I, art. 5.
10 C. Alvarez Ricart, *La mujer como profesional de la medicina en la España del siglo XIX*, Madrid, Anthropos, 1988, pp. 179–80.
11 See the accounts collected ibid., pp. 179–81.
12 R. Torres, 'Sobre parteras', *España Médica*, 1862, no. 7, p. 214. Cited in Alvarez Ricart, *La mujer*, p. 178.
13 'Decreto ley de libertad de enseñanza', *Gaceta de Madrid*, 21 octubre 1868, art. 6. The defence of individual rights suffered, however, from a strong gender bias.
14 Ibid., art. 3 and 6.
15 F. Herrera Rodríguez, 'La enseñanza libre de practicantes y matronas en el Cádiz de 1868', *Actas del VIII Congreso nacional de Historia de la Medicina. Murcia-Cartagena*, Murcia, 1988, vol. 1, pp. 222–8.
16 Advertisement in *El Progreso Médico*, 1869, vol. 2, p. 26. Cited in F.

Herrera Rodríguez, 'La titulación de matronas en la Facultad de Medicina de Cádiz durante el sexenio revolucionario', *Toko-Ginecología Práctica*, 1989, vol. 48, p. 231.

17 In addition to the school trained, another eight midwives were also examined at the university at this time, having studied with different town physicians in the province: Herrara Rodríguez, 'La titulación', pp. 235–6.

18 A. Fernández Dueñas, *La Facultad de Medicina de la Universidad Libre de Córdoba y su época (1870–74)*, Córdoba, Diputación Provincial, 1983, pp. 203–9.

19 F. Iracheta y Arguiñarena, *Examen de matronas conforme hoy son y conforme deben ser*, Madrid, Imprenta Médica de la viuda e hijos de Alvarez, 1870, pp. i–ii.

20 Ibid., p. i.

21 See reference in note 19. As far as we know, only the first 48 pages of this book are preserved (in duplicate) in the Archivo General de la Administración (hereafter AGA), legajo 6505. We are indebted to Consuelo Flecha for information about the existence of this book.

22 Iracheta y Arguiñarena, *Examen*, p. xv.

23 A. Medina, *Cartilla nueva, útil y necesaria para instruirse las matronas*, Madrid, Antonio Sanz, 1750. The style was common to other classical obstetrical manuals written by midwives, such as Siegemund, des Coudray or Coutanceau. For books written by midwives in early modern Europe, see G. Calvi, 'Manuali delle levatrici (XVII–XVIII sec.)', *Memoria. Rivista di Storia delle Donne*, no. 3, 1982, pp. 114–16; T. Ortiz and D. Sánchez, 'La experiencia escrita de las matronas, siglos XVII–XVIII', in P. Ballarín and C. Martínez (eds) *Del patio a la casa, las mujeres en las sociedades mediterráneas*, Granada, Universidad de Granada, 1996, pp. 239–47.

24 Iracheta y Arguiñarena, *Examen*, footnote on p. xv.

25 F. Alonso Rubio, *Manual del Arte de Obstetricia para uso de las matronas*, Madrid, Imprenta Nacional, 1866.

26 Iracheta y Arguiñarena, *Examen*, p. xv.

27 M. Vázquez y Muñoz, *Compendio de obstetricia para la enseñanza de comadrones y parteras*, Córdoba, Diario de Córdoba, 1871.

28 Iracheta y Arguiñarena, *Examen*, p. 19. Data on the *parteras* are scarce, but work is currently being undertaken on their competition with trained midwives in the early twentieth century.

29 Ibid., p. 1.

30 Ibid., p. 22.

31 'Ley provisional de matrimonio civil', *Gaceta de Madrid*, 21 junio 1870, cap. V, art. 49 and 52.

32 Iracheta y Arguiñarena, *Examen*, p. vii.

33 The advertisement appeared in the journal *El Anfiteatro Anatómico Español*, 1875, p. 342, and is reproduced by Alvarez Ricart, *La mujer*, p. 182.

34 Ibid.

35 Angel Pulido Fernández (1853–1932) completed his studies at the Madrid faculty of medicine in 1874. He was a military physician and became General Director of Health at the beginning of the twentieth

century; he edited several medical journals and local newspapers, was a member of the Spanish parliament and a senator. He was a founder member and secretary of the Spanish Society of Gynaecology set up in 1874: J. Alvarez Sierra, *Diccionario de autoridades médicas*, Madrid, Editora Nacional, 1963, p. 427.

36 A private school of medicine and surgery also operated in the museum. On this centre and its founder, see J.M. López Piñero, 'González de Velasco', in J.M. López Piñero *et al.*, *Diccionario histórico de la ciencia moderna en España*, Barcelona, Península, 1983, vol. 1, pp. 417–20.

37 In an article published in the same year she was referred to as a teacher at the school: P. Jáuregui, 'Una opinión', *El Anfiteatro Anatómico Español y el Pabellón Médico*, 1878, vol. 6, p. 96.

38 Ibid.

39 See E. Fee, 'Nineteenth-century craniology: the study of the female skull', *Bulletin of the History of Medicine*, 1979, vol. 53, pp. 415–33; G. Scanlon, *La polémica feminista en la España contemporánea*, Madrid, Akal, 1986, pp. 161–8.

40 Jáuregui, 'Una opinión', p. 96.

41 Iracheta y Arguiñarena, *Examen*, p. xiii.

42 Ibid.

43 Some of his opinions written in 1878 are reproduced by Alvarez Ricart, *La mujer*, pp. 82–5, 88–92 and 102–7.

44 'Reglamento para las carreras de practicantes y matronas', *Gaceta de Madrid*, 18 noviembre 1888. The quotation is from art. 5.

45 Brief mention of this journal was found in I. Segura and M. Selva, *Revistes de dones (1846–1935)*, Barcelona, Edhasa, 1984. The collection is partially preserved in the Madrid Municipal Publications Library, the Barcelona City Archives and the Catalonian Library in Barcelona.

46 Her death in 1895 was announced in the journal: *El eco de las matronas*, 1895, vol. 3, no. 41, pp. 285–7.

47 A news item in 1899 reported that nine students had passed the university examinations, one from the capital, and the rest from towns and villages in Catalonia province: *El eco de las matronas*, 1899, vol. 6, no. 14, p. 190.

48 'Real decreto sobre estudios que comprende la enseñanza de practicantes', *Gaceta de Madrid*, 27 abril 1901, art. 2.

49 'Real decreto de 31 enero 1902 sobre reorganización de la carrera de practicante', *Gaceta de Madrid*, 1 febrero 1902.

50 On *practicantes* during this period, see M. Amezcua *et al.*, *Sanidad y colectividad sanitaria en Almería. El colegio de practicantes (1885–1945)*, Almería, Colegio Oficial de Enfermería, 1994.

51 Data extracted from AGA, Sección Educación, *Libro de Registro de Títulos de Practicantes*, no. 105.

52 Between 1901 and 1912 only five women obtained the title of *practicante* authorized to carry out deliveries: ibid.

53 The figure for midwives comes from census data used by Clara Martínez Padilla in her forthcoming PhD thesis 'The health professions in Granada from 1874 to 1923'. The figure for physicians is taken from T.

Ortiz, *Médicos en la Andalucía del siglo veinte*, Granada, Averroes, 1987, p. 43.

54 The San Juan de Dios provincial hospital, the San Lázaro hospital and the *Hospital Real* (Royal Hospital), which housed a mental asylum, a home for waifs and strays, and a home for foundlings.

55 L. Seco de Lucena, *Anuario de Granada para 1893*, Granada, Imprenta El Defensor de Granada, 1893, p. 317; L. Seco de Lucena, *Anuario de Granada*, Granada, Imprenta El Defensor de Granada, 1901, p. 298; L. Seco de Lucena, *Anuario de Granada*, Granada, Imprenta El Defensor de Granada, 1917, p. 177.

56 In the eighteenth century it had also been obligatory for midwives working in medical institutions to live on the premises, as in the case of Luisa Rosado of Madrid: Ortiz, 'From hegemony', p. 103.

57 'Matrona', *El Defensor de Granada* (hereafter *DG*), 1885, vol. 6, no. 1820; L. Seco de Lucena, *Anuario de Granada para 1894*, Granada, El Defensor de Granada, 1894 p. 564.

58 'Asamblea provincial', *DG*, 1888, vol. 9, no. 2823.

59 Ibid.

60 *DG*, 1888, vol. 9, no. 3034. Vílchez was substituted by Rosario Favores Sevilla in 1894: 'Nombramiento', *DG*, 1895, vol. 16, no. 7186. In 1917 Eloísa Bueno García held the post: Seco de Lucena, *Anuario*, 1917, p. 177.

61 *Reglamento de los servicios municipales de Beneficencia y Sanidad aprobado por la Excma. Corporación en sesión de 7 de julio de 1893*, Granada, Imprenta de Francisco Reyes. Section 4 is dedicated to the *Casa de Socorro*.

62 Ibid., art. 140; L. Seco de Lucena, *Anuario de Granada*, Granada, El Defensor de Granada, 1906, pp. 485–6.

63 *Guía de Granada (Granada, Almería, Málaga y Jaén)*, Granada, El Defensor de Granada, 1911, p. 46.

64 'Asistencias de la Casa de Socorro en 1899', *La publicidad*, 1900, no. 4900.

65 'Beneficencia y sanidad', *DG*, 1905, vol. 26, no. 13462.

66 L. Seco de Lucena, *Anuario de Granada para 1895*, Granada, El Defensor de Granada, 1895, p. 654.

67 Archivo Municipal de Granada (hereafter AMG), Sección Beneficencia, legajo 1210.

68 *Reglamento de los servicios municipales*, cap. IV, sección sexta, art. 143.

69 Ibid., final appendix.

70 'Empleados municipales', *DG*, 1896, vol. 17, no. 9178.

71 'Personal del Ayuntamiento', *DG*, 1899, vol. 20, no. 11582.

72 AMG, Sección Personal, legajo 2017, *Expediente de nombramientos y ceses*, 1900.

73 *Memoria que acerca del estado de las clases obreras de la provincia de Granada presenta el Comité Ejecutivo de la Comisión Provincial*, Granada, Ventura Sabatel, 1884, p. 38.

74 J.W. Scott, 'La mujer trabajadora en el siglo XIX', in G. Duby and M. Perrot (eds) *Historia de las mujeres en Occidente*, Madrid, Taurus, 1993, vol. 4, pp. 415–24.

75 'Discusión de los presupuestos: Beneficencia y Sanidad', *DG*, 1904 vol. 25, no. 13422.
76 Seco de Lucena, *Anuario*, 1917, p. 179.
77 'Matrona', *DG*, 1889, vol. 10, no. 3183.
78 AMG, Sección Beneficencia, legajo 1210, *Sobre nombramiento de matronas de la Casa de Socorro*.
79 Advertisements for the surgeries of Pilar Ortiz Grimaud y Cristina Martín Rodríguez appear, for example, in *DG*, 1895, vol. 16, no. 7912; *DG*, 1896, vol. 17, no. 8072; *DG*, 1897, vol. 18, no. 9413.
80 See Alvarez Ricart, *La mujer*, pp. 59–170.
81 Ibid., pp. 150–1 and J. de Miguel, *El mito de la inmaculada concepción*, Barcelona, Anagrama, 1979.
82 *DG*, 1895, vol. 16, no. 7912.
83 *DG*, 1895, vol. 16, no. 7918.
84 *DG*, 1899, vol. 20, no. 11012.
85 *DG*, 1895, vol. 16, no. 7922.
86 Jáuregui, 'Una opinión', p. 96.
87 *El eco de las matronas*, 1898, vol. 4, no. 3, p. 34. Intrusion, or unauthorized practice, was the great obsession of the Spanish professions in the nineteenth century, particularly amongst the medical profession: A. Albarracín Teulón, 'Intrusos, charlatanes, secretistas y curanderos', *Asclepio*, 1972, vol. 24, pp. 323, 366.
88 As did Pilar Ortiz in 1895 (*DG*, 1895, vol. 16, no. 7922) and Juana Iglesias in 1903 (*DG*, 1903, vol. 24, no. 12953).
89 Figures calculated from a total of sixty midwives who appear in the *Album selecto de Barcelona Médica ante la Exposición Internacional*, Barcelona, Imprenta Romana, 1929, n.p.
90 Examples of this can be found in *DG*, 1895, vol. 16, no. 7922; 1904, vol. 25, no. 13168; 1905, vol. 26, no. 13468, and in *Album selecto*.
91 *Album selecto*.
92 D. Prieto, 'La profesión en el extranjero. Las matronas en París', *El Siglo Médico*, 1895, vol. 42, p. 662. See also the chapter by Thompson in this volume.
93 J. Valenzuela Candelario, 'El espejismo del ejercicio libre. La ordenación de la asistencia médica en la España decimonónica', *Dynamis*, 1994, vol. 14, pp. 269–304.
94 Jáuregui, 'Una opinión', p. 96.
95 T. Valera, 'Matronas titulares', *El Siglo Médico*, 1904, vol. 51, pp. 640–1.
96 In accordance with the new 'Estatuto Municipal', art. 207. Cited in J. de la Peña, *Legislación sanitaria vigente de Medicina*, Avila, Senén Martín, 1926, p. 584.
97 Ibid., p. 585.
98 *Practicantes* had professional associations and journals from the 1880s onwards: Amezcua *et al.*, *Sanidad y colectividad*. In 1895 the midwives of Granada first attempted to set up a professional association. It is not known if this attempt met with success: 'Las matronas', *DG*, 1895, vol. 16, no. 7998.

4

ROSALIND PAGET

The midwife, the women's movement and reform before 1914

June Hannam

In December 1906 *Nursing Notes*, the mouthpiece of the Midwives' Institute, carried a front page editorial entitled 'The nurse and the midwife as citizen'. In this it was asserted that far from a woman's place being in the home, if she carried out her role 'faithfully' as wife, mother or worker she should be 'alive to her responsibilities outside her own home' and be able 'to give out of her essential feminine qualities that help towards the general betterment of the whole nation which cannot be achieved by one sex alone'.[1] Such arguments, which contested the view that there was a separation between public and private spheres, were commonplace within the contemporary women's movement in Britain. The revival of the campaign for the vote in the decade before World War I brought the role of women as citizens to the forefront of political debate; it was argued that women should demand suffrage not only on the grounds of individual rights, but also because they were different from men and had a duty to contribute to social progress through promoting moral regeneration and reform.[2]

An important part of this discussion involved the responsibilities of middle-class women to the welfare of poorer members of the community, in particular women and children. This gained renewed importance after 1900 when the defeats of the Boer War focused attention on the high rates of infant mortality and poor child health which appeared to threaten Britain's standing as a leading imperial and economic power. In the ensuing debates over this issue mothers came to be seen as holding the key to future national greatness.[3] The 1906 article in *Nursing Notes* added to this discussion by emphasizing the specific role that the midwife could play as a professional worker and as a citizen and is worth quoting at some length. It was assumed that midwives had a greater sense of responsibility than other women because they could see how the 'mal-administration of municipal affairs', the inadequacy of the 'sanitary system' and the conditions under which people lived undermined their health. The duty of the midwife and nurse was to do something about this:

> by trying to add to her own stock of knowledge on social questions, by making herself a little centre of light and knowledge amidst the ignorance and misery she longs to mitigate, by making use of her power as a voter for County and other Councils, for Boards of Guardians, by acting as a medium between sanitary authorities and local agencies and the poor.[4]

It was as a 'Health Missioner' that the nurse and midwife could best play a part in reform and by doing so they would find their 'sense of citizenship grow and evolve day by day'.[5]

This quotation aptly illustrates the inter-relationship between the movement for women's suffrage, concepts of citizenship and social reform in the period before 1914. Historians have recently drawn our attention to the complexity of this relationship and have explored women's ideas about the best way to deal with social problems, the negotiations they made between a commitment to individual responsibility and a recognition that some state intervention was necessary, and the extent to which they influenced social policy.[6] The focus of attention, however, has been on female philanthropists and women active in political parties. Far less has been written about professional women and the extent to which they contributed to contemporary debates.[7] And yet this was a time when women were carving out a role for themselves as professional workers, and when even the women's movement was reluctant to challenge notions of women's special qualities and their role as wives and mothers. This set up particular tensions for women who chose paid employment.

It is the intention of this chapter to examine the ideas of one of the leaders of the Midwives' Institute, Rosalind Paget, concerning the relationship between women's suffrage and citizenship, paid employment and social welfare. Exploring the perspective of a woman who represented a group of female 'professional' workers should add to our understanding of both the women's movement and also the complex debate around social welfare in the period.[8]

The Midwives' Institute was established in 1881 with the aim of raising the efficiency and status of the midwife, to petition Parliament for recognition, and to establish a professional *esprit de corps*. Up to the early 1900s the Institute concentrated on achieving a Midwives Act. Thereafter it shifted its focus to dealing with the impact of the Act on practising midwives, and to acting as a pressure group for other pieces of legislation which could affect midwives. It hoped to encourage midwives to co-operate with each other and to that end provided a library and club room where they could meet, established a register for members, and arranged courses of lectures to prepare candidates for examinations and to facilitate discussion on the profession. It aimed also to act as a centre of information for the public. The Institute was governed by a Council, elected at the Annual General Meeting, which drew its membership from the most prestigious leaders and managers in the health field. In 1893, for example, they were nearly all matrons, superintendents or inspectors of the Queen Victoria Jubilee Institute for Nurses, and two doctors were among the vice-presidents. The Council addressed broad policy issues, but the day-to-day management of the affairs of the Institute was carried out by an executive committee which met once a month. There were numerous other sub-committees, including the Sectional Committee Midwives, which consisted of all midwife members of the Council and midwife vice-presidents. It met only when important matters relating to midwives were being discussed and communicated directly with the representative of the Institute on the Central Midwives Board.[9]

Rosalind Paget, a trained nurse and midwife, was one of a small group of well-educated, middle-class women who provided the driving force behind the development of the Midwives' Institute from the mid-1880s to the First World War.[10] There were only three presidents between 1890 and 1919. Zepherina Smith, the first treasurer of the Institute, acted as president from 1890 until her death in 1894. The daughter of a clergyman, she trained as a nurse in 1867 and gained the London Obstetrical Society certificate in 1873. She retired from nursing after her marriage to the surgeon Henry Smith in 1876, but was active in the affairs of the Institute. Jane Wilson, a founder member of the Institute and honorary secretary of the Workhouse Infirmary Nursing Association took over as president in 1894. She was succeeded in 1911 by Amy Hughes who had trained as a nurse at St Thomas's under Mrs Wardroper and then became a superintendent of the Queen

Victoria Jubilee Institute for Nurses. In 1897 the officers were strengthened when a close friend of Rosalind Paget, Paulina Ffynes Clinton, took over the role of secretary of the Institute which she carried out for twelve years. The two women had nursed together at the London Hospital, where Paulina was assistant matron, and shared a flat until Paulina died in 1918. Paulina Ffynes Clinton held the London Obstetrical Society certificate, was a trained masseuse, and joined the Institute in 1886. As secretary she received a small honorarium which amounted to £55 in 1910.

The officers of the Midwives' Institute were drawn from the same class background and had close friendship and family ties with the leaders of the women's movement and with those who took an interest in social welfare issues. Rosalind Paget herself came from a family which had an interest in both these areas. Born in 1855, she was the daughter of John Paget, a barrister and police magistrate who was a member of the commission set up to enquire into the Crimean War. Her uncle William Rathbone, a Quaker shipowner and Member of Parliament for Liverpool, had a lifelong interest in nursing reform and initiated a district nursing scheme in the city. He played a leading role in the formation of the Queen Victoria Jubilee Institute for Nurses and along with other members of the family gave practical help and advice to the Midwives' Institute.[11]

His daughter Eleanor also took an interest in social questions and women's rights. She was honorary secretary of the Liverpool Women's Industrial Council and was elected to the city council before 1914. An active suffragist, she became president of the National Union of Societies for Equal Citizenship after the First World War, served as an independent Member of Parliament and spearheaded the inter-war campaign for family allowances.[12] Rosalind Paget was in close contact with her cousin. In 1909, for example, they both gave papers at the Jubilee Congress on District Nursing held in Liverpool. Eleanor Rathbone spoke on 'sick room helpers' and Rosalind Paget, in a paper which acknowledged the influence of her uncle on her career, on 'midwifery and maternity nursing'.[13]

It was an uphill struggle to attract members in the early years and the organization was dependent on the unpaid work of its officers who gave both time and money to ensure the Institute's survival. The recruitment strategy of the Midwives' Institute up to 1914, as far as midwife members were concerned, was to take only fully trained women. In the 1880s such women had to be over 25, of 'good character' and holders of the London Obstetrical Society certificate. In 1885 there were only 25 members. After 1886 associate members could also be recruited, who were trained nurses and lay supporters. Yet membership still grew only slowly: in 1894 there were 240 members. Following the Midwives Act of 1902 there was greater interest in the Institute and by 1908 membership finally topped 1,000. In 1914 there were 1,235 members, but only 782 were midwives out of 5,500 trained midwives on the Roll.[14]

Rosalind Paget's role was particularly important. She provided continuity of leadership, holding the office of treasurer from 1890 to 1930, as well as acting as convenor of the Sectional Committee Midwives. Rosalind Paget was always at the forefront of any campaigns waged by the Institute: when the Midwives' Institute sought amendments to the Insurance Bill of 1911, for example, it was Rosalind Paget who contacted politicians, doctors and women's groups for support, drafted a letter to the press and tried to convene meetings of the Council and the Midwives' Advisory Committee so that members of the Institute could be consulted. In 1912 the Midwives' Institute was asked to nominate people onto provisional insurance committees in the counties and county boroughs. So little time was given for this task that Rosalind Paget and Paulina Ffynes Clinton had to do this work themselves within one week.[15]

Rosalind Paget also ensured that the Institute had links with other organizations. She had a close association with the Queen Victoria Jubilee Institute for Nurses. Appointed as its first chief officer in 1890, she resigned in 1891 but continued as a member of the Council with special responsibility for midwifery. It was the Queen's Institute nomination which secured her a place on the Central Midwives Board where she served between 1902 and 1924.[16] Rosalind Paget also attended and spoke at meetings of women's groups with an interest in midwifery, such as the Women's Liberal Federation, the Women's Co-operative Guild and the National Union of Women Workers, a body which aimed to promote the social, moral and religious welfare of women.[17]

It was not just the range of her activities which ensured Rosalind Paget's importance within the Institute, however, but also her political astuteness and communication skills. Rosalind Paget's financial reports were always delivered with humour as she tried to encourage members to pay their subscriptions on time. Each year she referred to the costs involved in sending out reminders: 'She hoped they would not consider her like the daughter of the horse-leech, who cried "Give, Give", she felt more like the absent-minded beggar who said "Pay, Pay!"'.[18] Contemporaries were unstinting in their praise of Rosalind Paget. When she attended the Annual General Meeting of the Association for Promoting the Training and Supply of Midwives, *Nursing Notes* claimed that:

> no questions ever seem to baffle Miss Paget, whose kind, practical advice was valued and appreciated not only by her questioners but by the Committee to whom she was giving invaluable assistance. There is a spirit attached to Miss Paget that carries conviction and a humour that is contagious.[19]

Edith Pye, who was elected as president of the Institute in 1929, referred to Rosalind Paget as the 'Florence Nightingale of midwifery' because of her determination to champion the cause of the trained midwife over a long period, often in the face of considerable hostility.[20]

The hard work of Rosalind Paget and the other officers played an important part in ensuring the survival and development of the Institute. What is less clear is how far they were successful in achieving their broader aims and objectives. Recent studies have questioned the extent to which pressure from groups such as the Institute was a major factor in affecting government legislation. Dingwall *et al.*, for example, argue that professional projects are only ever successful when they converge with state interests.[21] Discussion of the development of the Midwives' Institute has centred on a growing body of literature on nursing history and professionalization, although recent studies question the logic of professionalization and its relevance for female-dominated occupations such as nursing (and by implication midwifery) since it is a gendered concept and reflects the priorities of male occupations.[22] Little has been written, however, about the ideas put forward by the leaders of the Institute, in particular in the context of the women's movement and debates over social welfare.[23] And yet their views on the future of midwifery were affected by these debates and were often modified to suit their own needs as representatives of a group of female workers.

From its establishment in 1881 the leaders of the Midwives' Institute believed that the professional interests of their members and the Institute's broader concern with social reform were inextricably linked. They sought to raise the status of an existing area of women's work by securing legislation which would ensure that only women who were trained could call themselves midwives.[24] Once this had been achieved they worked to improve the training of the midwife and to ensure that she had a voice in any proposals to change maternity care. It was hoped that if the status of midwifery were raised, more educated, middle class women would be attracted to the work and thus poorer women would receive better treatment. Not only would midwives be more competent in terms of their skills, but they would also be able to influence mothers to adopt good moral habits and to look after their babies in the best possible way. These twin objectives convinced Rosalind Paget that, in campaigning for legislation, the Midwives' Institute looked beyond 'the narrow outlook of mere trade unionism'. Midwives were able to:

> consider what is the most effectual Bill for the protection of the lying-in woman as well as what is of advantage to ourselves, and we can feel assured that what is best for her will in the end be best for us.[25]

The leadership group remained similar up to 1914, but after 1900 there was more of an attempt to form stronger links with practising midwives, partly because membership was so low, and partly because the Institute felt that the backing of a broader cross-section of midwives would increase its effectiveness as a pressure group. Paget attempted in 1900 to have the election of two direct representatives onto the Council taken more seriously, and more use was made of these representatives. In London they set up centres where they could meet practising midwives and put them in touch with the Midwives' Institute. It was in the context of growing labour unrest after 1907, however, that the Midwives' Institute took further steps to make contact with a broader group of midwives. The leadership feared that midwives, especially in the provinces, would be attracted by trade unionism. In 1909, therefore, it encouraged the setting up of local associations which would affiliate to the Institute and send delegates to a Committee of Representatives. The Committee was to be the means through which practising midwives would make their views known to the leaders of the Institute and the representative on the Central Midwives Board, and was to give them the opportunity to take part in the nomination of that representative. Local secretaries and delegates to the Committee had to be members of the Midwives'

Institute, but other members of local associations did not. Some associations already existed and were encouraged to affiliate, whereas others were set up by Institute organizers. By 1914 there were fifty-three associations, most of which were supported by matrons, local inspectors of midwives and doctors. The leadership was at pains to point out that the Institute was not a trade union; it was a professional organization which put the good of the community alongside, and even above, the self-interest of the midwife.[26]

In a stimulating thesis Brooke Heagerty argues that the leaders of the Midwives' Institute sought a professional status for midwives by excluding working-class women from midwifery practice. Although they joined other feminists in the suffrage cause and fought against male domination of health care in the name of all women, as upper- and middle-class nurses and midwives they had more in common with men of their own class than with working-class women. They sought to encourage working-class mothers to adopt the middle-class values of thrift, self-help and an orderly family life as part of a broader interest in maintaining the hierarchical ordering of society and individual responsibility for social welfare. Heagerty suggests that implicit in such a strategy was an attack on working-class midwives who identified too closely with their clients. The Institute's support for the provisions of the Midwives Act which concerned training, the wearing of uniforms, strict supervision and morality was to ensure that midwives were distanced from their clients who were viewed as 'brutal, coarse and in need of reform'.[27]

In many respects this argument is a convincing one and is valuable in drawing attention to issues of class in shaping the outlook of the Midwives' Institute. A closer examination of the ideas of leaders such as Rosalind Paget, however, reveals a more complex set of notions about the relationship between the midwife and working-class mothers and between state responsibility and self-help. The issue of training provides one example of this complex interaction. Rosalind Paget always argued that poorer mothers should have the right to choose who would attend them in childbirth and that they could not make a wise decision unless they knew whether or not a midwife was trained. A major theme of her speeches and writings, therefore, was the importance of midwifery training:

> What did a woman who had refused to have a midwife say after the event? 'I was alone with the Almighty and it was little He

knew about the job.' You see that Providence demonstrates that trained midwives are a necessity.[28]

Her emphasis on training was not simply to improve the status of the midwife. She also wanted to ensure that poorer mothers received the best care possible in childbirth. In a speech to the National Union of Women Workers in 1896 which anticipated the national concern with motherhood after 1900, she noted how 'in many matters concerning the safety of life and health far less vital than the one under discussion, public opinion has demanded safeguards against ignorance and incompetence'. Doctors, dentists and chemists could not describe themselves as competent unless they were registered. This protected the whole community and yet 'the lives of the most important part of the nation – its mothers – are still entrusted to persons who may call themselves midwives, but who are, in many cases, absolutely untrained'.[29] At the same meeting she criticized middle-class women, who always used doctors when they gave birth, for taking little interest in the improvement of midwifery and for failing to realize the importance of midwives for working-class women.

Although keen to improve training, and frequently critical of the bona fide midwife, officers of the Institute constantly modified their demands when faced with a shortage of midwives willing to work with poorer women. Thus they criticized a proposal that midwives should be fully trained nurses on the grounds that such highly qualified women would be unlikely to practise midwifery amongst the poor. For similar reasons they showed sympathy for bona fide midwives who found the new regulations of the 1902 Midwives Act baffling and called for them to be given more assistance so that they could continue to attend poorer women.[30] The leaders of the Institute were certainly distanced from the practising midwife, even from those who were fully trained, and tended to have their closest contact with matrons, doctors and inspectors who sat on the Council. None the less, Rosalind Paget in particular recognized that this was a problem, as demonstrated by her efforts to encourage midwives to take the election of their direct representatives to the Council seriously so that she could benefit from their advice.[31] She was also concerned that younger members were not coming forward to take the place of officers such as herself: 'What more can the governing body of your Institute do to make it more popular among the new generation, who are now, in Ibsen's well-known phrase, "knocking at the door"'.[32]

Leaders of the Institute also had complex views concerning individual responsibility for social welfare, the role of philanthropy and state intervention. They shared the outlook of most women engaged in voluntary work in the late nineteenth and early twentieth centuries, that the influence of individuals working with families was an important force for social change. Rosalind Paget thought that midwives in particular could encourage mothers to live sober and responsible lives since they worked closely with them at a time when they were open to advice. Their potential for influence, however, meant that midwives also had to be of a good moral character. For that reason all the leaders of the Midwives' Institute supported the decision of the Central Midwives Board to remove a midwife from the roll if she became an unmarried mother. Rosalind Paget also argued that membership of the Midwives' Institute was a guarantee of good character and therefore midwives who belonged to the Institute would always be in demand.[33]

After 1900 infant welfare became an issue of national political importance as fears were expressed about Britain's ability to compete economically and militarily with other nations, in particular Germany. The physical efficiency of the population was thought to play a key role in this and the attention of policy-makers was drawn increasingly to the importance of the mother.[34] In this context leaders of the Midwives' Institute were concerned to emphasize the unique influence that midwives could exercise over mothers and to differentiate them from the philanthropist. Rosalind Paget suggested that the influence of the philanthropist came from a good moral character and caring, womanly qualities. In contrast, it was the midwife's scientific training which fitted her for this task, although it was crucial that her morals should also be of the highest standard. Rosalind Paget argued that training in ethical and social subjects was essential for the midwife since it enabled her to understand the influences on her work, to improve sanitary conditions, and to raise the friends of the patient to a 'better ideal of life'. This view was echoed in an editorial in *Nursing Notes* which claimed that midwives 'with their more or less scientific training . . . see the preventible nature of much of the evils it is their work to help in curing'.[35]

From the beginning of the campaign for the registration of

midwives Rosalind Paget in particular was critical of philanthropists when they touched on the role of the midwife. In a meeting at Somerville Women's Club in 1892, called to discuss the Midwives Bill, she was pleased to find that the 'old bugbear of the friendly neighbour' was not raised and instead of having to meet this 'philanthropic and sentimental objection, political questions, such as the unfairness of inserting a moral clause etc. in the Bill, came up'.[36] Her main concern was that midwives should be trained and licensed so that poorer women could receive efficient attendance at childbirth.[37] After the Midwives Act of 1902 Rosalind Paget was even more insistent that district nurses and midwives should not be associated with the dispensing of relief; their duty as 'good citizens and enthusiastic nurses' was to take account of the experience of others, including philanthropists, and to work in tandem with them, but also to recognize that their roles were distinct.[38]

In a context in which working-class mothers were constantly criticized for neglecting homes and children, the officers of the Institute displayed more complex attitudes towards the general lifestyle and morality of working-class women than those expressed by women from philanthropic backgrounds. They may have been critical of those mothers who turned to drink or neglected their families, but they were sympathetic to the problems that they faced when struggling on low incomes. They were reluctant, therefore, in the decade before the First World War to join in the general condemnation of mothers who returned to work. They feared that without employment mothers would turn to crime to feed their children: 'And who shall dare to be hard upon women driven by starvation? For we do not hear of state support for these mothers'.[39]

Leaders of the Institute argued that the midwife's position as a professional worker meant that she had a duty to provide an efficient service to all mothers, regardless of their moral standards. When several Queen's nurses expressed confusion about whether or not they should attend only respectable married women, Rosalind Paget was clear that the health and safety of the mother and child were paramount and that the mother's marital status was irrelevant. In 1907 she wrote an open letter to the effect that the issue had never been formally discussed by the Council of the Queen Victoria Jubilee Institute for Nurses, although she thought that it should have been: 'Our nurses have to nurse the sick poor ... it is not our business to judge the causes that have made our attendance necessary'. She asked who would treat unmarried mothers if a trained midwife did not do so. They might go to a workhouse or be left to the care of an untrained 'friendly neighbour', and yet the illegitimate child should have the 'very best chance possible'. The visit of a midwife could be 'the one influence for good' which might make the mother feel 'she has a responsibility towards the little being to whom she has given such an unfortunate start in life'.[40] Nevertheless, there were times when it was difficult to reconcile the needs of midwives as paid workers with the needs of poorer women and children. If midwives were too well paid, then poorer women would be unable to afford them. This is where social reform came in, because to improve midwives' working conditions, poorer mothers needed some form of economic assistance.

Rosalind Paget's view, which was shared by other leaders of the Institute, that midwives as a professional group could have a key influence on social change, was inextricably linked to support for women's suffrage and the need to foster 'active citizenship'.[41] The Institute supported the campaign for women's suffrage and Rosalind Paget took a prominent role in this. She provided the link between the Midwives' Institute and the Association for Promoting the Training and Supply of Midwives, a lay group set up to promote the training of midwives, which numbered many suffragists among its members. When the suffrage campaign revived after 1903 it was Rosalind Paget who urged all members of the Institute to take part in demonstrations for the vote, and in 1908 she led twenty members in a suffrage procession under the banner of Florence Nightingale.[42]

Her arguments in favour of the vote reflected those drawn on by the suffrage movement as a whole. She claimed that it took so long to achieve a Midwives Act because, as non-voters, women had little influence. By contrast, the fear that women would use their local votes explained the swift success of the campaign to persuade the London County Council not to delegate its supervisory powers to district councils.[43] Rosalind Paget returned to this theme at the end of the First World War when some women had at last been granted the parliamentary franchise. The Institute had gained a number of favourable clauses in the Midwives Act Amending Bill and in 1919 Rosalind Paget could not resist pointing out that:

much more consideration was given in many quarters to our question because it concerned women and that knowing that before very long they would have to consider the women's votes, and I think they looked forward to favours to come at the forthcoming General Election.[44]

Before the First World War meetings were held at the Nurses' Club to urge midwives to use their local votes, for it 'behoves every woman with a vote to remember her duties and responsibilities as a citizen'.[45] The sufferings of suffragette prisoners were described at meetings and in articles in *Nursing Notes* and, although the Institute could not fully support the militants, admiration was shown in 1908 for their self-sacrifice and whole-hearted devotion when there were those who 'will not cross the street to do battle for the cause'.[46] The Institute did not see the vote as leading to a rise in the wages of midwives and nurses, since their work was not an industry but a science, a profession, and an art. Its importance lay in the power it would give women to influence social improvement. The vote would be a first step 'toward enabling women to give their best help in forwarding social, moral, and economic reforms, which without their co-operation may be disastrously delayed. The history of the Midwives Act points this moral most strongly'.[47]

This considerable interest in women's suffrage contrasts with the position of the Women Sanitary Inspectors' Association which debated women's suffrage only twice. Celia Davies suggests that health visitors and sanitary inspectors used the same arguments as suffragists in developing their role as paid public health workers. They portrayed themselves as a mother's friend which implied special features and different training from men. This 'social maternalist' argument was often used as a broad justification for women's greater participation in political life and paid employment. None the less, Davies claims that the Women Sanitary Inspectors' Association did not 'seem eager to make explicit connections itself'.[48]

As already noted, midwives did see such a connection between reform and suffrage. This may have been because women had worked long as midwives and by the early twentieth century did not have to prove their suitability for the task. As independent practitioners, midwives were not subordinate to male doctors in their day-to-day practice, although they were closely supervised by the Central Midwives Board. They were acutely conscious that their Institute was 'managed by midwives for midwives' and was a 'self-governing body of professional women'.[49] The Institute believed that midwives could and should use their influence as citizens to achieve legislation which would improve maternity conditions – either by addressing the position of midwives, or by dealing with the adverse conditions under which women had to give birth. There were times, however, when there was a conflict between the perceived needs of midwives as paid workers and the Institute's sympathy with the plight of poorer women. Similarly, the class background of the leadership and their commitment to nineteenth-century liberal tenets also conflicted with proposals which aimed to increase government intervention in maternity care.

The main aim of the Institute was to preserve the independent midwife who could be chosen freely by the mother. It was argued that this was a system best suited to the interests of both the midwife and her client. Rosalind Paget made this point in 1898 in a scathing letter of reply to Dr Elizabeth Garrett Anderson who had accused midwives of campaigning for a registration act in order to enhance their own position by creating a monopoly. Rosalind Paget pointed to the wide range of restrictions which governed the practice of midwives:

> The fear of the competition of the midwife expressed by Mrs Garrett Anderson is exceedingly flattering, but from our view a little comical. The question is entirely one of supply and demand. The public will choose the attendant it prefers, quite irrespectively of the rights or sentiments of either doctor or midwife, and this we had all better recognise at once.[50]

It was for similar reasons that the leaders of the Institute were alarmed when they found that the first National Insurance Bill introduced in 1911 did not include any provision for midwife attendance. They believed that this would completely undermine the role of the midwife and therefore supported the campaign of the Women's Co-operative Guild to ensure that midwives as well as doctors could be chosen to attend births. They demanded also that midwives should be covered under the same terms as doctors and should be able to set fees according to their requirements.[51]

Although Rosalind Paget and other leaders of the Midwives' Institute were adamant that mothers should have freedom of choice, they were also aware of the financial difficulties poorer women faced in trying to meet midwifery costs, in particular when a midwife had to call in a doctor. They therefore supported a variety of schemes for the recovery of doctors' fees as long as these did not involve the Poor Law. They welcomed the provisions of the Insurance Act because the insured would have the right to financial assistance which would enhance their sense of responsibility. Rosalind Paget proposed to representatives on the Insurance Advisory Committee in 1912 that they should support the principle that the maternity grant should be given in cash, even if there were a risk of 'some abuse' because they should take every opportunity to uphold the independence and responsibility of the insured person, including single women. Representatives should not adopt the 'specious arguments of some rescue societies . . . the insured person and her employer have paid for their insurance: it is not a question of morals but of common honesty'.[52] Amy Hughes, Rosalind Paget and Paulina Ffynes Clinton drew up a circular to be sent to all midwife representatives on insurance committees giving them advice on what to support and concluded that the Insurance Act had changed the midwife's position for the better:

> In the past she has been most inadequately paid, she has been expected to do other people's philanthropy for them and has herself done in the aggregate a very large amount of charity work. This at least will be totally out of place with insured persons.[53]

In her annual report to the Queen Victoria Jubilee Institute for Nurses in 1914 Rosalind Paget was also pleased to note that midwives could recover fees from county councils.[54]

Despite these changes the remuneration of midwives was a problem which would not go away. Practising midwives complained that they needed higher fees and the leaders of the Institute were aware that without these it was unlikely that well-qualified, middle-class women would be attracted to the work. On the other hand, they feared that higher fees would simply mean that midwives would be 'wringing money from their poorer sisters' or 'driving them into the arms of the Poor Law'.[55]

A second difficulty related to low fees was how best to secure an adequate supply of midwives for the poor. Rosalind Paget feared that some women of good character could not afford the fees for training; government grants were difficult to obtain and therefore she advocated a system of county associations organized on similar lines to the Queen's Nurses which would encourage the efficient training and supervision of midwives. The Institute set up its own scholarship fund in 1904 to train midwives who agreed to work among the poor for two years. When she reviewed the operation of the scheme, however, Rosalind Paget had to conclude that 'there are few women thoroughly suited in every way and willing to work as midwives among the poor who cannot afford to pay for their own training'.[56]

Throughout the period under discussion, therefore, there were tensions between the interests of midwives as paid workers, a commitment to the independent practitioner, and support for the role of the midwife as an 'active citizen' and social reformer. The leaders of the Midwives' Institute sought ways to reconcile these tensions without undermining the position of the independent midwife. In doing so they put forward a complex array of views which cannot be neatly pigeon-holed and which formed part of, and were influenced by, more general debates about the relationship between state and individual responsibility for social welfare. The Institute officers were in favour of increasing the role of the state but only in so far as it created an environment conducive to individual responsibility. Thus they supported government legislation which gave financial assistance to mothers outside the Poor Law, enabling them to retain their self-respect, and refused to moralize about the unmarried mother. They saw a role both for the state and for midwives in fostering a sense of responsibility in mothers for the well-being of their children. Midwives could exercise this influence on individual mothers because they were trained, scientific in approach and had characters beyond reproach. As voters they could also ensure that legislation was passed which provided an improved environment and support for maternity care. In this dual capacity the midwife could be an 'active citizen' and a force for social progress.

The primary role of the Institute as representing the interests of a group of professional workers often conflicted, however, with these social welfare objectives. Thus, while the officers welcomed the growing interest shown by the Local Government Board, just prior to the First World War, in the provision of ante- and postnatal care through clinics, they feared that such centres might take clients away from midwives and that their role might not be recognized. Similarly, they had many demarcation disputes with the growing number of health visitors employed by local authorities who attended mothers soon after birth.[57] The main thrust of the arguments used was that the midwife was best placed to give antenatal and immediate postnatal care because of her medical training, experience and contact with the mother and that her involvement would be the best safeguard for the health of mothers and babies. Underlying these arguments was the fear that midwives would suffer financially if they were by-passed and mothers were treated by other health workers in clinics. By the end of the First World War, however, a shortage of midwives meant that leaders of the Institute expressed fewer concerns about midwives being displaced by others. They were more interested in how midwives would be remunerated for the extra time spent in antenatal care. The Institute favoured any schemes which protected the mother's free choice of midwifery attendant, her economic integrity and the independence of the midwife.[58]

Their commitment to the independent midwife, which was rooted in the leaders' support for *laissez-faire* economics, did hamper the extent to which the Midwives' Institute could make a positive impact on discussions about the future shape of health care and midwifery. They worked with pressure groups such as the Women's Co-operative Guild, which was keen to develop schemes for improved maternity care, but stopped short of accepting proposals which would have created a salaried midwifery service. When she attended a National Union of Women Workers conference in 1915 which focused on maternity and infant welfare, Rosalind Paget was unhappy to see it turn into a battle between individualists, who wished parents to have some responsibilities and appreciated the work of voluntary associations, and the socialists who thought the state should take control and pay for everything. 'They introduced an antagonistic and aggressive note' compared to others who were 'honestly trying to find a solution'.[59]

In the period before 1914 Rosalind Paget and the other leaders of the Institute sought to enhance the professional status of the midwife in a context in which policies to improve the nation's health and women's role in politics were hotly debated. The attitudes of the officers of the Institute on these issues were complex. They saw a role for both the state and midwives in fostering a sense of responsibility in mothers. As professionals, their influence was thought to be distinct from that of philanthropists since it was based on scientific training and was not concerned with moral rescue. They supported government legislation which aimed to improve maternity care and to provide financial assistance to mothers so long as it did not undermine the self-respect and the freedom of mothers to be attended by the midwife of their choice.

As voters they could ensure that legislation was passed which provided an improved environment and support for maternity care. In this dual capacity the midwife could be an 'active citizen' and a force for social progress. Ultimately, however, the commitment of the leaders of the Institute to the independent midwife practitioner reduced their potential to influence social reform. The mismatch between calls for a better trained, highly educated midwife and the low financial rewards made it difficult to attract women into the profession and retain them. Working-class women could not pay the fees necessary to provide midwives with an adequate salary and in the post-war years there was an increase in the number of midwives who did not work independently, but who were employed by local authorities, maternity centres and hospitals. This led Rosalind Paget to ask Dr Janet Campbell in 1923 whether 'she considered that the independent midwife was doomed, & she said she distinctly hoped not, as she considered in towns it was the best attendance for the mother'.[60] Having reached its apotheosis following the First World War the Midwives' Institute found itself increasingly on the defensive during the inter-war period rather than taking the lead in shaping the nature and practice of midwifery.

ACKNOWLEDGEMENTS

This is a revised version of J. Hannam, 'Rosalind Paget: class, gender and the Midwives' Institute', *History of Nursing Society Journal,* 1994/5, vol. 5, pp. 133–49.

NOTES

1 *Nursing Notes,* Dec. 1906.
2 For a discussion of the complexity of the views of nineteenth- and early twentieth-century feminists on concepts of equality and difference, see B. Caine, *Victorian Feminists,* Oxford, Oxford University Press, 1992, Introduction. See also J. Scott, 'Deconstructing equality-versus-difference: or the uses of post-structuralist theory for feminism', *Feminist Studies,* 1988, vol. 14, pp. 33–50.
3 For a discussion of the infant and child welfare movement and the development of an ideology of motherhood, see A. Davin, 'Imperialism and motherhood', *History Workshop Journal,* 1978, vol. 5, pp. 9–65; J. Lewis, *The Politics of Motherhood: Child and Maternal Welfare in England, 1900–1939,* London, Croom Helm, 1980; H. Marland, 'A pioneer in

infant welfare: the Huddersfield scheme 1903–1920', *Social History of Medicine*, 1993, vol. 6, pp. 25–50.
4 *Nursing Notes*, Dec. 1906, p. 173.
5 Ibid.
6 J. Lewis, *Women and Social Action in Victorian and Edwardian England*, Aldershot, Edward Elgar, 1991; G. Bock and P. Thane (eds) *Maternity and Gender Policies: Women and the Rise of European Welfare States 1880s–1950s*, London, Routledge, 1991.
7 Although, see C. Davies, 'The health visitor as mother's friend: a woman's place in public health, 1900–1914', *Social History of Medicine*, 1988, vol. 1, pp. 39–59 and H. Jones, 'Women health workers: the case of the first women factory inspectors in Britain', *Social History of Medicine*, 1988, vol. 1, pp. 165–81.
8 The midwife is described as a professional worker throughout this article since this is the term used by the leaders of the Institute.
9 For a more detailed account of the organizational structure of the Institute, see E. Brierly, *In the Beginning*, reproduced from *Nursing Notes*, Sept. 1924.
10 For more details of the officers of the Midwives' Institute, see B. Cowell and D. Wainwright, *Behind the Blue Door: The History of the Royal College of Midwives, 1881–1981*, London, Balliere & Tindall, 1981. Paulina Ffynes Clinton was secretary for much of the period.
11 J. Rivers, *Dame Rosalind Paget: A Short Account of Her Life Work*, London, Midwives' Chronicle, 1981.
12 For an account of Eleanor Rathbone's work, see H. Land, 'Eleanor Rathbone and the economy of the family', in H.L. Smith (ed.) *British Feminism in the Twentieth Century*, Aldershot, Edward Elgar, 1990, pp. 104–23 and J. Alberti, *Beyond Suffrage: Feminists in War and Peace*, London, Macmillan, 1989.
13 Jubilee Congress on District Nursing, *Report*, 1909, p. 159.
14 Midwives' Institute, AGM *Reports*.
15 Council minutes of the Midwives' Institute, 21 June 1912. For Rosalind Paget's activities on the Insurance Bill, see the Council minutes for 1911 and supporting papers.
16 Rivers, *Dame Rosalind Paget*; M.E. Baly, *A History of the Nursing Institute*, London, Croom Helm, 1987. The Midwives' Institute had to nominate a doctor to represent the organization on the Central Midwives Board.
17 For example, Rosalind Paget spoke at the 1896 Conference of the National Union of Women Workers on midwives' registration. She chaired the 3rd Annual Conference of the Association of Queen's Superintendents in the Northern Counties in 1903 and in 1909 attended the Congress of Italian midwives held in Milan: *Nursing Notes*, June 1903 and Oct. 1909. For details of the National Union of Women Workers, see P. Levine, *Victorian Feminism, 1850–1900*, London, Heinemann, 1987.
18 Annual General Meeting of the Institute, 1906.
19 *Nursing Notes*, Aug. 1910.
20 *Nursing Mirror and Midwives' Journal*, 11 July 1931.

21 R. Dingwall, A.M. Rafferty and C. Webster, *An Introduction to the Social History of Nursing*, London, Routledge, 1988.

22 For example, see A. Witz, *Professions and Patriarchy*, London and New York, Routledge, 1992.

23 An exception to this is J. Donnison, *Midwives and Medical Men: A History of Inter-Professional Rivalries and Women's Rights*, London, Heinemann, 1977, 2nd edn 1988, which discusses the battle for the 1902 Midwives Act and its relationship to issues of equal rights for women and the power of the male medical establishment.

24 For other areas of women's work see, for example, Davies, 'The health visitor' and Jones, 'Women health workers'.

25 'Midwives in Council Meeting', *Nursing Notes*, Nov. 1899.

26 For local midwives' organizational activities in Manchester, see the chapter by Mottram in this volume.

27 B. Heagerty, 'Class, gender and professionalisation: the struggle for British midwifery 1900–1936', PhD diss., University of Michigan, 1990, preface.

28 Speech to Midwives' Institute Jubilee AGM, 1931, quoted in *Midwives Chronicle and Nursing Notes*, Feb. 1982.

29 *Nursing Notes*, Nov. 1896, p. 47.

30 *Nursing Notes*, May 1903 and Nov. 1904.

31 *Nursing Notes*, Jan. and Feb. 1901.

32 Midwives' Institute, AGM, *Report*, 1910.

33 *Nursing Notes*, May 1914. Rosalind Paget was referring here to a scheme of the South Metropolitan Gas Company to use midwives from the Midwives' Institute for the wives of its employees.

34 Davin, 'Imperialism and motherhood'.

35 Rosalind Paget was speaking to a conference of the Association for Promoting the Training and Supply of Midwives; *Nursing Notes*, Oct. 1903, p. 144. The editorial was 'The nurse and the midwife as citizen', *Nursing Notes*, Dec. 1906.

36 *Nursing Notes*, April 1892, p. 44.

37 R. Paget, 'The registration of midwives', National Union of Women Workers, Annual Conference Report, 1896, pp. 159–67.

38 *Nursing Notes*, June 1903, pp. 85–6.

39 *Nursing Notes*, May 1908.

40 *Nursing Notes*, March 1907, p. 45. The *Nursing Notes* also complained about government plans which excluded Poor Law midwives from supervision by the Central Midwives Board, on the grounds that such mothers deserved the best skill and care regardless of marital status, *Nursing Notes*, Sept. 1906.

41 J. Lewis, 'Gender, the family and women's agency in the building of "welfare states": the British case', *Social History*, 1994, vol. 19, pp. 37–55.

42 *Nursing Notes*, April 1908.

43 *Nursing Notes*, July 1908.

44 Midwives' Institute, AGM, *Report*, 1919.

45 *Nursing Notes*, Feb. 1904, p. 20. See also Dec. 1903, Nov. 1906 and Nov. 1907.

46 *Nursing Notes*, April 1908, p. 73.
47 *Nursing Notes*, July 1908, p. 137.
48 Davies, 'The health visitor', p. 58.
49 E. Brierly, 'In the beginning: a retrospect', *Nursing Notes*, May 1923.
50 *Nursing Notes*, June 1898.
51 Heagerty, 'Class, gender and professionalisation', pp. 118–19. See also 'The National Insurance Bill', *Nursing Notes*, July, 1911 and Council minutes and supporting papers for 1911 and 1912 when Rosalind Paget spent a great deal of her time dealing with the Insurance Bill and its consequences.
52 Midwives Institute Council minutes, 22 April 1912.
53 Circular Dec. 1912, Council minutes, 2 Dec. 1912.
54 *Nursing Notes*, Aug. 1914.
55 *Nursing Notes*, April 1910.
56 Midwives' Institute, AGM, *Report*, 1912.
57 The anxiety of midwives on this issue can be seen in the supporting papers to the Council, letter from Florence E. Barrett, chairwoman of the Four Boroughs antenatal clinics committee, 28 Nov. 1918 and Rosalind Paget's undated reply.
58 'Municipal midwives', *Nursing Notes*, June 1917; 'The shortage of midwives', *Nursing Notes*, Sept. 1917; R. Paget, 'Midwives, are you awake!', *Nursing Notes*, May, 1918; 'The care of pregnancy – a suggestion', *Nursing Notes*, Dec. 1916; 'Maternity and child welfare', *Nursing Notes*, Nov. 1916; 'The relation of midwives to maternity centres', *Nursing Notes*, Oct. 1915.
59 *Nursing Notes*, April, 1915, pp. 92–3.
60 Midwives' Institute Council minutes, 6 July 1923.

5

THE 'ANTISEPTIC' TRANSFORMATION OF DANISH MIDWIVES, 1860–1920

Anne Løkke

In 1883 the physician Leopold Meyer (1852–1918) delivered a lecture to the Copenhagen Medical Society (*Det medicinske Selskab i København*) entitled 'On expanding the physician's role in birth attendance'.[1] Meyer proposed dispensing with midwives in larger towns and cities, replacing them with doctors assisted by nurses. Meyer had reached the conclusion that midwives should be removed during a recently concluded study trip to Germany, France, England, Ireland and the USA, where he had met leading obstetricians and gynaecologists. He vigorously attempted to convince his Danish colleagues that, like physicians in France, England and especially the USA, they should extend their work to attendance at normal births. Meyer argued that this was a better system than that of Denmark, where birth attendance was chiefly in the hands of midwives, doctors only being called in when serious complications arose. Meyer's central argument in proposing this change was that midwives would not be able to adopt proper antiseptic procedures, since, as non-academics, they were unable to fully understand their scientific basis.

Leopold Meyer's proposal met with overwhelming rejection by his fellow physicians. Not a single one supported his call for doctors to take on the tasks of midwives. Some felt that the idea had some merit, but that it was simply impracticable. Others maintained that the whole notion was ill-considered. The physicians' rejection of Meyer's proposal, however, was not based upon general satisfaction with midwifery practice. Throughout the nineteenth century the system of birth attendance was a recurrent subject of debate in medical journals and from 1870 onwards there was widespread

102

agreement that it was an anachronism. Participants in the debate, however, felt that improvements could be achieved by modernizing the occupation of midwife, not by removing it. Such modernization was actually set in motion, not against the wishes of physicians but to a large degree on their initiative and with their support. In time Leopold Meyer himself was to become one of the most important advocates of the midwife. When he became Professor and Head Obstetrician at the Royal Lying-in Hospital (*Den kongelige Fødselst-iftelse*) in 1897, and thus responsible for the education of midwives, he neither abolished the programme of education nor transformed it into a course for nurses. On the contrary, he devoted all his energy and innovative outlook to reforming the course and to the struggle to improve midwives' remuneration and their public image. In time and through experience, the only really enthusiastic proponent of physicians' takeover of birth attendance came to devote himself to improving the status of midwives. This indicates a vitality within the system of Danish birth attendance which could resist the imported idea of eliminating midwives.

In this chapter I shall attempt to place the modernization of Danish midwifery services at the end of the nineteenth century in context, based on an analysis of medical periodicals and medical legislation. How did midwifery services operate in the 1860s and 1870s, which actors and approaches set the process of change in motion, and what had been achieved by the first decades of the twentieth century? Why in particular was it apparently so self-evident to Danish physicians that midwives would continue to assume responsibility for normal births? To understand this discussion, it is important first to sketch in the background to the development of the professions of physician and midwife, and to review the organization of public health services.

MIDWIVES, REGULATION, AND THE HEALTH OF THE NATION

In Denmark, as in many other countries, birth assistance in the early modern period was a local affair. Female friends and neighbours assisted at births, with a 'helping woman' (*nærkone*) experienced in childbirth attendance or a midwife lending a hand.[2] The occupation of midwife is first mentioned in central legislation in a Church Ordinance of 1539, but its provisions do not appear to have had much practical significance.[3] Legislation of 1672, which outlined the principles of an official health system as a part of the early Absolute Monarchy's[4] efforts to create an orderly administration, would, on the other hand, come to be of great importance.[5] After 1672 only medical doctors, recognized by the professors of the medical faculty in Copenhagen, were permitted to call themselves '*medicus*'. The *medici* were accorded the exclusive right to prescribe internal medicines and were to supervise pharmacists and midwives. They were responsible for ensuring that towns were provided with good midwives, whom they were to instruct and examine. The decree thus ensured that, when a system of formal regulation was created, midwives were included among the country's official medical personnel. Since there were relatively few *medici* in Denmark, and very few outside of Copenhagen, the effects of the decree did not immediately become evident.[6]

Besides the *medici*, there were tradesmen–practitioners, subsequently barber–surgeons, who were also regulated around the same time. In the 1740s the education of surgeons was transferred to an academy, and from 1774 onwards they could acquire the right to practise on a par with the *medici*. In 1838 the two courses of study were combined, and after this date it is possible to speak of a single medical profession with one portal of entry.[7]

The failure to put the provisions of the decree of 1672 concerning the authorization of midwives into practice led to the passing of a special Act concerning midwives in 1714. This law, with its mixture of vision and realism, came to form the basis for the organization of birth attendance for the next two hundred years, and was still in place at the end of the nineteenth century.[8] The decree prescribed that all midwives should be examined by a *medicus* or surgeon and sworn in before the local authorities. The law provided uniform minimum standards for the entire country, with more rigorous rules for locations where a *medicus* could be found, and very detailed rules for Copenhagen, where the necessary prerequisites for strict administration prevailed. The aspiring midwives of Copenhagen thus had to be instructed by a *medicus* or surgeon, complete a period of apprenticeship with an experienced midwife, and finally sit an examination with a special Board of Midwifery.[9] Elsewhere in the country instruction and examination were to be carried out by the local *medicus*, or, in the absence of one, the nearest surgeon. The law required midwives to serve rich and poor alike, seek the assistance of other midwives for difficult births, and to call upon a *medicus* if their patient's life was threatened. Midwives were not permitted to administer abortive substances or medicines which would speed labour, and all midwives were made subject to regulations adopted by the Board of Midwifery in Copenhagen. Furthermore, midwives were prohibited from offering medical assistance unless their patients were in extreme circumstances and no *medicus* or surgeon was available.

The decree thus established a hierarchy and a distribution of responsibility between the *medicus*, surgeon and midwife, wherever the former were to be found. If there were no authorized doctors the regulation authorized and obliged the midwife to act as 'a person with medical knowledge'. In effect this was a general dispensation to almost all midwives outside the large towns to practise in a medical capacity. The Act of 1714 confirmed the notion that the occupation of midwife should be subject to similar conditions for admission and authorization to that of the two other groups of medical practitioners (in contrast to wise men and women and other traditional healers, who were not authorized, and who after 1794 ran the risk of being prosecuted as quacks).

The number of midwives passing their examinations in Copenhagen is known from 1743 onwards, and an increase can be seen from 51 during the years 1743–49, and 58 in 1850–59, to 214 in 1790–99. By 1800 a total of 677 midwives had passed examinations since 1743, 476 of these during the years 1770–1800. Thus by the turn of the century there was a significant number of qualified midwives spread through the country.[10]

At the end of the eighteenth century, the government embarked upon a massive campaign to increase the wealth of the King and the country by improving the common good. Ambitious agricultural reforms were carried out, the Poor Law authorities were reorganized (1803), and basic education for children was made compulsory (1814). In the field of public health, expensive reforms were initiated which aimed to stimulate population growth by improving access to authorized medical assistance and expanding the public health administration. In 1787 a school for midwives was set up at the Royal Lying-in Hospital in Copenhagen.[11] In 1803 the Royal Board of Health (*Det kongelige Sundhedscollegium*) was established as the supreme authority in public health administration; it was also directly responsible for midwives.[12]

In 1810 detailed midwifery regulation was introduced with the purpose of ensuring that the most ambitious provisions of the 1714 Act would be implemented throughout the entire country.[13] The country was now divided into midwife districts. Each district was required to appoint a district midwife educated at the Lying-in Hospital and to pay her a fixed salary which would be supplemented by fees paid by her patients for each birth. The district midwife was obliged to present herself unhesitatingly to every parturient woman who requested her help, and she was forbidden to leave a woman once labour had begun.[14] If a trained midwife could not be recruited directly, the *physicus* (superintending medical officer) was required to authorize a local midwife to carry out deliveries, and, at the same time, to send a local woman for training at the Lying-in Hospital. The midwife authorized by the local *physicus* could continue to practise in the district after the arrival of the trained midwife. Unauthorized midwives were not prohibited from practising, but women making use of their services were required to pay the authorized midwife all the same.[15] The idea of training local women and of authorizing existing midwives, if they were popular among the population, was based on experience gained since the eighteenth century; the rural population had simply rejected strangers as midwives. Training local women with local knowledge reduced hostility to the system of district midwives. There were struggles, but these were mostly financial, many parishes being slow to adjust to the idea of paying a basic salary to the district midwife. By around 1840, however, the public had become used to the system and competition from unauthorized midwives had largely disappeared.[16]

PHYSICIANS AND MIDWIVES

While the principles upon which the Danish public health service were based had been formalized around 1700, it was not until the beginning of the nineteenth century that support became available to pay for the education and employment of a sufficient number of educated doctors and midwives to implement these principles. By around 1820 the build up of the public medical administration was complete. The country was divided up into nine medical regions (*physicater*) each with its own superintending medical officer (*physicus*). The *physicats* were divided again into 67 medical districts (*lægedistrikter*), each with a district medical officer (*distrikts-læge*) and further sub-divided into midwife districts, about 650 in number.[17] The total number of doctors and midwives is shown in Figure 5.1. As can be seen from Figure 5.1, even by the mid-

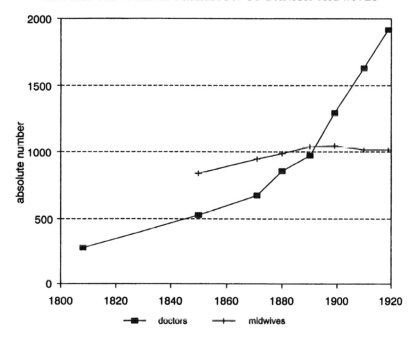

Figure 5.1 Number of doctors and midwives in Denmark, 1800–1920
Sources: V. Falbe-Hansen and W. Scharling, *Danmarks Statistik bd. V,* Copenhagen, 1881, pp. 80–2; J. Lehmann *et al.* (eds) *Denmark: Its Medical Organization, Hygiene and Demography,* Copenhagen, 1891, p. 54; *Medicinalberetning for Kongeriget Danmark for Aaret 1891,* Copenhagen, 1893, p. 190; *Statistiske undersøgelser nr. 19, Befolkningsudvikling og Sundhedsforhold 1901–60,* Copenhagen, Det statistiske departement, 1966, p. 165.

nineteenth century there were still far more midwives than doctors. Excluding Copenhagen, in 1850 there was one doctor for every 4,300 inhabitants compared with one midwife for every 1,700. Most midwives lived in the countryside, while doctors resided primarily in the towns.[18]

From a legal standpoint there was no doubt that the public medical officers[19] were the superiors of the midwives, and that midwives were to cease independent medical practice when an authorized doctor moved into the area. By mid-century, however, many midwives working in the most distant outposts of the official health system had become accustomed to working independently as birth attendants as well as providing general medical care;[20] they had little contact either with public medical officers or other doctors, who were normally beyond the reach of the rural population.

In 1860 midwives were still more numerous than doctors, but the latter were quickly catching up. The increase in their number meant that private medical practitioners began to settle in districts where no doctor had previously practised. An increasing number of doctors found themselves in a situation where they had to compete with a midwife, who had previously been the only authorized medical person in the locality.

Under pressure from the Danish Medical Association (*Den almindelige danske Lægeforening*), the Royal Board of Health decided in 1861 to tighten control over midwives. Superintending medical officers (*physici*) were required to call midwives to annual meetings and midwives were to give a detailed report of all the births they had attended in an official register.[21] In 1877 the Royal Board of Health adopted a new 'Instruction to Midwives' which reflected the more frequent contact which was taking place between doctors and midwives: 'If a physician is called in, she [the midwife] is to do everything according to his instructions, support him as best she can in any operations, which he may need to perform.' According to the same instruction, midwives were also obliged to report any cases of puerperal fever to the district medical officer.[22]

MIDWIVES' DUTIES AND IMAGE

Legislation is one thing, reality another. It is difficult to be precise about the kind of duties midwives actually performed, their status in the local community, how they regarded puerperal fever, and the conflicts they were involved in. Medical periodicals and the annual reports of the Royal Board of Health do, however, give us some insight into such matters.

In a lecture of 1873 N. Salomon, medical officer at the military hospital of Aalborg (1823–85), and from 1877 until his death a member of the Royal Board of Health, provided a comprehensive description of the activities of the midwives in his region, with the intention of encouraging discussion on the question of whether puerperal fever could be reduced by limiting the scope of midwives' activities. Dr Salomon divided the duties of midwives into three categories: first, assistance directly preceding, during and after the delivery, second, attendance on the mother and swaddling the child one or two times daily for eight to ten days after the birth, and, third, midwives' work with other patients when no physician was available or when they acted on the instructions of a physician.[23]

While Dr Salomon was of the opinion that daily visits to the new mother could be omitted, he felt that the medical services midwives provided to other patients were indispensable to the rural population, and, as they accounted for such a large proportion of midwives' incomes, they could not be prohibited. As an extra sphere of activity, Salomon mentioned that a number of midwives in the rural areas still laid out the dead, a practice that he wished to see prohibited immediately.[24]

Throughout the nineteenth century the economic situation of midwives was described as poor, their reputation as ambiguous. According to the world-view of the rural population, the midwife balanced herself on a fine line between the 'impure' and the 'exalted', as a result of her contact with the great forces of birth and death. As far as the urban middle class was concerned, the midwife also had a double role. With her knowledge of the female body and its workings, she brought reassurance in the embarrassing situation where the middle-class woman was forced to succumb to her own physicality. The midwife was a much appreciated female helper during a fundamental rite of passage in the female life cycle, but at the same time a representative of the 'unclean', which the middle-class woman sought to distance herself from at all costs as soon as the birth was over. In 1884 L. Meyer encapsulated this sentiment: the midwives are not held 'in any great esteem; but, surprisingly enough, despite this there is no lack of confidence shown in them' and another physician added that 'the female population seems to pay peculiar respect to the midwife [but] once a woman has taken her leave of the midwife, the latter is rejected. Her company is no longer desired, her position is not esteemed.'[25] As late as 1895 midwives were complaining of the double standard of morality, a mix of confidence and disrespect, with which they were treated:

> Those who in the most serious and overwhelming moments of their lives can place their life and death into our hands and cry out for our understanding and concern one moment, the next moment can with the greatest ease speak both without understanding and with contempt of the work of midwives.[26]

ANNE LØKKE

PHYSICIANS, MIDWIVES AND ANTISEPSIS

The debates between physicians concerning midwifery in the medical journals of the 1870s and 1880s often centred around the 'antiseptic campaign' against puerperal fever. The Lying-in Hospital in Copenhagen had been plagued by epidemics of puerperal fever throughout the nineteenth century, and the mortality rate reached extremely high levels in the 1860s. In 1868 the physician G.G. Stage defended his medical thesis on the occurrence of puerperal fever outside of Copenhagen. By investigating puerperal fever in areas where physicians for the most part were not involved in birth assistance, he avoided casting blame on them for spreading the infection. He thus created the possibility of reaching attentive ears amongst the physicians. His principal conclusions were twofold: that puerperal fever occurred very rarely outside of the Lying-in Hospital, and that it could be spread by midwives.[27]

Stage's thesis allegedly encouraged A. Stadfeldt (1830–96), who had recently been appointed head obstetrician at the Lying-in Hospital, to begin to experiment in 1869 with antiseptic procedures at deliveries. In 1867 Lister's article on antisepsis had been published in translation in the *Ugeskrift for Læger.*[28] Positive results were observed by the beginning of the 1870s and were published in 1876.[29] By the beginning of the 1880s Danish obstetricians were dizzy with success. Mortality due to puerperal fever at the Lying-in Hospital no longer exceeded puerperal fever mortality elsewhere, and also outside of the Hospital the rate was falling (see Figure 5.2).

For the midwives, however, Stage's thesis put them under suspicion. For most of the population, mortality rates at the Lying-in Hospital had no direct meaning. On the other hand, the public did catch on to the claim that the midwife could carry infections. The Royal Board of Health had already been thinking along these lines, linking the spread of puerperal fever to midwives. In 1850 they had granted superintending medical officers the right to suspend midwives for a specified period if 'circumstances give cause to imagine that the midwife may be spreading the infection'.[30] Suspension could be regarded as a sort of quarantine arrangement, the traditional response of the public health authorities to the imminent threat of infection. Stage's 1868 thesis had an important effect: the population and public health authorities no longer imagined, but rather regarded it as a certainty, that midwives could

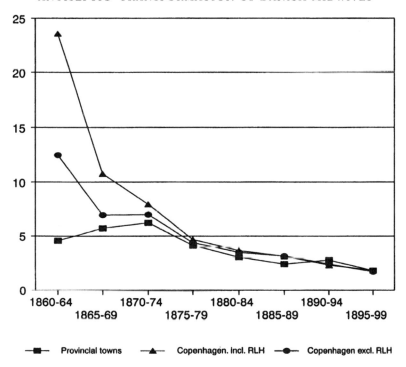

Figure 5.2 Deaths from puerperal fever in Denmark, 1860–99 per 1,000 births

Source: *Tidsskrift for Jordemødre*, 1903, vol. 13:6, p. 75.

Note: RLH = Royal Lying-in Hospital

spread puerperal fever. This led to an immediate surge in the number of midwife suspensions.[31] A midwife later described the 1860s as 'the time when we began to hear talk among the people that it was the birth assistants who were the actual cause of puerperal fever'.[32] A midwife who had been suspended after being linked to puerperal fever was avoided by the public. What she needed was knowledge and a means to cleanse herself in the eyes of the population she served. There was no help to be found in the *Textbook for Midwives* (*Lærebog for jordemødre*), the only professional literature for midwives available; the 1870 edition recommended general cleanliness but gave no detailed instructions on how to avoid the spread of infections.[33]

111

The dissemination of knowledge on puerperal fever and antisepsis

The Royal Board of Health made use of the public health authorities to request public medical officers to spread the latest knowledge to all midwives as early as 1871. This took the form of a printed leaflet, 'Directions for the prevention of puerperal fever' ('Vejledning til Forebyggelse af Barselfeberen').[34] The printed leaflet was potentially a useful channel of communication, as literacy was a precondition for admission to midwife training. The text of the leaflet was brief, it supplied no scientific explanations, but described the disease in a universe of clean and unclean, immediately accessible to midwives whose cultural roots were among the 'lower grades' of society. To begin with, the directions claimed that the disease could be transmitted by any 'unclean' and 'dirty' objects, persons and especially hands. Instructions followed on cleaning methods: boiling instruments in lye solution, and washing hands in soap, bleaching solution and carbolic acid. Clothes were to be disinfected by heating them in an oven with carbolic solution or sulphurous fumes. The directions forbade midwives from bringing their own sponges to wash the parturient to a delivery, and from laying out women dying in childbirth.

Dr Salomon's lecture of 1873 and the resulting debate in the local Aalborg medical association show that provincial doctors also had to rely upon the directions of 1871 for an understanding of puerperal fever. The Royal Board of Health had not provided doctors with better or fuller information than midwives.[35] After 1876 doctors could read about the results of new experiments in the medical journals, but as early as 1881 the midwives were also brought up to date with new directives from the Royal Board of Health. These instructions also made use of a concrete, visually expressive language, which was easy to remember, and at the same time well adapted to produce feelings of repugnance with regard to the danger of infection. The instructions explained how the 'poisonous substances of disease' were present in patients suffering from puerperal fever just as in other patients having 'malignant boils' and diseases with 'foul-smelling' excretions or 'reeking' discharges. The midwife should thus avoid contact with such patients. Similarly, all corpses, spoiled meat and other rotting substances were described as dangerous for the parturient and thus taboo for the midwife. The regime to be followed was carefully outlined, and in plain terms, just as in 1871, but it was more precise, for example, with regard to the preparation of carbolic solution. The word 'disinfection' was introduced and explained as meaning to 'kill any infectious substance possibly present'. The directions were without doubt written by Stadfeldt, who had become a member of the Royal Board of Health in 1877. It bears the signs of years of experience in explaining the antiseptic regime so that it would be comprehensible within the frame of reference of midwives, who were recruited from the lower rural and urban classes.[36]

It was customary around this time to compare Denmark with Prussia, and great emphasis would later be placed on the fact that the first Danish directives appeared seventeen years before the first Prussian ones.[37] There were also important differences in the contents of the directives. The Prussian version was comprised of orders and prohibitions written in a detailed, technical, scientific language which failed to place these commands into any comprehensible context. The Danish instructions were less detailed with reference to regime, but aimed at establishing a frame of reference within which the rules of practice were given a symbolic meaning. The metaphorical emblems evoke a physical feeling of infectious substances as lurking representatives of evil, while soap and water, nailbrushes and carbolic acid were presented as weapons placed at the midwife's disposal in the struggle against this evil. On another occasion, Stadfeldt argued that midwives were quick to learn to master antisepsis 'once they understood the principle of antisepsis and once their feeling of obligation and their own benefit were involved'.[38]

The effects of the directives were monitored systematically in the statistics of puerperal fever mortality which were published both in the annual medical reports of the Royal Board of Health and in medical journals. The results can be seen in Figure 5.2. The statistics had the effect of consolidating political support, and it was not without a sense of pride that it was stated, in a review of the situation in 1902, that Danish midwives had mastered antisepsis much more rapidly than their German counterparts.[39]

Disinfection or suspension?

For doctors practising in rural districts the directions concerning puerperal fever issued by the Royal Board of Health emphasized the necessity of establishing a solid basis for co-operation between themselves and midwives. The provisions on suspension in particular were a potential cause of conflict, because suspension highlighted the power relationship which existed between doctors and midwives. In 1877 a district medical officer asked for authorization to suspend midwives immediately if puerperal fever occurred among their patients.[40] This brought a sharp response from one of his colleagues, who advanced for the first time an opinion which would dominate the debate in the 1880s. The suspension of midwives, he believed, could and should be avoided, because it strained the relationship between midwife and doctor. It was often unjustified, and, with the coming of disinfection, a new scientific means became available which was of more value than suspension. In the eyes of the public, suspension made the midwife unclean; this undermined public respect for the profession and was detrimental to the midwife's economic situation. He proposed that the Royal Board of Health should instead work towards increasing respect for midwives by reviewing the entrance requirements to their school and increasing their income. He urged physicians to devote their efforts to making it possible for a midwife to become 'a clean and disinfected collegial assistant' to the physician, who should be respected 'as one who carries out a very onerous task, and bears great responsibility for the safety of families in this nation'.[41]

In 1881 a considerably younger private practitioner conceded that he did not have command of the local situation. For him the obligation to report instances of puerperal fever brought him problems, because the position of the midwife in his district was more secure than his own.[42]

> The most honoured Royal Board of Health appears to assume that the midwife is to be regarded as the physician's assistant in maternity cases, and the young physician may share the same conception when setting out, but practice soon teaches him that there is a difference between young apprentice mistresses and practising Madams ... and it might prove useful to recommend to every young physician setting out to a rural practice to treat the midwife with kid gloves, as his future practice will be determined to a great extent by his relationship to the latter and it is easy to see how defenceless he is when confronted by a midwife who silently works contrary to his efforts or ignores his existence.[43]

The obligation to pass information on could not help but cause conflict, since any reporting of puerperal fever by a physician would deprive a midwife of both income and esteem. The physician's proposal to resolve the problem followed the same lines, however, as that of the district medical officer mentioned above: to emphasize disinfection, instead of suspension, together with a rise in the basic salary of midwives.

THE DEBATE IN THE MEDICAL ASSOCIATION 1883

In 1883 the 'Shortcomings of our midwifery care and ways to combat them'[44] was the subject of discussion at the annual general meeting of the Danish Medical Association, which was attended by 101 out of an approximate total of 850 physicians nationally. All of the District Associations (*kredslægeforeninger*) were represented.[45] The debate at the meeting is thus a fairly reliable indication of the overall picture of the provincial doctor's conceptions of midwifery practice.[46]

The introductory lecture was delivered by a private medical practitioner, J. Brodersen. His central thesis was that midwifery in Denmark was well constituted and by no means inferior to that of other countries; on the contrary, the schooling of midwives took ten months in Denmark while in Germany, for example, it lasted for only five to six months. He wanted the occupation of midwife preserved and improved.[47] Improved primarily because he regarded it as problematical that the midwives belonged to the lower class. The midwives' 'shockingly low' wages[48] and the minimal entrance requirements to the school of midwifery meant that midwives were recruited from the worst situated of the common people. As a result of this, Dr Brodersen felt, most of the midwives lacked an appropriate social and cultural background, '*almindelig dannelse*'.[49] This had proved especially unfortunate in recent years, Brodersen continued, because an understanding of antisepsis demanded *dannelse*. Their lack of *dannelse* meant that the midwife pupils could not take full advantage of their instruction at the Lying-in Hospital. After leaving the school a midwife as a rule returned to her place of origin, and only a short while after 'she will, to a large extent, have returned to the old prejudices and misconceptions with which she has been brought up'.[50]

Brodersen wanted to recruit midwives who, like the rural doctors,

115

were 'a cut above' the level of the population amongst whom they worked. First and foremost, the occupation should be made accessible to the unmarried daughters of the urban upper-middle classes through removing the requirement that the midwife should be married and have given birth herself. In addition, midwives should be better paid, as this would attract the daughters of better-off tradesmen and farmers. Last but not least, some form of secondary school diploma should be required for entrance to the school for midwives. In addition, Brodersen felt that the public medical officers should tighten their control over midwives and that midwives' activities should be limited to birth assistance only.

The ensuing discussion was dominated by the *physici* Knudsen and Trautner. They agreed that midwifery could be improved, but felt that primarily this required support of the occupation from the authorities and the medical profession. Knudsen did not agree that midwives required '*almen dannelse*' since 'what is *dannelse*? what is *dannelse* for us is not *dannelse* for midwives'. Yet he wished midwife recruits to be both intelligent and interested in their profession, and not compelled to work to support their families; he felt that it was a positive step to accept unmarried pupils at the school. As regards remuneration, in many areas the situation of midwives would be greatly improved, Knudsen believed, if they merely received what was their due from the local authorities. Knudsen concluded by maintaining that 'in present times those in the occupation of midwife are regarded as a pariah caste' with only duties and no rights. Midwives cannot go on strike and may be suspended merely on the suspicion of carrying puerperal fever.

> If we take all of this into consideration, I believe I may justifiably say that the occupation of midwife is one of repression and subjugation, and that it will only be elevated in its own eyes and the eyes of the public through the determined and understanding direction of the state and the Authorities.[51]

This debate revealed the strengths and weaknesses of the midwifery system which the Absolute Monarchy had bequeathed to its successors.[52] The two *physici* almost automatically took up positions as defenders of the profession of midwife. Midwifery was their responsibility and any criticism was thus also a criticism of their conduct in office. The fact that midwives were recruited from among the 'commoners'[53] and were thus bearers of a different culture was a premise for the claim to maintain patriarchal power and the concern of the *physici* regarding the midwives. What Brodersen interpreted as a deficiency in the cultural background of midwives, that is, that the midwives, immediately upon returning home, would conduct their practice according to local customs, was without doubt one of the bases of the success of Danish midwifery. Their training and the time spent together with pupil midwives from other areas opened the midwives' eyes to the possibility of customs different to those they had been brought up with. Yet abiding by local traditions assured them public support. The *physicus* Knudsen was very explicit in his statement that folk culture included aspects which were important for the quality of birth attendance which the classes with '*dannelse*' did not possess. Knudsen's insight can be regarded as a direct heritage of the tradition of officialdom under Absolutism, which was embedded in a hierarchical yet negotiable relationship with folk culture. The higher royal officials sent to the provinces did not adapt to local folk culture, but acquired a very intimate knowledge of it, and this assisted them in their administrative activities. Practising physicians of Brodersen's sort, on the other hand, regarded themselves as men of the new era and regarded the 'commoners' as uneducated and old-fashioned; it was therefore the duty of the physician not to manage the existing conditions, but to change and improve them. With such a conviction it was naturally intolerable that midwives authorized by the state should not operate within the same bourgeois natural scientific conception of the world as did the physician himself.

THE DEBATE ON PHYSICIANS VS. MIDWIVES

Leopold Meyer's proposal to the Copenhagen Medical Society, described at the beginning of this chapter, that physicians should take over birth attendance, triggered off a debate on the issue in 1884. This debate introduced new factors, as it was conducted between obstetricians: four young residents with experience gained through appointments at the Lying-in Hospital, one of Copenhagen's most sought-after private obstetricians, E. Ingerslev, and Professor Stadfeldt of the Lying-in Hospital. Last but not least a midwife's voice was heard.[54]

All of the participants in the debate rejected, as mentioned earlier, the idea of eliminating the occupation of midwife, and all of them supported the proposal raised at the annual general meeting of the Danish Medical Association, that an attempt should be made to raise the status of the occupation of midwife through changes in recruitment and an improvement in remuneration. They agreed that 'bad' midwives existed, as did bad physicians, but the majority of midwives were capable women who acted in accordance with what they had learned at their training school.[55]

The key reason for their rejection of Meyer's proposal was, however, that none of the participants in the debate could imagine a physician being willing to carry out the tasks which they saw as being at the core of the midwife's work:

> If the physician is to assume the duties of the midwife, he must also assume what is to my mind the most important obligation of our midwives, i.e., that they, once they have been summoned to attend a woman in labour, may not leave her until the birth is completed. In this provision lies, in my opinion, the telling point of justification for our midwives; even such an enthusiastic obstetrician as Dr Leopold M. would certainly think twice before spending two entire days in a sixth floor apartment with windows only to the back in Adelgade, where he would receive neither light, fresh air or food.[56]

If the physicians were to take it upon themselves to attend women in labour for half a day or entire days at a time they would neglect the rest of their practice, while only a very small part of the population would be able to pay the physician a suitable fee for his trouble. If the physician was not on hand at the moment he was needed, his superior qualifications would hardly result in an improvement in birth attendance. Apart from this, Stadfeldt added, it was an advantage that the midwife was a woman, because women were more poorly paid than men; thus society could get more birth attendance for the same amount of money by employing women. Birth attendance was supposed to benefit the entire population, and those with more limited means should also be able to afford it.

Ingerslev, with his flourishing private obstetrical practice, was adamant in his rejection of the idea of physicians taking over birth attendance. He demanded statistical proof that morbidity and mortality amongst parturients and infants were lower when birth assistance was in the hands of male practitioners rather than educated midwives. He referred to statistics which already showed a decrease in mortality due to puerperal fever, despite the fact that midwives had only had knowledge of antisepsis for a few years. This, he concluded, indicated that there were no grounds for contending that midwives could not master antisepsis successfully.[57]

Fru J. Wegener, head midwife at the Lying-in Hospital was the first midwife to make her voice heard in the public debate. She took the same line as other participants, but also emphasized the sometimes improper use of antiseptics amongst physicians. She added that most physicians lacked sufficient knowledge of normal births, as a result of which they often intervened in normal labour with substances to speed the birth or applied forceps, with the delivery concluding in an 'unfavourable result'. Wegener was of the opinion that the 'patience and perseverance' which the midwife demonstrated when assisting impatient or nervous parturients would seldom be possessed by physicians.[58]

Professor Stadfeldt unhesitatingly attributed this 'something' which the midwife, but not the physician, could bring to a birth, to her sex. He was of the opinion that most Danish women preferred to be assisted by a woman. This was not because 'our women are so silly or prudish that at the serious moment of giving birth they would in principle push away male assistance', but because the midwife as a woman had a better basis for offering empathetic and patient assistance than a man. Women were right to prefer a midwife, he concluded, assuming *nota bene* that this meant a well-educated and conscientious midwife, who sought the help of a physician if any situation arose that she could not handle.[59] He was also of the opinion that women were from the start better qualified than men to become efficient antiseptic users, as antisepsis was basically a regime of cleanliness, which could be viewed as an extension of women's housework. Stadfeldt concluded that if more 'intelligent' assistance was desired at deliveries, the best way to achieve this would be to educate female obstetricians.

The obstetricians' defence of the occupation of midwife appeared to follow the same lines of argument as that of the public medical officers: the instruction of midwives was their responsibility and criticism of it was therefore also a criticism of the physicians. It is clear that it was a major factor in the professional identity of the obstetricians to develop a system of birth attendance which would produce positive results in the form of low infant and maternal mortality rates. Since all the obstetricians furthermore had witnessed through practical experience that the high quality of Danish birth assistance was achieved through the constant attendance of the midwife on the woman in labour, a task the physicians themselves did not wish to take on, they could not argue for the elimination of the role of the midwife without contradicting the desire to maintain a well-functioning system of childbirth attendance.

One of the young residents at the Lying-in Hospital argued, however, for an approach whereby the struggle between conflicting loyalties in maintaining the system of birth attendance and the physicians' efforts to professionalize could be avoided, by gradually accustoming the population to use more 'professional' personnel for normal births. There would thus be room for well-educated, properly remunerated midwives who were responsible for the labour-intensive part of the birth process, while physicians would have a hand in the final stages of normal births, as a guarantee of greater security for those of the population who could afford it.

LOCAL CONFLICTS – CENTRAL AUTHORITY

It thus difficult to speak of *one* type of relationship between physicians and midwives in the 1880s. There was at least one central relationship and a number of local ones. The Royal Board of Health, the public medical officers, and the physicians at the Lying-in Hospital naturally displayed a paternal concern for and power over the midwives, secure in their conviction of their own professional, social and economic superiority. Private practitioners, in comparison, could find themselves in a situation of direct competition with midwives, not only in connection with birth attendance, but more generally as healers and advisers on health. Most general practitioners, however, seem to have been able to deal with this situation, as their numbers grew in proportion to the population, while the number of midwives stagnated. A few conflicts, however, grew to such an intensity that they found their way into the pages of the medical journals.

In 1885 a conflict developed which made it clear that the support a local practitioner could expect from the Royal Board of Health was limited. A rural private practitioner had complained to his superintending medical officer (*physicus*) of a district midwife who he maintained had not followed his advice in a case involving bottle-feeding. After the *physicus* had spoken to the midwife he came to the conclusion that she had not exceeded her competence, but he cautioned her not to contradict the prescriptions of physicians.[60] This did not satisfy the private practitioner. He wanted the midwife punished, but instead he received a sharp reply from the secretary of the Royal Board of Health: in cases of disagreement of such an everyday character the individual physician should, it was stated, know how to conduct himself:

it is, after all, the ability of the physician to assert his authority over the patient which is, in the end, the decisive factor; if this ability is present . . . then the availability of external coercive measures toward the midwife is inconsequential.[61]

The Royal Board of Health's position can be interpreted as encapsulating the view that each individual physician, by virtue of his greater knowledge, complete autonomy, and superior results should be well armed to win the struggle for patients' favours. If a physician could not do so, the medical profession would scarcely be doing itself a service by offering him too much support. The Royal Board of Health had, through its restrictions and control, made sure that midwives were no threat to the medical profession as such.

TRANSFORMATION IN THE 1890s

In 1890 a decisive change occurred, when midwives were given a public voice in print. Inspired by similar journals in other countries, Th.B. Hansen (1852–96) assistant obstetrician to the Lying-in Hospital from 1887 to 1890, established a journal for midwives, the *Tidsskrift for Jordemødre*. The journal was intended to bolster the status of the midwife. It was to penetrate the isolation surrounding individual midwives, and serve as both a forum for the interests of the occupation and its professional development. The first issue contained a warm recommendation from Professor Stadfeldt.

During its early years the journal supported the picture presented by the public medical officers, of midwives constantly struggling against poverty, and having a static position within the authority structures of a class-bound society, lacking faith in their own capacity to bring about improvements. An anonymous midwife wrote in 1892:

Hon. Doctor. I am very pleased to see the concern you feel for matters of midwifery and how eager you are to assist them, for which I thank you greatly; this is, however, a difficult task you have taken upon yourself, and the obstacles will come from the midwives themselves.

121

She mentions the ignorance which resulted from having limited means and the poverty which forced midwives to compete instead of co-operating. Another wrote that, while she thought it a good idea to found midwives' societies, midwives did not have the necessary information and education to be able to direct a meeting, since, as the result of their birth, upbringing and marriage, they belonged to the class of 'commoners'.[62] She later became an assiduous correspondent and dedicated organizer of midwives.

Changes were in fact already under way. Better-situated unmarried women were applying to the school for midwives and their wages improved slightly in 1893. In 1895 the period of study was lengthened to a full year, a compulsory interim examination was introduced, and instruction in anatomy and physiology was reformed. In 1891 midwives founded their first local society and in the course of the 1890s more would be set up, by 1902 providing the basis for the formation of a national association of midwives. Professor Leopold Meyer became the first president of the association![63]

More self-confident contributions were not long in appearing in the journal. In 1894 ten midwives published sharp replies to the translation of an article written by Professor Winter, the editor of the German midwives' journal. The article dealt with the relationship between midwives and physicians. Winter was of the opinion that in recent years German midwives had acquired an inappropriate degree of self-confidence. This had led to competition and enmity between physicians and midwives. Winter urged German midwives to keep silent and to obey the doctor, even if he was acting improperly. If a physician failed to disinfect himself it was an impudent and intolerable act of excessive self-esteem to hand him a nailbrush and carbolic solution and request that he used them. If puerperal fever should occur and the midwife was blamed, she had to trust that the superintending medical officer would defend her. Midwives should not campaign for their rights but put their faith in their superiors.[64] The Danish readers were of the opinion that the relationship between physicians and midwives was far better in Denmark, but should conflicts over disinfection arise the midwife was responsible to 'God, the authorities, the mother and child', which prohibited her from acting as Professor Winter desired. The editor, who was after all a physician, replied that the article had been published to show what a respected German medical man, who was well inclined toward midwives, felt he was justified and even obliged to request of them. The editor considered it natural that the midwives were aroused and hoped that the article would prevent similar developments taking place in Denmark.[65]

From the mid-1890s onwards articles began to appear centring on the modernization process that the occupation of midwife was undergoing. Under the heading 'Then and now' a midwife who had qualified in 1865 recalled the speech delivered by the minister following the examination:

> From now on we had left the ranks of the women, as humility, modesty, and all of these other charming virtues accorded to the chaste woman, were now behind us, and as we now, in caring for others, sought to reach the world of men, although we naturally could not manage this . . . No, we had to be satisfied with standing between the two, being neither man nor woman. A strange, bisexual social existence, don't you think? . . . Years passed before I could gladly accept this occupation which I had chosen for myself.[66]

Others wrote that there was still shame attached to the profession, and proposed campaigning against this prejudice amongst the public and midwives themselves, for example, by writing about childbirth in the press. Embarrassment was the main theme of the keynote speech delivered at the first general meeting of midwives: 'As long as it is no shame for a married woman to give birth to her child, it should hardly be considered a shame to be the one who, with all her special feminine capabilities, stands at her side'.[67] In 1897 a midwife noted that, in the eyes of the general public, midwives were no longer regarded as an inferior class of beings.[68] It was an indication that things had already moved on.

By the turn of the century midwives' contributions to the journal show that at least some of them were using cleanliness and order to indicate their position *vis-à-vis* both the traditions of folk culture and the middle classes' puritanical regard of bodily functions. They symbolically tied themselves to medical science and a modern, rationalist view of the world:

> The midwife arrives to perform her duty in her simple dress, clean and neat, bringing her large white apron which she dons for the task. All those present see how carefully she cleans the woman, before and after the birth, taking care to see to it that no permanent stains are left on the bedclothes.[69]

Another article related how the midwife should bring order, calm and propriety to the birthing room, seeing to the removal of men, children and the neighbourhood women. To have too many women assisting was described as disturbing; one in the kitchen and another in the labour room was sufficient. In other articles, young midwives explained how to put an end to local preferences for standing and sitting labour positions, which they considered to be old-fashioned. The women should be persuaded to give birth in bed lying, hygienically, on an oilcloth.[70]

The narrowing of the scope of the midwife's work was discussed as a positive step towards enlightenment and the common good. One midwife related that her predecessor had been physician, veterinary surgeon, and cook. On another occasion mention is made of the fact that cupping, blood-letting and laying out the dead were well-paid aspects of the work of earlier generations of midwives, and that the latter especially was hardly a suitable activity to combine with the tasks of a midwife.[71] The dominant trend during the journal's first decade was to describe the developments taking place as progress and liberation from the tyrannical traditions of older world-views. The identity of the modern midwife was constructed on cleanliness and order, and also the recognition of every child's right to life. Tales of midwives of former times, who were willing to register unwanted births as stillborn, were told with aversion.[72]

Around 1910 the break with the culture of the 'commoners' had progressed so far that midwives could be regarded from the vantage point of the physicians as 'the outposts of natural science among the populace'.[73] It would only be in a much later period that it was recognized that some positive aspects of traditional birthing practices could be lost through modernization. For the midwives who brought about the process of modernization, it was a relief to be able to exchange their ambiguous position, which their connection to life's most incomprehensible miracle had invested them, in preference for science, anatomical explanations, hygienic white aprons, and carbolic solution.

THE TWENTIETH CENTURY

In 1914 a new law was adopted as the basis of midwifery practice, the first since 1714. This was primarily a case of belatedly adjusting the provisions of the legislation to accord with the customs and practice that had developed during the intervening two hundred years. The new Act confirmed that it was the responsibility of the authorities to ensure that all the country's citizens, even those without financial means, had access to skilled birth attendance.[74] In addition the Act provided for an improvement in midwives' wages, with guarantees of payment and pensions. As the motivation for consolidating midwifery, the committee set up to make recommendations wrote that the medical profession did not wish to take upon itself the task of assisting at normal births, since this did not fit well with the rest of their practice.[75]

No significant conflicts appear during the first half of the twentieth century. By 1920 it was common, in the most affluent homes, to have the family doctor, a midwife and a nurse attending at a birth. For the great majority of the population, however, a midwife was unassisted at all normal births. The definition of 'normal' was just as dependent upon the distance to the nearest doctor as it was to the type of irregularity.[76] Not until the 1930s, when many women began to demand analgesics in childbirth, did physicians begin to attend regularly at normal births. This was a development which proceeded even more rapidly towards the end of the 1940s, when more and more local health insurance associations were forced to acquiesce to the demands of women's organizations and cover the expenses of both a midwife and a physician. By this point, however, midwives were so well educated and highly esteemed that the division of labour was generally such that the midwife directed the birth while the physician sat on the sidelines and waited.[77]

Until around 1950 most births took place in the home, although complicated cases were to an increasing extent transferred to a hospital. Only after 1973, when the combination of district midwife and privately practising physician was replaced by publicly employed midwives in the maternity wards of hospitals, did the remaining third of Danish births move to the hospital.

CONCLUSION

Amongst feminist historians, the almost total takeover of childbirth by obstetricians in the USA is well known and generally interpreted from a gender perspective. In Denmark such a takeover did not occur. Birth attendance in normal cases is still handled by midwives towards the end of the twentieth century. The great transformation in Danish childbirth services cannot thus be characterized as the replacement of one profession by another or its masculinization, and did not take place around the beginning of the twentieth century. The deciding change in Denmark followed the Act of 1973, and can be described as hospitalizing, depersonalizing and 'technologizing'. It resulted in an almost complete break with what had been the central principle of Danish birth attendance since the 1714 Act, that is the constant attendance of a local midwife during the entire labour and birth with the purpose of providing what was referred to in the 1800s as that special feminine patience and empathy which was assumed to strengthen the capacity of the parturient to have a normal delivery.[78]

There is in fact no doubt that Danish midwifery underwent a crisis in the 1870s. The crisis was not caused by antisepsis, but antisepsis became the catalyst which brought the crisis to light. The crisis itself can be described as a general crisis of development, because processes of modernization were under way in so many other areas of society, while midwifery was solidly anchored in the structure of Absolutist officialdom and the social structure and cultural forms of the early nineteenth century. This anchoring had been of central importance for the population's acceptance of trained, authorized midwives during this period. But what had been uniquely suitable during the first half of the nineteenth century became outmoded with the rise in general prosperity and the gradual development of a scientific, rationalist world-view amongst the majority of the well-to-do.

If the crisis appeared primarily in connection with the antiseptic campaign against puerperal fever, this is related to the fact that the teachings on infection struck at the midwives' centuries-old, but still precarious balance between being valued helpers and representatives of life's dark forces. So long as giving birth was regarded as an unavoidable contact with chaos, disintegration, disorder and creation, which society could attempt to protect itself from by means of taboos, it was unproblematic and inescapable that the status of the midwife would be ambiguous. There was also a certain logic in her belonging to the lower class, which in general came into contact with things unclean.[79] At the moment when it became regarded as a fact that the midwife was a potential bearer of infection, the balance tipped and birth attendance had to adapt to keep in step with the times. As has been shown, Danish midwives emerged on the other side of the crisis with their status restored, their right to practise independently at normal births maintained, and, not least, without being removed altogether in competition with physicians.

I have tried to show in the foregoing discussion that the fact that the crisis had these consequences in Denmark is related to the development of officialdom under the Absolutist monarchy. Under Absolutism the concern for population growth led to the recruitment of midwives in the official system of health care as a part of the area of responsibility of *medici* as early as 1672. The organization of district midwives ensured that the entire population, in towns as well as thinly populated rural districts, both wealthy and poor, had access to birth assistance of a high quality for a relatively modest charge. Both the population and the physicians – not least the public medical officers – had become accustomed to regarding proper birth assistance as consisting of a well-trained midwife being present continuously from the time the pains became regular until the mother and child had been washed and dressed after the birth, in most places followed by one or two daily visits for eight to fourteen days. The discussions in the medical journals indicate that no Danish physician wished to assume this work, even if they were paid three times what the midwives received. That the taking over of birth attendance by the medical profession would have meant a lowering of its quality is not, however, an explanation for why it did not happen.

What was significant was that an important and influential portion of the medical profession was obliged to look after the nation's best interests as royal officials. For the public medical officers and the professor of the Lying-in Hospital envisaged their professional identity as responsible wielders of power in the name of King and country, and this had more significance than their conception of themselves as representatives of the medical profession as a whole. Provision of effective childbirth services was an indication of their success as medical officials, and this gave them a major stake in determining what form of birth attendance, under the conditions of the time, was optimal as measured in infant and maternal mortality. Thus there were representatives within the medical profession, who as part of their own career objectives, worked to see that midwives maintained their role and would quickly be brought up to date on the newest indications of medical science for the prevention of puerperal fever infection. That Professor Stadfeldt possessed a tremendous talent for making the instructions on and techniques for disinfection meaningful outside the world of natural science, so that the midwives did in fact master them, was naturally fortuitous. No more of a coincidence, however, than that just this obligation, of building bridges between the academic medical world and the folk culture to which the midwives belonged, had been part of the professional obligations of professors at the Lying-in Hospital since the establishment of the school for midwives.

That the well-off portion of the population also without hesitation wanted to keep the midwife as the central helper in normal births, possibly with a physician standing by, can also be ascribed to the rapidity with which midwives took on the process of modernization. The population had scarcely realized that there was a problem before the transformation was well under way, and here the midwives themselves took an active part. They sought out, mastered and demonstrated the new knowledge, so that antisepsis, which had initially appeared as a threat to their occupation was quickly turned into a weapon in the struggle for its reputation. Thus as early as the 1880s midwives could already show positive results in the statistics on maternal mortality and in the course of the 1890s presented themselves as envoys of progress, natural science and rationality in contrast to the stagnation and superstition of former times. The relatively high level of education of the midwives and their accompanying literacy served without doubt as good premises for this active adaptation to contemporary demands.

The medical establishment which the officialdom of Absolutism had bequeathed to its successors in Denmark ushered in a system of birth assistance which Irvine Loudon has designated as the most secure available according to the requirements of the time.[80] This does not, however, mean that all liberal national governments actively or passively tolerated or condoned the suppression of midwifery by physicians, or that strongly hierarchical official government bureaucracies in general developed a system of birth attendance based on midwives. The Netherlands, with a government system less influenced by centralized bureaucracy, and a liberal society, entered the twentieth century with a system of birth attendance dominated by midwives, while the regime of officialdom throughout Prussia limited the activities of midwives. This is an argument for a concrete analysis of the development of birth attendance in all national settings, because its development takes place in an interplay of local and national power relationships.

ACKNOWLEDGEMENTS

This chapter was translated from Danish by Keneva Kunz.

NOTES

1 'Om en Udvidelse af Lægens Virksomhed som Fødselshjælper', published in *Hospitalstidende* ('Hospital Journal'), 1884, 3rd series, vol. 2, pp. 145–53.

2 There are examples of both 'helping women' (*nærkoner*), who occasionally assisted at births, and midwives for whom birth attendance was their occupation: I. Dübeck, 'Jordemødre i retshistorisk belysning', *Historie*, 1973, vol. 3, pp. 337–90; E. Ingerslev, *Fragmenter af Fødselshjælpens historie* ('Fragments from the history of birth assistance'), Copenhagen, 1906.

3 Dübeck, 'Jordemødre', p. 339.

4 The Absolute Monarchy was introduced in 1660 and abolished in 1848–49.

5 'Forordning om Medicis og Apothekere' ('Decree concerning doctors and pharmacists'), 4 Dec. 1672. Cited in C.P.N. Petersen, *Den Danske Medicinallovgivning*, vols 1–2, Copenhagen, 1833–36. Laws and decrees in force in the years 1836–72 can be found in F.A. Uldall, *Haandbog i den gjeldende civile Medicinal-Lovgivning for Danmark*, Copenhagen, 1855 and F.A. Uldall, *Den civile Medicinallovgivning i Kongeriget Danmark*, vols 1–2, Copenhagen, 1863–72. The period after 1872 is covered by 'Den civile Medicinallovgivning' published by the Royal Board of Health.

6 It was not until after 1700 that *medici* were educated on a fairly regular basis at the University of Copenhagen: J. Brix, *En sammenlignende studie af udviklingen indenfor lægestanden i kongeriget og hertugdømmet Slesvig indtil år 1864*, Aabenraa, Forlaget Lycke, 1992, pp. 159, 191–2.

7 '*Læge*' is the Danish word for the group of doctors qualified to practise both medicine and surgery. This is equivalent to the American usage of 'physicians' (and English 'doctors'); no difference can be inferred from this term between medical scientists, clinicians, and general practitioners.

8 'Forordning 30 Nov. 1714': Petersen, *Medicinallovgivning*, vol. 1, 1833. The next Act concerning midwifery would be passed in 1914.

9 Comprised of the professors of the medical faculty in Copenhagen, the King's own Royal Physician, and the City *Physicus*.

10 Dübeck, 'Jordemødre', p. 350. This can be compared with the end of the nineteenth century, when the entire country was densely served by midwives, with some 330 to 350 examinations taking place each decade. Annual lists of names can be found from 1890 onwards in the *Tidsskrift for Jordemødre* ('Journal for Midwives').

11 The Lying-in Hospital was founded in 1750 as a free maternity service where midwives assisted women without charge and in confidence. In 1787 it was given the status of a Royal foundation with the twofold purpose of providing a place for unwed mothers to give birth and a

place of training for midwives and doctors: A. Stadfeldt, *Kjøbenhavns Fødselsstiftelse 1787–1887*, Copenhagen, 1887.

12 'Royal Ordinance of 13 May 1803': Petersen, *Medicinallovgivning*, vol. 1, 1833.

13 'Regulation of 21 Nov. 1810': ibid., vol. 2, 1834.

14 Instructions of an unknown date, but published in 1797, and continued in an almost identical 'Instruction of 3 May 1836': Uldall, *Den civile Medicinallovgivning*, 1835, p. 43.

15 It is still unknown if or how this rule was put into effect, but only a few complaints are recorded in the Royal Board of Health archives of authorized midwives not receiving their fee.

16 The Royal Board of Health examined the situation of midwives in 1852 and found no complaints of unqualified competition: *Det kongelige Sundhedscollegiums Forhandlinger for Aaret 1852*, Copenhagen, 1853, p. 258. In 1892 it was reported that there had been no conflicts between unauthorized and authorized midwives 'during the last half century': J. Lehmann *et al.* (ed.) *Hygiene and Demography, Denmark its Medical Organization, Presented to the Seventh International Congress of Hygiene and Demography London 1891*, Copenhagen, Gjellerup, 1891, p. 49.

17 V. Falbe-Hansen and W. Scharling, *Danmarks Statistik*, vol. V Copenhagen, 1881, pp. 77, 82. The figures are for the years 1825 and 1829. All figures are exclusive of Copenhagen. The number of midwife districts is not known precisely before 1850 when they totalled 686. Copenhagen had approximately ninety midwives and a much greater concentration of doctors than the rest of the country.

18 Ibid., pp. 76–83.

19 I use public medical officer as a blanket term for both *physici* and *distriktslæger* (district medical officer). In the nineteenth century there is no Danish equivalent to the term public medical officer.

20 Kanc. Skrivelser (Chancellery records), 28 Nov. 1829, 7 Dec. 1843 and 9 Sept 1850 confirmed that midwives had the right to give medical treatment based on their training, when no authorized doctor was available: Petersen, *Medicinallovgivning*; Uldall, *Den civile Medicinallovgivning*.

21 Prior to this only stillbirths had to be reported by the midwife: *Ugeskrift for Læger* ('Weekly Journal for Physicians'), 1861, 2nd series, vol. 35, p. 378.

22 'Instruction', 28 Sept. 1877 (*Den civile Medicinallovgivning*).

23 N. Salomon, 'Om Jordemødrenes Forretninger med specielt Hensyn til Barselsfeberen', *Ugeskrift for Læger*, 1873, 3rd series, vol. 17, pp. 254–60.

24 Ibid., p. 253.

25 *Hospitalstidende*, 1884, 3rd series, vol. 2, pp. 153, 209.

26 *Tidsskrift for Jordemødre*, 1895, vol. 6:1, p. 6.

27 G.G. Stage, *Undersøgelser ang. Barselfeberen i Danmark udenfor Kjøbenhavn* ('Investigations concerning puerperal fever in Denmark outside of Copenhagen'), Copenhagen, 1868.

28 *Ugeskrift for Læger*, 1867, 3rd series, vol. 4. p. 361.

29 In connection with the International Congress on Hygiene in Brussels:

'Les Maternités, leur organisation et administration, illustrées par la statistique de 25 ans de la maternité de Copenhague'. Danish summary in *Ugeskrift for Læger*, 1876, 3rd series, vol. 22, pp. 225–32.

30 'Just. min. skr. 14 Nov. 1850' (Records of the Ministry of Justice): Uldall, *Den civile Medicinallovgivning*.

31 *Det kongelige Sundhedscollegiums Forhandlinger* ('Proceedings of the Royal Board of Health'), medical report, with an annual section on puerperal fever. The rules concerning suspension were made more precise in *Just. Min. Skr.* ('Records of the Ministry of Justice'), 27. Feb. 1873.

32 *Tidsskrift for Jordemødre*, 1896, vol. 6:8, p. 115.

33 A. Stadfeldt, *Lærebog for Jordemødre*, Copenhagen, 1870, p. 23. The professor and head obstetrician at the Royal Lying-in Hospital was responsible for publishing a textbook for midwives, which would contain everything a midwife ought to know. The first edition was published in 1790. In the 1880 edition the risk of infection was mentioned and methods of disinfection covered. The edition of 1891 was completely rewritten in the light of the new understanding of the subject.

34 'Circular of the Royal Board of Health 12 May 1871': Uldall, *Den civile Medicinallovgivning*. H. Blomquist, 'For det Almene Vel', *Fortid og nutid*, 1991, vol. 4, p. 245 indicates that this was written by Stadfeldt.

35 *Ugeskrift for Læger*, 1873, 3rd series, vol. 17, p. 250ff.

36 'Circular of the Royal Board of Health 10 May 1881', *Den civile Medicinallovgivning*, 1881. The Danish word for the social stratum from which midwives where recruited is '*almue*'; the closest translation is 'commoner', but used in the nineteenth century it referred to people from the lower rural and urban classes, who still were bearers of a folk culture with deep roots in the countryside of the sixteenth to eighteenth centuries.

37 The Prussian directives appeared in 1888: 'Vejledning for Jordemødre i Preussen til Forebyggelse af Barselfeber', *Tidsskrift for Jordemødre*, 1891, vol. 1:6, pp. 75–8.

38 A. Stadfeldt, 'Om Jordemødrenes sociale og økonomiske Stilling' ('On the social and economic situation of midwives'), *Berlingske Tidende*, 2–4 April 1884, I–III, cited I.

39 E. Ingerslev, 'Den puerperale Mortalitet -Barselfeberdødeligheden – i Provinsbyerne og København 1860–1899', *Ugeskrift for Læger*, 1902, 5th series, vol. 9, pp. 35–6.

40 A. Berg, 'En lille Barselfeberepidemi', *Ugeskrift for Læger*, 1877, 3rd series, vol. 23, pp. 449–53.

41 H. Matthiessen, 'Nogle Bemærkninger i Anledning af Dr. A. Bergs: En lille Barselfeberepidemi', *Ugeskrift for Læger*, 1877, 3rd series, vol. 24, p. 49.

42 In a circular of 10 May 1881 the Royal Board of Health made it the task of all physicians in the country to see to it that midwives followed the rules for the prevention of puerperal fever. The article is written under the pseudonym of 'Conor', and the identity of the actual author has not been discovered, but it is likely that he was one of the younger physicians: 'Nogle Bemærkninger om Jordemoderinstitutionen og

dens forhold til Lægestanden', *Ugeskrift for Læger*, 1881, 4th series, vol. 4, p. 77–81.

43 Ibid., p. 78.

44 In Danish, 'Manglerne ved vort Jordemodervæsen og Midlerne derimod'.

45 Out of approximately 1,000 physicians in 1890, 564 were members. In the provinces the majority of medical practitioners were members, but in Copenhagen only one-third: *Hygiene and Demography*, pp. 33–5.

46 Supplement to *Ugeskrift for Læger*, 1883, 3rd series, vol. 25, pp. 56–79.

47 Ibid., p. 56.

48 District midwives at this time received between 100 and 160 kroner per year, a modest house rent-free, some fuel and fodder for a cow, plus remuneration for each case of labour which was fixed by the Ministry of Justice at between 1 and 8 kroner according to the social position of the parturient. The economic position of a district midwife was comparable to an unskilled male worker; a female unskilled worker received approximately half the midwife's income. A district medical officer was paid around 1,000–1,900 kroner per annum, in some cases an official residence, plus a fee paid by patients per consultation: *Hygiene and Demography* pp. 31, 53; F.L.E. Smith *et al.* (eds), *Den danske lægestand*, Copenhagen, 1885, pp. 275–83.

49 '*Dannelse*' is equivalent to the German '*bildung*', '*Almindelig dannelse*' to '*allgemeine Bildung*'. This refers not to formal education, but formal education is one aspect of it, because it means well brought up in middle- or upper-class culture. See also note 36.

50 Supplement to *Ugeskrift for Læger*, 1883, 3rd series, vol. 25, pp. 58–60. See also the chapter by Marland in this volume.

51 Ibid., p. 75.

52 Officialdom and the structure of medical care were not significantly affected by the abolition of the Absolute Monarchy in 1848–49.

53 See note 36.

54 L. Meyer *et al.*, 'Om en Udvidelse af Lægens Virksomhed som Fødselshjælper', *Hospitalstidende*, 1884, 3rd series, vol. 2, pp. 145–53, 205–10, 224–30, 258–62, 262–9, 316–18, 319–24, 372–5; Stadfeldt, 'Om Jordemødrenes sociale og økonomiske Stilling', I–III.

55 Meyer *et al.*, *Hospitalstidende*, p. 207.

56 Ibid., p. 207.

57 Ibid., p. 269. For the incidence of mortality amongst trained midwives compared to doctors, see the chapter by Loudon in this volume, and for anxieties on puerperal fever in Manchester and connections with midwives, see Mottram in this volume.

58 Meyer *et al.*, *Hospitalstidende* p. 317.

59 Stadfeldt, 'Om Jordemødrenes sociale og økonomiske Stilling', I.

60 C. Struckmann, 'Et Spørgsmaal vedrørende Jordemoderens Kompetence ligeoverfor den private Læge', *Ugeskrift for Læger*, 1885, 4th series, vol. 11, pp. 583–9, vol. 12 pp. 34–5, 92–3, 220–1.

61 E. Madsen: 'Om Jordemoderens Kompetence ligeoverfor den private Læge', *Ugeskrift for Læger*, 1885, 4th series, vol. 12. p. 68.

62 Anonymous, 'Letter to the editor from a rural district midwife',

Tidsskrift for Jordemødre, 1892, vol. 2:10, p. 123; M. Nielsen (district midwife), Letter to the editor, 'Om Jordemoderforeninger', *Tidsskrift for Jordemødre*, 1892, vol. 3:2, p. 23.
63 The history of the organization of midwives is described in H. Cliff, 'Nød und fattigdom fik jordemødrene til at organiscre sig' ('Poverty and desperation forced the midwives to organize'), *Tidsskrift for Jordemødre*, 1987, vol. 97:11, pp. 4–14.
64 Prof. Winter, 'Jordemoder og Læge', *Tidsskrift for Jordemødre*, 1894, vol. 4:9, pp. 101–10.
65 Letters to the editor and editorial comment, ibid., pp. 117–21.
66 M. Nielsen, 'Før og nu', *Tidsskrift for Jordemødre*, 1894, vol. 5:1, pp. 10–11.
67 'Report on the first Danish midwife meeting', *Tidsskrift for Jordemødre*, 1895, vol. 6:1, p. 6.
68 K. Høgsberg (district midwife), 'Jordemødrenes Kaar', *Tidsskrift for Jordemødre*, 1897, vol. 8:2, p. 17.
69 M. Nielsen (district midwife), 'Lidt om Renlighed', *Tidsskrift for Jordemødre*, 1898, vol. 8:11, p. 128.
70 O. Gebaur, 'Om Jordemoderkaldet', *Tidsskrift for Jordemødre*, 1902, vol. 12:4, pp. 45–47, 57–60; M. Nielsen, 'Fra Praksis, Fødsel af Trillinger', *Tidsskrift for Jordemødre*, 1898, vol. 8:5, pp. 54–5; Y (anonymous), 'Fra Provinsen', *Tidsskrift for Jordemødre*, 1903, vol. 13:11, p. 144.
71 'Report on the meeting of the Danish organization of midwives 1905', *Tidsskrift for Jordemødre*, 1905, vol. 16:1, p. 11; Y, 'Fra Provinsen', p. 144.
72 M.T. Nielsen, 'Om Udstedelse af Dødsattester', *Tidsskrift for Jordemødre*, 1903, vol. 13:10, p. 134.
73 A district medical officer, reviewing the activities of midwives during the previous twenty years: R. Oppermann, 'Barselsfeber og dens Forebyggelse', *Tidsskrift for Jordemødre*, 1922, vol. 32:11, p. 167.
74 *Medicinalkommisionens Betænkning angaaende Jordemodervæsenet* ('Remarks of the medical commission on midwifery'), Copenhagen, 1913, p. 9.
75 Ibid., p. 18.
76 Midwives were not permitted to use forceps, only to sew perineal tears and do everything they could manage with their own hands.
77 The course of study for midwives became a two-year programme in 1927, and a three-year one in 1939: H. Cliff, *Jordemoderliv* ('A midwife's life'), Copenhagen, Borgen, 1992, p. 27.
78 How midwives experienced this transformation is dealt with ibid., and the hospitalization of births by S. Vallgårda, 'Hospitalization of deliveries. The change of place of birth in Denmark and Sweden from the late nineteenth century to 1970', *Medical History*, 1996, vol. 40, pp. 173–96.
79 See T. Vammen, *Rent og urent. Hovedstadens piger og fruer 1800–1920* ('Clean and unclean. The maids and mistresses of the capital 1880–1920'), Copenhagen, Gyldendal, 1986.
80 See I. Loudon, 'Maternal mortality: 1880–1950. Some regional and international comparisons', *Social History of Medicine*, 1988, vol. 1, pp. 183–228 and the chapter by Loudon in this volume.

6

STATE CONTROL IN LOCAL CONTEXT

Public health and midwife regulation in Manchester, 1900–1914

Joan Mottram

For good or for evil the measure has reached the statute-book.[1]

Midwives in England and Wales were made subject to state control under the Midwives Act of 1902, which aimed 'to secure the better training of Midwives and to regulate their practice'.[2] Prior to the Act, midwifery had been almost completely free from restriction.[3] Anyone, whatever their skills or education, could take sole charge of a birth, even if it turned out to be complicated or dangerous. 'Unless they do something so outrageous as to bring themselves within reach of the criminal law they cannot be meddled with', a leading campaigner for state regulation fumed in 1898.[4]

Once the Act was implemented, midwives on the official Roll had to comply with the rules of the Central Midwives Board (CMB). They were required to follow antiseptic procedures, prohibited from laying out the dead and restricted to attending 'normal' births. Cases developing complications had to be relinquished to a doctor. Failure to comply with the regulations could result in penalties ranging from a reprimand to removal from the Roll. Much, however, depended on the local authority concerned, and perhaps especially the Medical Officer of Health.[5]

The operation of the Act at local level was delegated to county and county borough councils with powers to inspect midwives, investigate charges of incompetence and suspend them from practice. Some authorities operated the Act efficiently, others did little. In remote areas with few midwives, control was often lax. In districts where doctors were hostile to midwives, the Act could be used, as Donnison noted 'to harass midwives rather than to encourage their improvement'.[6] However, little is known about how individual authorities used their supervising powers, or how midwifery fitted into contemporary practice of 'public health'.[7]

This chapter focuses on Manchester, which was cited by the University's Professor of Obstetrics, as an example of 'the administration of the Act at its best'.[8] This opinion was endorsed by the *British Medical Journal*.[9] The response of midwives was more mixed, and so were the relevant statistics.

MANCHESTER AND THE 1902 ACT

Manchester, with a population of 543,872 in 1901, was the centre of a huge conurbation with a legacy of public health problems stemming from early and rapid industrialization. In the Edwardian period the city was striving to maintain its former reputation, as the Ship Canal was opened in 1894, the city encouraged new industries, and it was self-consciously innovative in public health.[10]

The University boasted the largest provincial medical school. Its Professor of Obstetrics and Gynaecology, William Japp Sinclair, knighted in 1904, had an international reputation. Closer to home he was a controversial figure.[11] At the turn of the century, Sinclair and others were engaged in the complex negotiations which resulted in the relocation of the Manchester Royal Infirmary from the city centre to a suburban site alongside the University. Sinclair was also involved in debates over St Mary's, the major voluntary hospital for women and children, where he obtained a senior post on its amalgamation with his smaller maternity hospital. Shortly before the merger, St Mary's moved into new premises close to the city centre, to be near to the districts served by its domiciliary midwifery service. The enlarged charity used this building for obstetrics, and erected a new hospital near the University, for gynaecology and paediatrics.[12]

This considerable investment in three new hospital buildings demonstrated the power of the city's leading medical professors and their links with large industrial capital. The University 'wire-pullers', not least Sinclair, were also well connected with the City Council and its enterprising Medical Officer of Health, James Niven, who was noted for his ambitious scheme to clean up Manchester's milk supply, in collaboration with Professor Sheridan Delépine, Director of the University's Public Health Laboratory. Contaminated milk was blamed for causing infant diarrhoea, a major cause of infant deaths and Delépine's research also linked contaminated milk with tuberculosis in infants. The City Council, through sending him samples of milk for testing, became an important source of funding for Delépine's work.[13]

Niven's more general concern for infant welfare was indicated by his encouragement of health visiting but until the Midwives Act was passed, he does not appear to have been closely involved with the midwife question. In contrast, Professor Sinclair was conspicuous in the conflict that developed on the issue amongst the medical profession of the North-West, when the campaign urging the regulation and upgrading of midwifery gathered momentum during the 1890s.[14]

The maternity hospitals and a wide variety of medical institutions operating in a highly competitive market provide much of the context for local debates on midwife reform. Compared to smaller towns, Manchester had a high proportion of qualified midwives, not least because the maternity hospitals trained and employed midwives.[15] As in smaller towns, there was direct opposition between midwives and general practitioners; but in Manchester, as in London, obstetricians, especially Japp Sinclair, called for midwives to be registered and placed under medical control.[16]

The registrationists were strongly opposed by general practitioners (GPs) from Manchester and surrounding industrial towns, who saw their livelihoods threatened by midwives, medical clubs and hospitals offering midwife training. The GPs mobilized in the Lancashire and Cheshire Branch of the British Medical Association (BMA); the largest provincial branch, with 1,039 members in 1896, and most active against the midwife. Some members were so anti-midwife, that they campaigned to have the midwife abolished and replaced by an 'obstetric nurse', who would be prohibited from taking sole charge of a delivery. Such extreme views and the robust tactics of the anti-midwife faction, who tried to prevent teachers of midwives, notably Sinclair, from issuing midwifery diplomas, created a huge controversy in the branch, and in the pages of the *British Medical Journal*.[17] The anti-midwife GPs were also active in medical guilds formed in the 1890s to act as trade unions, protecting their members' incomes. The Manchester Guild was the major provincial lobby.[18]

Towards the end of the century midwives in Manchester also began to organize, independently of the London-based Midwives' Institute, which was leading the registration campaign in alliance with a group of obstetricians. The Manchester Midwives' Society, which appears to have been a short-lived initiative, was established by women with a formal training, living near anti-midwife doctors and fearful that registration as proposed by the Institute would involve deskilling and medical control. The Society wanted midwives to be independent and highly trained; it recruited sixty members, mainly from Lancashire and Cheshire, but also from as far afield as Glasgow.[19] The Institute described the Society's stance as 'pretentious'.[20]

Manchester might well serve as a case study of the midwives' controversy, but that is not my main focus here. Rather, I wish to indicate how the organizational politics evident before 1902, and the interests involved after 1902, shaped the realization of the Midwives Act in the city.

MANCHESTER MIDWIVES POST-1902

Through his appointment to the CMB, as a nominee of the Privy Council, Japp Sinclair played a large part in the way the Midwives Act was put into practice at the national level. He was disappointed by the Act, which he found a 'sadly defective piece of legislative work', deeply biased towards the midwife and 'ominously silent' where the interests of the medical profession were concerned.[21] He nevertheless thought it might accomplish a great deal. On the Board he fought his corner fiercely, often in opposition to the Midwives' Institute representative up until 1905, Charles Cullingworth, his predecessor in the Manchester chair of obstetrics.[22] Sinclair was also involved in the implementation of the Act in Manchester, where his colleague, the MOH, James Niven, was mainly responsible for its administration. Niven described the measure as 'an entirely workable and potent engine' for midwife improvement.[23]

Of the 18,000 births taking place in Manchester each year, around 60 per cent were attended by midwives or handywomen. During the registration campaign, working-class midwives, especially the untrained, had been portrayed as dangerous Gamps, responsible for causing unnecessary maternal and infant deaths, transmitting puerperal fever, causing blindness in babies, and terrible injuries, through their drunken bungling.[24] The Gamp/Mother Midnight figure associated with infanticide and abortion, resonated with *fin de siècle* preoccupations with sexual licence, corruption and decay.[25]

After 1902 the image of the Gamp-like lower-class midwife contrasted sharply with depictions of her reformed successor, the unmarried, professional, educated 'new midwife', a near relative of the 'New Woman'.[26] During this period, notions of womanhood were being challenged by the suffragette movement, which had strong roots in Manchester. It was at their home in the city that the Pankhursts launched the Women's Social and Political Union in 1903.

This was also a period when new notions of motherhood came to the fore, as the infant welfare movement gathered momentum. The dangers posed by the Gamps, with their potential for carrying death and disease into the homes of the poor, appeared particularly acute as attention focused on the saving of infant lives, and on the future and quality of the race.[27] Such issues were central to the public health concerns of the period, which concentrated on personal services and advice rather than on environmental measures. Manchester was already well advanced in responding to these concerns, as shown, for example in its pioneering health visiting programme, and it is crucial to realize the extent to which the reform of midwifery fitted into this broader model.[28]

The fact that the supervision of midwives was given to Medical Officers of Health has sometimes seemed little more than an administrative convenience. But, as the Manchester case shows, it could be much more: an active MOH, backed by the Professor of Obstetrics, could focus on the control of puerperal fever, so making disease control a matter of regulation of services. Niven was deeply interested in the interplay of disease control and domestic circumstances, while Sinclair was an author on puerperal fever and one of the creators of the 'Semmelweis legend'.[29]

The unreformed midwife was seen as most likely to do harm in the poorest, most insanitary districts, where mortality and morbidity rates were highest, and where the residents were assumed to be feckless and unfit, breeding sickly infants and endangering the quality of the race. Niven was already targeting the worst areas, sending in sanitary inspectors and health visitors to clean up homes, while the diseased and afflicted were encouraged to move out. Sufferers from tuberculosis were sent for treatment at sanatoria, epileptics were sent to rural colonies and 'feeble-minded' children to schools in the countryside.[30]

Some homes continued to be seen as 'foci of disease'. To reduce infection the city's water supply had been improved and Niven, with

Delépine, tried to clean up its milk supply. In 1903 Niven pioneered investigations into the relationship between fly prevalence and infant summer diarrhoea.[31] Flies, milk and water were potential carriers of disease (rather like Gamps).[32]

To prevent the Gamps from spreading disease and destruction, Niven wanted to transform them into smart, hygienic professionals, similar to health visitors. Niven reorganized the city's health visiting programme in 1907, arranging for health visitors to be paid from the rates, and for all new appointees to be qualified nurses. But midwives had an advantage over the health visitor as they were engaged by a family and invited into their home, whereas the health visitor was not always welcome.[33]

The presence of Niven and Sinclair, the city's status as a major urban centre, and the size and diversity of its medical community, all contributed to the way in which the Midwives Act was implemented. A further factor was the role of doctors hostile to midwives. They continued to organize to protect themselves, in the Medical Guild (to 1909) and in the BMA, not only in relation to midwives, but in connection with a range of other issues. They agitated strongly, for example, against the 1907 Notification of Births Act, which Niven was keen to introduce, as part of the infant welfare campaign. Niven was hopelessly outnumbered. The activists, with overwhelming support from Manchester's medical profession, delayed the measure's adoption in the city until 1912, when their opposition was finally overruled. Manchester doctors were known for their objections to disease notification; their opposition to early notification of births was argued on the grounds of protecting patient confidentiality, but financial reasons were also crucial. Niven responded by organizing a voluntary system of early notification using midwives.[34] This arrangement was dependent on the goodwill of registered midwives, and was only possible due to the procedures which brought them under State control.

To administer the Midwives Act, the Manchester County Borough Council established a Midwives Supervising Committee, chaired by a doctor, and with a medical sub-committee. The latter included Margaret Bell, Dr Scotson (a general practitioner supportive of the Medical Guild), and two obstetricians, Arnold Lea, a CMB examiner and author of *Puerperal Infection* (1910), and Ernest Annaker, formerly of St Mary's.[35] The extent to which the medical profession was involved in administering the Act was reinforced by the appointment of a doctor, Margaret Merry Smith (MB, ChB, DPH), as Midwives Supervisor, at an annual salary of £250. The medical press called for doctors to be given these posts but many authorities chose a less qualified individual who would be cheaper for the ratepayers.[36] Lancashire County Council appointed a midwife at £104 per annum, a more typical salary;[37] her task was to oversee large numbers of midwives, spread over a very wide area (by 1909 the County had two inspectors to supervise 871 midwives).[38]

We shall see later how the Manchester Midwives Supervising Committee dealt with the question of midwives and infection, but can first note its reaction to the common grievance of general practitioners, that the Act of 1902 made no provision for the payment of doctors for midwifery call-outs to poor women. Many families could barely find the fee for the midwife, let alone a doctor, but midwives were obliged to call in a medical practitioner to take over in certain circumstances, particularly if complications arose.[39] In some areas doctors became so frustrated at being called out to mothers too poor to pay that they refused to attend.[40] The delay in finding a doctor willing to oblige could cause unnecessary suffering and risk to life.[41] In some cases doctors could claim from the Poor Law, the State system of poor relief, but this was time-consuming and unpopular with families wishing to avoid the stigma of pauperism.

In Manchester poverty was exacerbated by the extent of casual labour; around half the population in central districts were employed on a casual basis. Unemployment in the early 1900s was high; unemployment riots in 1905 were said to 'have no parallel in the history of the city since the dreadful days of Peterloo'.[42] It was against this background that the Medical Guild petitioned the Council to pay doctors midwifery call-out fees under the Public Health Act. Following deputations from the Guild and a large conference of interested parties, Niven eventually devised a scale of charges and a scale for means-testing families, and the scheme was adopted as a temporary arrangement.[43]

The Guild's initiative was prompted by reports of the operation of a similar scheme in Liverpool. Cardiff and St Helens also made provision for the payment of doctors, but Salford, Manchester's smaller neighbour, refused repeated requests to follow suit. Consequently, Salford doctors boycotted the 1902 Act, thus creating particular problems for its midwives, who attended three-quarters of the town's births.[44] In Manchester, the payment of fees resulted in more frequent calls for medical assistance, while in Salford and many other areas, midwives faced continuing difficulties in finding doctors to attend.[45] The issue was not resolved until the Act was amended in 1918.

IS SHE SAFE?: UPGRADING THE GAMPS

Manchester was also unusual in the extent of its midwife supervision. Niven encouraged as many midwives as possible to apply for registration, so they could be scrutinized.[46] The crucial deadline was 1 April 1905, after which all registered midwives had to pass an examination.[47] Until then, women with no formal qualifications who had been in practice for a year prior to the Act were allowed, on proof of satisfactory character, to register as 'bona fides'. After April 1910 women not on the register were prohibited from practising 'habitually and for gain', except under the direction of a qualified doctor, but this was difficult to enforce.[48]

There were 151 registered midwives in the city in 1905, of whom 92 could produce evidence of formal training. The untrained, including seven who could not read or write, registered as 'bona fides'. Dr Merry Smith provided tuition that was appreciated by those keen to make up for their lack of learning, but her efficient oversight was not always welcome, especially by those with qualifications who resented supervision.[49] Smith inspected every midwife at home, she checked the sanitary state of the house and if necessary called in the cleansing department. If there was no bath, one had to be obtained: Manchester midwives had to have a bath at least twice a week. Smith also ensured they had the regulation washable dresses, separate storage (not in the rules) for their duty clothes, an obstetric bag, and appliances such as a catheter.[50]

The CMB rules restricted midwives to a very low level of technology, but for poorly educated women, unaccustomed to hygienic procedures, the requirement to carry equipment, however basic, could create problems. Smith found only twenty-two women had a complete set of appliances in good order. The remainder had an inadequate supply, or 'kept the appliances in a dirty condition, and used the bag for any rubbish they chose to carry around'. One woman, described as 'personally dirty', had trained in a hospital four years previously and was carrying on a 'fairly large practice'. She used a small handbag with a filthy, bloodstained lining; the bag was allegedly soiled throughout, the scissors bloodstained, the thermometer broken and she had no vaginal douche or catheter.[51]

The lack of catheter and vaginal douche was perhaps fortunate. Smith noticed that most of the midwives used a particular type of syringe for both rectal and vaginal injections. The same syringe was commonly used, without intervening sterilization or disinfection, to give enemas, to douche normal or septic cases, and cases of emergency, ante- and postpartum haemorrhage.[52]

Smith's training was supplemented by printed instructions compiled by the Midwives Supervising Committee, expanding on the CMB rules.[53] The instructions emphasized the need for hygiene and drew attention to the midwife's bag, on which the CMB rules said little. Smith taught that it should be disinfected inside and out at least once a week. She arranged with a firm of chemists to supply a bag to her design, in canvas or leather, with two detachable waterproof linings and a complete set of appliances; the canvas bag complete cost 23s 6d and the leather 25s 0d, which was double the price of some bags available. Many of the midwives bought the one recommended and refused to consider a cheap drill bag instead. The bag was used to impress Smith; with the washable dresses, it may have also served to project a new professional image. Medical instrument suppliers advertised a range of midwives' bags, with an increasing variety of appliances after 1902.[54]

Smith's instructions were based, as were the regulations, on contemporary theories of disease transmission. Since the 1880s maternity hospitals had dramatically reduced their mortality rates from puerperal infection through the adoption of antisepsis. The results were so remarkable that, according to Irvine Loudon, while the maternal mortality rate from all causes for England and Wales as a whole remained steady at 40–50 per 10,000 births, in lying-in hospitals the rate, by the end of the century, had fallen to 20 or less per 10,000. Loudon notes, 'There seemed no reason why such levels should not be obtained in home deliveries. Antisepsis and asepsis were neither complex nor difficult to put into practice'.[55] A great deal depended, however, on the birth attendant's attention to detail.

The rules stressed the role of 'decomposing matter' (such as dried blood, lochia or liquor amnii), the smallest particle of which could set up puerperal fever. The 'matter' could be transmitted from a healthy mother by the midwife, under the fingernails, for example, where it could decompose readily, and endanger the next mother attended, thus turning the midwife into a life-threatening hazard.[56]

142

To prevent this, midwives had to be extra-hygienic in the lying-in room. The Committee stipulated the length of time they had to soak their hands in antiseptic solution and the strength of the four types of antiseptics required for cleansing themselves, their equipment, and the mothers' external organs, which had to be cleaned and swabbed with antiseptic solution each time an internal examination was made.[57] During the birth, once the baby's head emerged, the eyelids had to be bathed in a 'suitable antiseptic solution', to prevent ophthalmia (a procedure described by one expert as 'useless').[58] Immediately after the birth, once the cord was cut, the mother's parts had again to be disinfected. Manchester midwives were also advised to apply an antiseptic pad to the vulva; and, before the infant was given attention, all soiled materials had to be removed from the room.[59]

Compared to procedures recommended for maternity hospitals these precautions were rudimentary. (*Nursing Notes*, the journal of the Midwives' Institute, exclaimed with horror at the scrubbing of the mother's genitals recommended in a textbook by Henry Jellett of the Rotunda Hospital, Dublin.)[60] But busy general practitioners often did much less to prevent infection, and not all the midwives were convinced of the value of the procedures.[61]

In the postnatal period midwives had to visit for ten days. The Manchester Supervising Committee provided them with instructions on infant care, and they also had to be alert to puerperal infection and signs of infantile ophthalmia. Medical experts claimed that ophthalmia neonatorum, which was blamed for causing around one-third of all cases of blindness, could be prevented by early treatment but there was no consensus on the role of the midwife in the prevention and treatment of the disease. The Manchester midwives were reminded to call for medical aid immediately upon noting the slightest inflammation. In 1908, when ophthalmia neonatorum was the subject of a BMA national investigation, the Supervising Committee consulted the Eye Hospital. Two years later, the city successfully applied for the disease to be made notifiable under the Infectious Diseases Notification Act; in March 1911, on the recommendation of the BMA, an eye nurse was appointed to visit cases, and a second nurse was soon taken on.[62]

On puerperal fever, the CMB rules outlined the presenting symptoms and the steps which midwives had to follow to detect the disease. But it was difficult to diagnose, and Niven found the regulations insufficient. He required midwives to record temperature and pulse at each visit, a practice later incorporated into the CMB rules.[63] Smith had to teach most of the women how to use a clinical thermometer, take the pulse, and keep records.[64] But Niven was still not satisfied, as midwives delayed or failed to report cases, which could contribute to transmission of the disease and affect recovery adversely.[65]

Poor mothers suffering from severe puerperal fever were sent to the city's isolation hospital, at Monsall, where bacteriological tests were immediately carried out. Usually, the uterus was curetted and treated with undiluted Izal, a germicide; until 1907 'antistreptococcic' [sic] serum was often administered. In cases near to death, more drastic measures, often involving surgery, were carried out. Those who survived generally remained in hospital with their baby for several weeks, but their chances of recovery were higher than at home.[66]

Their chances were also better if the disease was detected promptly. Smith found that doctors as well as midwives failed to notify cases.[67] 'Puerperal infection' was a notifiable disease but notification was avoided by fudging the terminology. This led Niven, with advice from Sinclair, to produce a working definition of the disease, wider than that used by the CMB and BMA. He also tried to persuade Manchester doctors to accept this definition, to ensure no cases were missed, even if some turned out to be false alarms.[68]

The reluctance of midwives to report puerperal fever was increased by the threat of suspension and the disinfection required on reporting a case. Manchester midwives had to have *two* antiseptic baths. Then, in Smith's presence, their hands and arms were washed for five minutes in soap and water, then for five minutes in lysol solution, followed by soaking in a corrosive sublimate solution: 1–1,000 for ten minutes. Their nails were scrubbed in the disinfecting solution and their bag and appliances sterilized. Their clothing and bedding were taken to be 'stoved' and they were suspended from practice. Suspension varied from a day or two, to several weeks; after 1910 it was usually for a few hours.[69]

Such treatment was meant to save lives, but it could appear excessive especially to women unused to antiseptics. Before Smith's arrival, it was mainly the city's hospital midwives, working on the district, who used hygienic precautions.[70] Women in independent practice were less strict; indeed, some believed the level of asepsis practised in maternity hospitals was harmful. Mrs Green, a midwife with a diploma from Japp Sinclair's hospital, was highly critical of doctors who irrigated with bichloride solution immediately after delivery. In a paper to the Midwives' Society, she complained that this procedure washed away the plastic lymph that nature poured out to protect lacerated tissue, rendering the exposed parts more liable to infection. She believed that to prevent infection it was important for the midwife to work *with* 'Dame Nature' to restore the mother's vital forces, rather than using chemicals. It is not known how many midwives supported this anti-interventionist view but the Midwives' Society did not find it remarkable.[71]

Smith's efficient oversight, which included detailed investigations into all stillbirths occurring in midwives' practices, met with some resistance, especially from the certificated women, who she noted, 'often proved the most resourceful as a barrier to progress'. Smith noted false entries in record books, carelessness in practical hygiene, and delays in reporting puerperal infection. Two of the women were found to have well-equipped bags, ready for inspection, at home: the bags were never taken to confinements.[72]

Women who did not conform to the rules could be removed from the Roll, or they could withdraw voluntarily. In 1907 for example, three 'bona fides' were struck off the Roll and a fourth had her name removed at her own request. One of those struck off continued to attend a large number of deliveries.[73] But Smith could report improvements too, not only amongst the midwives, but in the preparations women made for a birth. Initially she noted, 'Midwives are often summoned hastily to a labour which is almost over. In many cases no adequate preparation has been made to provide the necessary clean garments, and the bed and woman herself are dirty'.[74] In 1908 she recorded that better provision was being made 'in the way of clean clothing, etc.'. The improvements were most obvious among women attending the recently established Mothers' Guild, which taught hygiene and mothercraft, and provided cheap meals for expectant and nursing mothers.[75]

There were still cases, though, where the mother had made no preparations whatsoever. The problem for a midwife in such circumstances was that if anything went wrong, she could be blamed. To protect themselves, midwives began to report families living in insanitary conditions. But there were also mothers with high expectations of hygiene and care, and they in turn began to report midwives with whom they found fault.[76] This suggests that some working-class mothers were coming to see home birth as requiring advanced preparation and a level of hygiene that made the lying-in room more like a hospital.

Manchester's policy of paying medical fees also encouraged the calling in of doctors. In 1907 medical assistance was summoned by midwives in 1 in every 7.3 labours in Manchester, compared to 1 in every 17 in Salford.[77] The payments for call-outs helped to improve doctor–midwife relations, but an increase in medical assistance did not always mean better maternity care. The Medical Officer at Monsall Hospital reported terrible injuries caused by general practitioners' use of instruments.[78] Busy doctors admitted they applied instruments in a hurry and their hygiene was perfunctory.[79]

Statistics published by the Manchester MOH allowed comparisons to be made between the rate of infection in births attended solely by midwives and those relinquished to doctors. The extent of infection in cases attended by doctors put the profession on the defensive and led to accusations that it was not doctors who were causing infection but midwives and women looking after mothers in the postnatal period. The development of infection several days after parturition in some cases lent support to such claims.[80]

In the first few years following the 1902 Act, the Manchester death rate from puerperal fever appeared to decline but the incidence of the disease did not. In 1912 the city's attack rate was three times as high as that for England and Wales and much higher than that of other towns. Niven suggested this could be due to the 'activity of administration' and the notification of many cases which would not have been notified some years previously, but this could not provide the entire explanation. He admitted that the city suffered 'severely from septic disease' probably due to the standard of living, and that asepsis in midwifery was perhaps not practised as generally as desirable.[81]

In the previous year the city had increased its work relating to the Midwives Act. In addition to the two ophthalmic nurses, two 'special nurses' were appointed to investigate puerperal fever cases, stillbirths and the deaths of new-born infants, and to visit cases such as patients with mammary abscess, or new babies with skin affections. They also investigated the practice of midwifery by uncertified women, and women banned from the Roll.[82] By 1915 Niven could report, 'In Manchester the older type of uneducated women – the "Sarah Gamps" – has been practically eliminated. The present midwives are, on the whole, a much better type of woman in every respect, and are better trained'.[83]

CONCLUSION

Most of the historical literature on the 1902 Act has concentrated on the standing of doctors and midwives. We have seen that these issues were indeed important in the implementation of the Act in Manchester; doctors resisted, they forced payment and local compromises. Some midwives also resisted regulation, but with much less organization and power than the doctors.

But we have also explored another dimension of implementation, one absent from most studies of the Act, though central to other histories of Edwardian health and medicine: the 1902 Act was administered by Medical Officers of Health. As such, at least in Manchester, it became a central plank of public health programmes. Midwives, like health visitors, were to take 'public health' into working-class homes – to teach hygiene and to exemplify high standards during the birth, when the mother was especially exposed to infection. This message would subsequently be reinforced by the advice of health visitors.[84] But midwives were themselves the objects of regulations on hygiene. Because they moved between danger-sites, it was crucial that they and their equipment were kept scrupulously clean. While midwives were agents of the new public health, they were also among its objects.

ACKNOWLEDGEMENTS

The author wishes to thank Roger Cooter and John Pickstone for helpful comments on previous drafts of this chapter, and Bill Luckin and Michael Warboys for advice and encouragement. Thanks also go to Maxine Rhodes and Janet Blackman for their invitation to present an earlier version at the Northern Women's History Network conference at Hull University in March 1994.

NOTES

1 *Lancet*, 27 Dec. 1902, p. 1783.
2 The Act, 2 Edw. 7, c.17, received the Royal Assent on 31 July 1902 and came into force on 1 April 1903.
3 On the lack of midwife licensing in England, compared to the continent, see I. Loudon, *Death in Childbirth: An International Study of Maternal Care and Maternal Mortality 1800–1950*, Oxford, Clarendon Press, 1992, p. 425. On Church licensing, see J. Donnison, *Midwives and Medical Men: A History of the Struggle for the Control of Childbirth*, London, Heinemann, 2nd edn, 1988, 18–22, 236–7; D. Evenden, 'Mothers and their midwives in seventeenth-century London', in H.

Marland (ed.) *The Art of Midwifery: Early Modern Midwives in Europe*, London and New York, Routledge, 1993, pp. 9–11, *passim*; D. Harley. 'Provincial midwives in England: Lancashire and Cheshire, 1660–1760', ibid., pp. 27–44.

4 C.J. Cullingworth, 'The registration of midwives', *Contemporary Review*, 1898, vol. 73, pp. 393–402, on p. 396. On the campaign for state regulation, see Donnison, *Midwives and Medical Men*; B. Cowell and D. Wainwright, *Behind the Blue Door: The History of the Royal College of Midwives 1881–1981*, London, Ballière & Tindall, 1981, pp. 11–36; R. Dingwall, A.M. Rafferty and C. Webster, *An Introduction to the Social History of Nursing*, London, Routledge, 1988, pp. 154–8; A. Witz, *Professions and Patriarchy*, London, Routledge, 1992, pp. 104–27.

5 Donnison, *Midwives and Medical Men*, pp. 182–3; Dingwall *et al.*, *Social History of Nursing*, pp. 159–60.

6 Donnison, *Midwives and Medical Men*, p. 182.

7 Dingwall *et al.*, *Social History of Nursing*, p. 160.

8 W.J. Sinclair, 'The Departmental Committee on the Midwives Act and general practitioners' interests', *British Medical Journal* (henceforth *BMJ*), 23 Jan. 1909, pp. 245–6, on p. 246.

9 'The Midwives Act in Manchester', *BMJ*, 24 July 1909, p. 236; 'The Midwives Supervising Committee', *BMJ*, 23 Sept. 1911, p. 706.

10 A. Kidd, *Manchester*, Keele, Ryburn, 1993, pp. 115–28.

11 'Sir William Japp Sinclair, M.A., M.D., M.R.C.P.', *The Journal of Obstetrics and Gynaecology of the British Empire*, 1912, vol. 22, pp. 171–4; 'Sir William Sinclair, M.D., M.R.C.P.', *BMJ*, 14 Sept. 1912, pp. 665–6.

12 J.V. Pickstone, *Medicine and Industrial Society: A History of Hospital Development in Manchester and its Region 1752–1946*, Manchester, Manchester University Press, 1985, chapter 9; J.H. Young, *St Mary's Hospitals Manchester 1790–1964*, Edinburgh and London, E. & S. Livingstone, 1964, pp. 66–88.

13 M. Armitstead, 'The life and work of James Niven', University of Manchester DipPH dissertation, 1958; 'The late Dr. James Niven', *Medical Officer*, 1925, vol. 34, p. 160. On Niven and Delépine, see D. Dwork, *War is Good for Babies and other Young Children*, London, Tavistock, 1987, p. 73.

14 W.J. Sinclair, 'The Midwives Bill, 1902', *BMJ*, 7 June 1902, pp. 1450–2, on p. 1451.

15 Young, *St Mary's*, pp. 4–8, 57–8, 84. Sixty per cent of Manchester midwives had a formal qualification in 1905: J. Niven, 'The Midwives Act, 1902', *Public Health*, May 1906, p. 506.

16 Sinclair, 'Midwives' Bill', p. 1451; Donnison, *Midwives and Medical Men*, p. 171.

17 BMA, Lancashire and Cheshire Branch, Minutes, 1894, pp. 231–68; Sinclair, 'Midwives Bill', p. 1451; 'Registration of midwives', *BMJ*, 21 July 1894, p. 154; 'Lancashire and Cheshire branch', *BMJ*, 20 Oct. 1894, p. 896; 'Midwives' registration and the Lancashire and Cheshire branch', *BMJ*, 27 Oct. 1894, p. 952; 3 Nov. 1894, p. 1015; 10 Nov. 1894, pp. 1080–1, *passim*. Donnison, *Midwives and Medical Men*, pp. 145, 148, 171.

18 Manchester Medical Guild, Annual Reports; *Medical Guild Quarterly*, 1898–1908; 'The organisation of the profession', *Lancet*, 7 Oct. 1899,

pp. 980–2; J. Brand, *Doctors and the State*, Baltimore, Johns Hopkins University Press, 1965, p. 157.

19 Midwives' Society, *Transactions 1897–98*, Manchester, 1898; *Slater's Manchester, Salford, and Suburban Directory*, Manchester, Slater, 1897, 1898; Donnison, *Midwives and Medical Men*, pp. 151, 153.

20 Witz, *Professions and Patriarchy*, p. 125. See also Cowell and Wainwright, *Blue Door*, p. 31.

21 W.J. Sinclair, 'The Central Midwives Board', *BMJ*, 4 June 1904, pp. 1341–3, on p. 1341; Donnison, *Midwives and Medical Men*, p. 171; Sinclair, 'Midwives' Bill', pp. 1450–2.

22 Sinclair, *BMJ*, 'The Central Midwives Board', p. 1342; *Nursing Notes*, July 1904, p. 123; CMB Minutes, DV1/1 1903 – 5, DV1/2 1905 – 7, DV1/28 1 Oct. 1905, p. 3, 26 Oct. 1905, p. 12 (Public Record Office).

23 Niven, 'Midwives Act', p. 514. Sinclair and Niven had co-operated as far back as 1884, as founder-editors of *The Medical Chronicle*: 'Sir William Sinclair', *BMJ*, 14 Sept. 1912, p. 665.

24 Cullingworth, 'Registration', p. 396; N. Leap and B. Hunter, *The Midwife's Tale: An Oral History from Handywoman to Professional Midwife*, London, Scarlet Press, London, 1993, pp. 6–7.

25 J.R. Walkowitz, *City of Dreadful Delight: Narratives of Sexual Danger in Late-Victorian London*, London, Virago, 1992, pp. 100–2.

26 'The midwife of the future', *Nursing Notes*, Jan. 1903, p. 63.

27 Dwork, *War is Good for Babies*, pp. 3–21; H. Marland, 'A pioneer in infant welfare: the Huddersfield Scheme 1903–1920', *Social History of Medicine*, 1993, vol. 6, pp. 25–50.

28 Dwork, *War is Good for Babies*, pp. 125–6; C. Davies, 'The health visitor as mother's friend: a woman's place in public health, 1900–1914', *Social History of Medicine*, 1988, vol. 1, pp. 39–59.

29 W.J. Sinclair, *Semmelweis: His Life and Doctrine. A Chapter in the History of Medicine*, Manchester, Manchester University Press, 1909.

30 J.A. Barclay, 'Lango Epileptic Colony, 1906–1984: a contextual study of the origins, transformations and demise of Manchester's "colony for sane pauper epileptics"', PhD thesis, University of Manchester, 1989; Pickstone, *Medicine and Industrial Society*, pp. 226–31. On sanatoria see also M. Worboys, 'The sanatorium treatment for consumption in Britain, 1890–1914', in J.V. Pickstone (ed.) *Medical Innovations in Historical Perspective*, London, Macmillan, 1992, pp. 44–71.

31 Dwork, *War is Good for Babies*, pp. 48, 72–3.

32 J.W. Leavitt, '"Typhoid Mary" strikes back. Bacteriological theory and practice in early twentieth-century public health', *Isis*, 1992, vol. 83, pp. 608–29.

33 Niven, 'Midwives Act', p. 508; J. Niven, *Observations on the History of the Public Health Effort in Manchester*, Manchester, John Heywood 1923, p. 185. For the 'antiseptic campaign' of Danish midwives, see the chapter by Løkke in this volume.

34 Niven, *Observations*, p. 185; 'Manchester and Salford, The Notification of Births Act', *BMJ*, 14 Sept. 1907, p. 696; 2 Nov. 1907, pp. 1271–2; 21 Dec. 1907, p. 1801; 8 Feb. 1908, p. 350; 11 Feb. 1911, p. 322; 4 March 1911, p. 520; 24 Aug. 1912, p. 456; 21 Sept. 1912, p. 738; 17 Jan. 1914,

p. 167. On birth notification, see Marland, 'A pioneer in infant welfare'; J. Brand, *Doctors*, pp. 182–3.

35 Midwives Supervising Committee, 'The Midwives Act, 1902', Manchester, 1906, pp. 4–5; Manchester City Sanitary Committee Minutes, vol. 7, 27 July 1904, p. 142. The 'somewhat special character' of the Committee was noted by the Departmental Committee on the Working of the Midwives Act, 1902: *Report of the Departmental Committee on the Working of the Midwives Act, 1902*, Cd 4822, London, 1909, vol. 1, 5982; A.W.W. Lea, *Puerperal Infection*, London, Hodder and Stoughton, 1910; CMB, *First Annual Report*, London, 1909, list of examiners.

36 P. Rose, 'Inspectors of midwives', *BMJ*, 2 June 1906, p. 1318; H.T. Sells, 'Inspectors of midwives', *BMJ*, 9 June 1906, p. 1376.

37 Lancashire County Council (LCC), Midwives Act Committee Minutes, 30 Oct. 1904; *Nursing Notes*, Oct. 1904, pp. 155, 171. In 1906 the County raised the salary to £120: LCC, Midwives Act Committee Minutes, Jan. 1906, 19 July 1906. The average salary of inspectors was £75 to £100 p.a.: 'The Midwives Act, 1902', *BMJ*, 28 Oct. 1905, p. 1135.

38 'The Midwives Act in Lancashire', *BMJ*, 27 Feb. 1909, p. 561.

39 *Report on the Midwives Act*, vol. 1, 5393–4, 5435–44.

40 Ibid., 604–22, 1513–725, 1989–91.

41 Donnison, *Midwives and Medical Men*, p. 84; *Report on the Midwives Act*, vol. 1, 1909, 5960.

42 Kidd, *Manchester*, p. 177; A.J. Kidd, 'Charity organization and the unemployed in Manchester c. 1870–1914', *Social History*, 1984, vol. 9, pp. 45–66, on pp. 56–8.

43 Manchester Midwives Supervising Committee Minutes, vol. 1, pp. 10, 35, 40, 56–8, 62; *Manchester MOH Annual Report 1905*, Manchester, 1906, p. 235.

44 'The Midwives Act in Salford', *BMJ*, 12 Oct. 1907, pp. 1010–11; 'Salford and the Midwives Act', *BMJ*, 16 May 1908, pp. 1202–3; 'Payment of medical men summoned by midwives', *BMJ*, 28 March 1908, p. 777; 'The Midwives Act', *BMJ*, 9 Jan. 1909, p. 115; 'The Midwives Act in Salford', *BMJ*, 25 Dec. 1909, p. 1822; *Report on the Midwives Act*, vol. 1, 5884–6016.

45 *Report on the Midwives Act*, vol. 1, 5930.

46 Niven, 'Midwives Act', p. 500.

47 A candidate 'was not passed on a percentage of figures, but is rejected only where she appears to be likely to be dangerous to the life of a lying-in woman', CMB, *First Annual Report*, 1909, p. 7. Examiners were advised to ask themselves, 'Is she safe?': J. Towler and J. Bramall, *Midwives in History and Society*, London, Croom Helm, 1986, p. 194.

48 Dingwall *et al.*, *Social History of Nursing*, p. 161.

49 *Manchester MOH Annual Report 1905*, pp. 257–8.

50 Niven, 'Midwives Act', pp. 515–17; Corporation of Manchester, Midwives Supervising Committee, *Instructions to Midwives*, Manchester, n.d. [1905]; 'Instructions to midwives', *BMJ*, 27 Jan. 1906, pp. 222–3.

51 *Manchester MOH Annual Report 1905*, p. 247.

52 Ibid.

53 Manchester Committee, *Instructions to Midwives*; 'Instructions to midwives', *Lancet*, 20 May 1905, p. 1368; *BMJ*, 27 Jan. 1906, pp. 222–3.

54 *Manchester MOH Annual Report 1905*, p. 248; 'Practical notes by a practical midwife on a midwife's equipment', *Nursing Notes*, July 1904, pp. 112–13; advertisements in *The Midwives Record*, for example, March 1907, p. 12.

55 C.J. Cullingworth, 'The undiminished mortality from puerperal fever in England and Wales', *Transactions of the Obstetrical Society of London*, 1897, vol. 39, pp. 91–114, on pp. 93–4, 108; I.S.L. Loudon, 'Childbirth', in W.F. Bynum and R. Porter (eds) *Companion Encyclopedia of the History of Medicine*, London and New York, Routledge, 1993, pp. 1058–61.

56 CMB Rule E1. On theories of transmission of puerperal infection, see Loudon, *Death in Childbirth*, pp. 49–83.

57 Manchester Committee, *Instructions to Midwives*, pp. 4–7.

58 'Instructions to midwives', *BMJ*, 27 Jan. 1906, p. 222.

59 Manchester Committee, *Instructions to Midwives*, pp. 6–8.

60 *Nursing Notes*, Aug. 1902, p. 98; H. Jellett, *A Short Practice of Midwifery for Nurses*, London, Churchill, 1901.

61 Loudon, *Death in Childbirth*, pp. 218–21.

62 'Instructions to midwives', *BMJ*, 27 Jan. 1906, p. 222; *Manchester MOH Annual Report 1908*, Manchester, 1909, pp. 235–7; *Manchester MOH Annual Report 1911*, Manchester, 1912, p. 183; 'Ophthalmia neonatorum', *BMJ*, 8 May 1909, pp. 1138–9.

63 In June 1907 the CMB decided to call the attention of local supervising authorities to the proposal: CMB Minutes, DV1/2, p. 499. It was incorporated into the rules in 1911.

64 *Manchester MOH Annual Report 1905*, p. 247.

65 In 1905 notification in several cases 'occurred immediately preceding the death of the patient': *Manchester MOH Annual Report 1905*, p. 253.

66 *Report of Midwives Supervising Committee 1905*, pp. 14–18; *Manchester MOH Annual Report 1906*, Manchester, 1907, pp. 254–6; *Manchester MOH Annual Report 1907*, Manchester, 1908, pp. 199–203; *Manchester MOH Annual Report 1911*, pp. 171–2.

67 *Manchester MOH Annual Report 1905*, p. 253.

68 *Report of Midwives Supervising Committee 1905*, pp. 6–8.

69 *Manchester MOH Annual Report 1905*, pp. 255–6. See also the chapter by Løkke in this volume.

70 *Nursing Notes*, July 1904, p. 115.

71 'Aseptic midwifery', *Midwives Society, Transactions*, pp. 15–16.

72 *Manchester MOH Annual Report 1905*, pp. 255, 259; *Manchester MOH Annual Report 1907*, p. 287.

73 Manchester MOH Annual Report 1907, pp. 296–7.

74 *Manchester MOH Annual Report 1905*, p. 258.

75 *Manchester MOH Annual Report 1908*, pp. 253–4.

76 *Manchester MOH Annual Report 1907*, p. 288; *Manchester MOH Annual Report 1908*, p. 242.

77 'The Midwives Act in Salford', *BMJ*, 19 June 1909, pp. 1505–6.

78 In 1907, in eight cases delivered by forceps and later admitted to Monsall with puerperal fever, six had extensive laceration of the cervix and vagina, and one had lacerations which extended to and opened

up the general peritoneal cavity: *Manchester MOH Annual Report 1907*, pp. 300–1.

79 Loudon, *Death in Childbirth*, pp. 219–21.

80 'Puerperal fever in Manchester', *BMJ*, 28 Sept. 1907, p. 844; 'The Midwives Act in Manchester', *BMJ*, 24 July 1909, pp. 236–7; 'The Midwives Supervising Committee', *BMJ*, 23 Sept. 1911, p. 706. The Medical Officer at Monsall thought the incubation period probably did not exceed 48 hours, so where a longer interval elapsed between the last medical examination and onset of symptoms, 'the doctor must be held blameless – except, perhaps, in so far as his responsibility for the acts of the nurse goes': *Manchester MOH Annual Report 1906*, pp. 323–4; *Manchester MOH Annual Report 1907*, pp. 299–301.

81 'Prevalence of puerperal fever', *Medical Officer*, 1913, vol. 10, p. 183.

82 *Manchester MOH Annual Report 1911*, pp. 180–3; *Manchester MOH Annual Report 1913*, Manchester, 1914, p. 17.

83 *Manchester MOH Annual Report 1915*, Manchester, 1916, p. 109.

84 *Manchester MOH Annual Report 1905*, p. 260; *Manchester MOH Annual Report 1907*, p. 297.

7

THE MIDWIFE AS HEALTH MISSIONARY

The reform of Dutch childbirth practices in the early twentieth century

Hilary Marland

When Dr Clemens Meuleman, between 1913 and 1932 director of the midwives school in Heerlen in the south of the Netherlands, interviewed candidates for admission as pupils, he was looking for more than bright, well-schooled, healthy and sturdy young women. He was also seeking malleable girls, straightforward, agreeable, perhaps a little rough at the edges, who would be transformed during their years of training into 'modern' midwives, their roughness smoothed out, educated in more than midwifery, taught the principles of hygiene and the importance of being scrupulously neat and clean, professional deportment, how to speak, dress and behave.

The midwife was to be lifted out of society, reformed and transformed, and put back amongst people of her own class, ready to work as a childbirth missionary, influencing the practices and beliefs of the women she was to deliver. An almost exclusive preference was given in Heerlen in the southern province of Limburg to good Catholic girls. First and foremost it was a school dedicated to the promotion of Catholic motherhood and encouraging the birth of Catholic babies.[1] But, aside from religious qualification, the three other midwifery schools in Amsterdam, Rotterdam and Groningen shared in the requirements demanded by Dr Meuleman. Girls were to be in their early twenties, unmarried (or widows), who enjoyed good health, and who would be tested to ensure that their 'general development and understanding' were sufficient for a thorough scientific and obstetric training. They were to be in possession of references confirming their 'irreproachable

153

moral behaviour'.[2] Competition for admission could be stiff, in many years there were far more candidates than places, so the school directors could pick and choose. These highly selected young women passed through a rigorous two-year training, after 1921 three years, before re-emerging ready to act as childbirth attendants, to guide and educate the women they were to deliver. This chapter will explore these attempts at transformation, the sending forth of midwives to reform childbirth practices the errors of tradition which so intrigued and concerned medical men.

CONTINUITY AND CHANGE IN DUTCH CHILDBIRTH

In 1900 around two-thirds of Dutch women were attended in childbirth by midwives, though during the last quarter of the nineteenth century an increasing number arranged to be delivered by general practitioners, particularly in the countryside.[3] For some women the choice was made for them, as many regions, particularly rural ones, had a doctor or a midwife, but not both. And large numbers of villages had no midwifery practitioner whatsoever, leaving women to turn to traditional attendants or the help of family and neighbours.[4]

Most babies were born at home, the growth of hospital obstetrics being very limited in contrast to the rapid growth of other institutional medical facilities around the turn of the century.[5] Poor women in Holland were not, as in many other countries, shunted into maternity hospitals or poor relief facilities.[6] Medical intervention in childbirth was stepped up during the first decades of the century; pain relief was introduced on a small scale, and medicines used increasingly to control bleeding, to hasten delivery and the expulsion of the placenta. But, with birth taking place in a domestic setting and with the new techniques being largely placed in the hands of midwives, such forms of intervention were self-limiting.[7]

The majority of women giving birth in the Netherlands in the early twentieth century then would stay at home, attended by either a midwife or a general practitioner, and supported by friends and neighbours. But change was taking place in the organization of maternity services, deep-rooted and radical change, as the midwife, the main key to obstetric care, received her training in an increasingly specialized environment. Though midwife training had been offered in clinical schools during the mid-nineteenth century, the numbers passing through this two-year training were limited and the teaching was unsatisfactory, and most midwives were still trained by apprenticeship, variable in intent and standards, and largely uncontrolled.[8] In 1861 a state midwives school was established in Amsterdam, followed two decades later by a second in Rotterdam, and in 1913 a Roman Catholic school was founded in Heerlen. In Groningen in the north, training was provided for small numbers of pupils under the auspices of the university medical school. These schools, catering for the training of midwives and maternity nurses, introduced rigorous admission procedures, based on interviews and examinations, a training course incorporating a good deal of theory, with practical experience being obtained in attached clinics.

The midwife was effectively drawn out of the domestic sphere, placed in an institution, separated from home and family, and brought under the influence of the medical staff and mistress-midwife. Weak candidates, mistakes, were weeded out and dismissed. No longer were midwives trained largely in a home environment, attending deliveries with experienced midwives as they went about their day-to-day practices. No longer did the pupils fall under the influence of older experienced women, but largely that of male teachers and school directors, who would teach them everything that they believed they needed to know. The only strong female influence in the schools was the towering figure of the mistress-midwife, in charge of the pupils' well-being and deportment, who was typically a young woman and a product of the modern schooling system.

The situation was replete with paradoxes. The midwife schools set up clinics where women could be delivered in hygienic and safe conditions; the Heerlen clinic, for instance, admitting several hundred women annually, was not only by far the largest maternity facility in the south, but one of the largest in the country.[9] The clinic specialized in gynaecological cases, and complicated deliveries, at the same time providing training to the midwife pupils, who, once qualified, would primarily be attending at normal births. The pupils who, once set up in practice, would deliver women in their homes in a predominantly female milieu, attended few home deliveries before qualifying, and received most of their training in a modern institutional setting dominated by men.

The midwife schools were set up with the purpose of solving the problem of a shortage of trained midwives, particularly in the countryside of the south. The difficulties of adequately servicing rural districts were unconscionable for the reformers. In the obstetric blackspots, a shortage of trained midwives, doctors and maternity nurses, combined with poor services, particularly a lack of infant clinics, and with great poverty, inadequate sanitary provision, poor housing conditions, and atrocious standards of domestic hygiene. Poor maternal health and high infant mortality were linked to the employment of women in factories, and their rapid return to work following delivery, and to the large numbers of babies born out of wedlock, and to another factor detrimental to mothers and their infants, the survival of traditional childbirth practices and the interference of traditional attendants.[10] Because birth almost always took place at home, in comparative privacy and ordered to a large extent by neighbours and female relatives, these practices could continue unchecked. They tended to be worst in the poorest and 'most backward' areas, where their combination with poverty and uncleanliness led to a deadly cocktail. In the years 1901–05 the infant mortality rate in North Brabant[11] at 183 per 1,000 live births was the highest in the country, and compared with a national rate of 136, and 92 in the province of South Holland.[12]

It was largely to combat such death rates that the Heerlen midwives school opened in 1913, the conclusion of a campaign to set up a school in the south which dated back to the 1880s.[13] In 1910 more than a third of women in Limburg and North Brabant gave birth without midwifery help.[14] In Limburg the situation was described by Meuleman, the school's first director, as 'pitiful', with only 58 midwives for a population of over 300,000, and neither a doctor nor midwife in 123 out of 176 parishes.[15] The school was to train 'thoroughly developed midwives, theoretically and practically, for the care of childbearing women and their children',[16] targeting isolated areas and the mining and factory districts. Most reformers took it as read that midwives would also offer care to 'healthy' infants, especially in rural districts, though some general practitioners opposed what they saw as an incursion on their work.[17] The doctor would still attend some confinements and man the infant welfare clinics, but it was the midwife, who had more extensive dealings with women during childbirth, more time, and who was better equipped to deal with the home front, who would be influential in steering poor mothers away from dirty and superstitious practices towards practical and hygienic methods. The modern midwife would oust the interfering neighbours, mothers and 'busybody grannies, who had always had at least 18 children themselves and who thus always knew better',[18] the untrained midwife, and the *baker*, the traditional dry nurse, all guilty parties in allowing outmoded and dangerous childbirth practices to continue.[19]

The duty of the midwife was to 'protect' the mother. One Catholic doctor, J.L.B. Gribling, practising in Oudenbosch in North Brabant and campaigning for a second midwife school in the south, described the task of midwives as threefold: to protect the mother, to protect the baby, and to educate and enlighten the mother.[20] Mothers, not just the unmarried ones, but all mothers, were seen as victims of poverty and the strains of child-rearing and hard work. One important purpose of the Heerlen school was to rescue unmarried mothers, bring them into the clinic to deliver, protect them from recrimination and abuse, keep them with their babies, and prepare them to go back into society. The clinic would also protect married mothers from their husbands, families, overwork, poor conditions, and detrimental birthing practices. Treading a fine line, the school was to encourage 'Catholic motherhood', yet squeeze out the customs and behaviour associated with 'bad Catholic practices'. While the fears of having a large family compared with the attractions of having just one or two children were recognized by Gribling, the midwife was, he stressed, not in any way to encourage the use of birth limitation.[21] Rather, she was to ameliorate the conditions and weariness associated for many mothers with incessant pregnancy, birth and child-rearing.

The occupation of midwifery – divided up between traditional practitioners and their modern trained counterparts – contained much potential for conflict, aside from the constant competition for custom between general practitioners and midwives.[22] By the early twentieth century the lines of division between 'qualified' and 'unqualified' were, however, fairly clear, and the number of births attended by unlicensed midwives, though still considerable in some regions, was in decline.[23] But tensions went deeper. For pupil midwives were being drawn from a background where, potentially, practices frowned upon by the schools still held sway. Raised in households where there was little money to spare, with a limited schooling, and in districts where traditional beliefs were strong, they were instructed to lay these aside in favour of modern methods and scrupulous hygiene. The Heerlen school was 'to raise the position of midwives, would develop her ethics more highly'.[24] The school-trained midwife was to be a crusader in the fight against weariness, ignorance, dirt and poverty.

CHILDBIRTH TRADITIONS: CURIOUS, PRIMITIVE AND DANGEROUS

At the same time as the midwife was being brought into the schools to be reformed and trained as a health missionary, medical men were showing considerable interest in the folklore customs and traditional practices surrounding childbirth,[25] which manifested itself in books, theses and medical journals, and as papers presented to medical and learned societies.[26] All-embracing surveys of health maintenance, sickness and death,[27] tended to give pregnancy, birth and infancy special treatment, turning up numerous accounts of popular beliefs on ways of improving fertility or getting rid of unwanted babies, of predicting the sex of the child, of easing birth pains, of improving breast milk, strictures on maternal diet and behaviour, and stories of monster births.

In Limburg the aid of various saints and more dubious 'helpers' was called upon to ease labour, prayers and relics were carried on the woman's body throughout pregnancy, while the influence of the moon was also important. Prayers could stop bleeding following birth, but vinegar, cold water, spiders' webs and ergot were also efficacious.[28] *Verzien*, the influence of maternal imagination and behaviour on the unborn child, to which all kinds of birth defects – birthmarks, deformed limbs, and hare lips – were attributed, stimulated particular interest.[29] Starmans tells the story of a child in Heerlen born with one arm. The grandmother had anticipated this 'because the father had been shot in the arm when smuggling' when the mother was carrying the child. Mothers were also recorded as giving birth to children with curious blemishes, in the form of the cows and mice which had frightened them whilst pregnant.[30]

For some authors, their curiosity was motivated by an interest in folklore, myth and history. By the late nineteenth century they were looking back with longing to the 'golden age' of the Dutch *kraamkamer* (birthing chamber); for the rich, the elaborately prepared rooms, with special cradles, linen cupboards, drinking glasses, feasts, highly organized rules and protocol surrounding birth and lying-in, celebrated by the genre painters of the seventeenth century, and mirrored in less elaborate customs and form by the poor.[31] Yet for many there was a more practical purpose in what they wrote, as they condemned popular practices as regrettable and harmful survivals. With regard in particular to the well-being of infants, it was 'no longer a question of a list of errors to be denounced, but rather one of combating an entire system'.[32] It is this strand of traditional practice, the aspect of 'popular error' and attempts at its solution, that I will be focusing on here.

Traditional childbirth practices were associated with ignorance, dirt, and poverty and were barriers to modern, safe childbirth. New practices – such as the misuse of manufactured baby milk and careless hygiene with feeding bottles – were tacked on to traditional ones. They were linked to a disposition to resort to quack doctors and old wives in cases of sickness, and with undesirables present at the birth, the untrained midwife, the *baker*, old wives and neighbours, mothers and grandmothers. These practices were firmly linked to female culture and knowledge, and to the yet darker aspects of herbal medicine, dabbling with fertility and abortion. The use of traditional helpers was also closely linked to cost; the *bakers* not only did the housework and cared for the children, but were substantially cheaper, and in the south close to the Belgian border unqualified obstetric attendants took care of well over half of the deliveries.[33] These 'errors' were rife in both Protestant and Catholic regions, but the Catholic south, where infants perished in far greater numbers, attracted most attention.

In his recent article on the influence of religion on health, Van Poppel[34] has cited the work of P.J.M. Aalberse, who discussed the special relationship between high infant mortality and Catholicism at the beginning of the century.[35] Some Catholics, Aalberse concluded, did not breast-feed 'because of a misplaced sense of shame or even worse, because of the tradition of binding young girls' breasts . . . so that these women are systematically being made unable, in their youth, to feed their own babies'.[36] Meurkens too in his study of the Brabantine Kempen describes the claustrophobic sense of 'shame' which developed during the second half of the nineteenth century amongst Catholics, the obsessional repression and shrouding of the female body, which made it impossible for women to breast-feed.[37] Another possible influence on infant survival rates, according to Aalberse, was the prohibition of marriage during fasting and Advent, which meant that births occurred later in the year, closer to the coldest and hottest months with the highest levels of infant mortality. Several commentators referred to poor schooling in the Catholic areas, smoking and drinking, habits strongly associated with Catholicism, and the acceptance of pain and suffering encouraged by the Catholic faith which contrasted with the health-promoting actions of Protestants.[38]

Those promoting a midwives school in the south were particularly aware of such regional problems, but at the same time required that Catholic midwives would be the ones to solve them. The necessity of this was geared to the importance of having midwives of the same faith attend women in childbed. The number of midwives required was closely calculated – in 1925 to a total of 335 – as leading figures in the Catholic Church allied themselves closely to the school directors in promoting Catholic motherhood and guiding the work of Catholic midwives.[39]

In 1927 one general practitioner, H.R. Folmer, reflected on his experiences thirty years previously, when 'as an inexperienced doctor' he came from Amsterdam, fresh from his medical training, to the 'then still primitive region and people' of Zuid Beveland in Zeeland. He reflected on the curiosity, disbelief and despair which confronted doctors witnessing traditional practices for the first time.[40] Most pregnant women in Folmer's district reached full term without being examined by a doctor or midwife. When the doctor was summoned to the birth, he found the labour room ready, 'on the table stood a little cup of linseed oil. The first examination took place in a standing position. The woman stayed as long as possible on her legs'. However

> most impressive was the labour on the ground . . . on an improvised bed . . . a stool, with its legs in the air . . . forming a back support. During the contractions a broad folded sheet was lain on the loins, which two women pulled upon. Before the feet of the woman in labour was a foot-warmer, as the seat of the attendant.[41]

This, Folmer surmised, had the practical purpose of keeping the bed clean. But there were also symbolic associations, and for the mother to achieve a 'roomy opening' everything in the house must also be wide open and loose, 'doors, cupboards and drawers open'.[42] If a doctor could not attend – and he was often held up simply by the distance and poor roads – an 'old woman' would step in, an active participant in the birth; 'assistance then consisted largely of pulling and stretching the soft parts' by a tippling or cigar-smoking midwife.[43]

After the delivery the woman was not washed, the filthy bed sheet was tucked up to form a kind of nappy and left on for several days, tightly bound, to prevent the womb from flying to the throat. The new-born was washed down in a mixture of linseed oil and *brandewijn*, and bound into a stiff package, 'that was cleaned only once a day'.[44] The mother was to be beware of cold and draughts; though permitted to do heavy household tasks, she was not to venture outside, even in the summer. But most dangerous of all was to open the linen cupboard, for the damp cold air from the linen would attack the 'open body'.

Folmer's concern with conditions seems genuine; his opportunities for practice-building and profit would after all be modest amongst such a clientele. Similar practices were recorded by a great many observers. The emphasis given on opening everything during the birth and shutting it again immediately after, muffling the mother and baby up and excluding all fresh air, continued well into the 1930s in country districts.[45] This practice could result in serious infections, including lung disorders, and dehydration, while diarrhoea was a natural accompaniment of dirt and poor feeding practices. Writing about the period which also saw the introduction of the first *consultatiebureaus* (infant welfare clinics) and the school-trained midwife, Folmer's observations starkly demonstrate the 'otherworldliness' of the modern methods.

Others went further than observation, offering advice on how old traditions could be done away with and replaced. In 1922 P.A. Barentsen, a general practitioner working in the predominantly Catholic region to the east of North Brabant, spelt out some of the problems faced by the local population which impacted on death rates.[46] As well as 'folk' survivals, Barentsen discussed the absence of all the socio-economic prerequisites necessary for good health. There was great poverty, but very few charitable institutions, housing conditions were appalling with 'house and stable under one roof', the water supply was defective, hygiene non-existent.

These conditions were more or less standard in the district where Barentsen practised, yet there was great variation in the mortality rates of infants. In the village of Bergeyk almost 9 infants out of 100 died in their first year, in Liujksgestel 10, in Westerhoven 14, in Eersel over 16, and in Borkel 18.[47] How could this be explained? Simple, according to Barentsen. It was due to the varying influence of the doctor and *baker* in different communities, and childbirth and childcare practices. Many of the actions of the *baker* threatened the child's well-being or at least did not improve its chances. A weak child was spoon-fed brandy to revive it, her heart massaged with alcohol, little attention was given to the eyes when washing, and, though lots of soap was employed in cleaning the infant, little water was used, the child's legs were stretched out and she was tightly swaddled, arms included, from the armpits to the feet. Hungry babies were fed sugar and water; a dummy was always used. After birth Catholic infants were rushed as soon as possible to be baptized, regardless of their state of health. Children were not put quickly enough on the breast, with the consequence that many were not breast-fed at all. In any case, the duration of breast-feeding was generally short. Babies were fed diluted cow's or goat's milk, and 'pap'. As soon as possible, infants were given food from the 'middagpot' (midday pot). If the child became sick, and most did, their mothers resorted to the baker, an old woman, or the quack doctor for help.[48]

Barentsen summarized that the influence of the doctor versus the baker was crucial in determining death rates, and in overcoming the ignorance of the population and the vicious cycle of poor feeding and overfeeding, sickness, crying and more overfeeding. He cited the proximity and cost of a doctor as one of the four factors that could strongly influence the survival of infants. The second factor was the position of the woman in the family. Many North Brabant women had to work hard on the land to maintain the family economy. These women could devote little time or energy to the preparation of food, to domestic hygiene or the care of their babies, who were quickly put on the bottle – warmed up repeatedly and fitted with long feeding pipes – or left to the dubious attentions of their grandparents or siblings. The third factor hinged on the sex of the children. Girls, Barentsen believed, simply had a better chance of survival than the precious boy babies; less was done to ensure their well-being, and this was seen as a plus under the regimes he observed. Fourth, alcohol abuse led to the neglect of children in many families.

We cannot determine how far what Barentsen describes is typical or extreme. He had little good to say about the Catholic areas he was commenting on,[49] but the fact that up to one-fifth of the babies born in his district died before their first birthdays does to a considerable extent speak for itself. Barentsen saw part of the answer to what seemed to be insurmountable problems in the employment of trained midwives, subsidized by the province or state, so that they would be affordable to the poor families they attended, but local women who could understand and speak the dialect. The midwife would be responsible not only for managing the birth, but also for ensuring the infant's well-being in its earliest days, to give advice, and to protect the mother from the influence of grandmothers and *bakers*.

THE MIDWIFE: FROM SUBJECT OF REFORM TO MISSIONARY

The Heerlen school tried to fill this need. The 'modern midwife' product of the school would be a campaigner, challenging ignorance and introducing cleanliness and modern methods of maternal and infant care into the home. But before she could reform others, she herself was to be reformed. Like the Bible nurses, health missionaries who entered the homes of the Victorian poor in Britain,[50] midwives must be prepared and equipped for their task, fitted out not with Bibles and tracts, but soap, nailbrushes, dressings, sterilizing equipment, and a clean, white apron.[51]

To enter the schools the midwife had to pass a number of tests. Her credentials had to be good. Much correspondence could change hands between parents, guardians or sponsors and the school directors before a formal application for admission was even submitted. Some candidates were turned away because they were too young or were advised to obtain additional schooling; some opted to do this on a private basis, and letters from local teachers asking how they could best prepare their pupils also appear in the pupils' files. Candidates were required to obtain recommendations from their vicar, mayor or another local notable, who would answer questions concerning their moral behaviour, religious life and family background. An admission examination would be taken to test writing abilities, comprehension, mathematics and creativity (not too much), and candidates were interviewed at the school. Many dropped out of the running at this stage; in some years the schools had four times more applicants than places.[52] In 1913 Heerlen received applications from thirty candidates, after the written examination fifteen were dismissed, and only nine were finally admitted.[53]

Concern was expressed not only about individual candidates but also general standards of admission. The schools found it necessary to instruct their pupils in the three Rs to equip them for theoretical training. While there had been an extension in the secondary schooling offered to girls in the last part of the nineteenth century,[54] the system seemed to have failed those who wished to train as midwives; many had been taken out of formal schooling by their families to help in the home or to earn a living before they had learnt enough. It was clearly a struggle to obtain the learning necessary for admission, many candidates putting together a patchwork of several years in primary school with private tuition. Once admitted, the course was demanding, with a good deal of theory being taught from difficult textbooks, and it was physically exhausting. The course covered the theory and practice of midwifery, antenatal care, anatomy, physiology and hygiene, and some nursing. After a third year was added in 1921, greater emphasis was placed on the care of healthy infants. In addition to the lessons, the pupils helped at deliveries, largely in the attached clinics. Though there was domestic help in the schools, the midwives also were required to undertake a great deal of household labour: 'You cleaned everything: floors, rooms, beds, tables, sheets, plates, surfaces and people. You dusted and swept, scrubbed and wiped classrooms, dining rooms, delivery rooms and the clinic.'[55]

Stress was placed on appearance and deportment. School reports gave marks and comments on dress, attitudes towards superiors, fellow-pupils and patients, and manners. Some pupils were criticized for being brusque, conceited or quick-tempered. In Heerlen religious instruction topped the list of subjects in year reports. The midwives were kept out of trouble through work. Hours were long, most days from dawn to dusk, with extra study periods, few holidays or days off. Almost without exception the girls lodged in the school under the strict supervision of the mistress-midwife: 'You were treated like a child, a difficult child. You must do what they said.'[56] The Amsterdam school instituted Swedish gymnastics to complete the processes of improving body and mind. Boyfriends were forbidden and the pupils' movements curtailed even when they were allowed out. Discipline was 'strict, strict, strict', but perhaps as much related to the need to keep the pupils healthy to carry out their heavy tasks as to guarding their moral characters. New pupils were to bring bills of clean health from their doctor, and certificates showing that they were free from tuberculosis and had good teeth! According to one mistress-midwife a strict regime was absolutely necessary. Some girls came from families where discipline was lax: 'Now they were learning a profession that demanded responsibility.

Order, discipline, hygiene.'[57] In many ways midwife training resembled that of nurses,[58] the mistress-midwife more than the equal of the hospital matron. Yet, unlike nurses, once qualified most midwives would work more or less independently, outside of institutions, and often in considerable isolation.

Doctors campaigning for better services and an improvement in maternal and infant health saw the school-trained midwife as an ally. The midwife came out well in government reports, but they stressed, along with the school directors, the need to attract a better class of pupil, and, in the meantime, to transform the rougher material into educated ladies. Klaas de Snoo, director of the Rotterdam school, expressed a wider felt anxiety in 1912, fear of malaise and that the midwife would die out: 'We have need of her: 59 per cent to 60 per cent of women deliver under the direction of midwives.' Even if doctors would take over more deliveries, the midwife would still be needed, 'if it was only because most women, especially in the towns, would not be able to pay the fee demanded by doctors'.[59] It was important, De Snoo argued, to raise standards of recruitment and training. Ten years on, De Snoo described how, 'The girls, who for a large part stem from the lower social classes, are raised during their apprenticeship to a higher level of civilization.' It came as a constant surprise to him that society accorded more status to the nurse, the mere helpmate of the doctor, than the independent midwife. This, he assumed, stemmed largely from the fact that the initial recruitment of nurses was from a higher social milieu.[60]

Girls entering the schools usually had experienced no previous employment, or at least not on a formal basis. Many, however, had helped in the family home or worked as domestic servants in other households. A small number were qualified nurses, and a handful were described as dressmakers, children's nannies, teachers, or shop assistants. Their fathers typically were farmers, shop assistants or small shopkeepers, artisans or craftsmen of some sort.[61]

By the 1920s and 1930s the midwife candidates began to be drawn from a broader social spectrum, as the costs of training fell increasingly on their families.[62] A small proportion of pupils were funded by the provincial authorities; in return, following the completion of their training, they would work as a town midwife for a period of two years, being permitted to buy themselves out of this obligation for the sum of 200 guilders.[63] By the 1920s 200 guilders a year was being demanded in school fees. In addition, money had to be found for uniform, books, and pocket money. Somehow families scraped the necessary money together to pay the fees. A few pupils even took out life insurance policies to fund their training. Johanna Maria Dijkstra, a former cashier at the Catholic-owned department store Vroom en Dreesman, came up with this option in 1933 when commencing her training in Heerlen, but, with the help of her local church council, she was finally able to persuade the town authorities to fund her for one year.[64] Most of the pupils would need to earn a proper living from their work once qualified; only very few could enjoy the luxury of a vocation. Though many of the pupils would eventually marry, many also continued with their work, in some cases being the main bread-winner. While midwife training was a costly business, often involving a struggle to raise funds, the rewards were apparently sufficient to make it a viable option.[65]

Refresher courses were considered vital not only to bring mid-wives up to date with the latest techniques and knowledge, but to remind them of their duties with regard to the care of mothers and babies, to put them back on the right track. In 1912 a report of the government's advisory body on health, the *Gezondheidsraad*, concluded that it was necessary that:

> the practising midwife is taken once a year from the treadmill of her activities to refresh her knowledge and her skill in a civilized and cultured milieu; that she, for the largest part originating from the working class, sometimes falls under the influence of the continual association with her class, with the consequence that she takes up prejudices ... after a while she can no longer resist the old wives' tales and so-called 'experience'.

For a short time she should return to the fold 'to come back to a circle of colleagues of a higher class, to draw from new pupils and to put on stronger armour against the all-threatening influence of the daily grind'.[66] Refresher courses were consistently put forward as being very useful, but were rarely put into effect.

The midwife schools nurtured a feeling of community within the school, with stress on uniform, badges, group photographs and graduation ceremonies. After the midwives left the schools, contact was maintained through reunions, and at the Heerlen school in particular pleas for support for various fund-raising campaigns. The school directors helped their pupils to obtain their first jobs, encouraged and advised them, sometimes going to great lengths to secure them appropriate posts. The medical directors in Heerlen sent telegrams of congratulation to midwives celebrating their 30th or 40th jubilees in practice.[67] The testimonies of the midwives express a debt of gratitude to the school directors, their mentors and guides, and they were enthusiastic about their study years in Heerlen. The correspondence is often friendly and confiding, the midwives telling stories of their practices, incomes, struggles, illnesses, marriage, the birth of children, decisions to trade in a bicycle for a motor car, but always respectful. Questions of gender mingled with those of status in defining the midwives' position *vis-à-vis* the school directors, and status would also play a role in determining midwives' relationships with the women they delivered.

BRIDGING THE GAP: THE MIDWIFE MISSIONARY OR MEDIATOR?

Influencing the midwife pupil in the training schools was well and good, but what happened when she stepped though the school gates, diploma in hand, to start up in practice? Had she been so well drilled that she carried all the baggage of modern midwifery with her? Had the midwife schools been preaching to the converted in the first place? Or were midwives prepared to compromise when actually confronted in practice with poor, unhygienic conditions, dealing with a clientele who had their own expectations of how birth and infant care should be conducted?

The fact that most babies were born at home is of great importance, potentially giving free rein to traditional ways of managing birth, but also leaving room for negotiation – and conflict – between the woman in childbed, her family and helpers, and the midwife. Because birth took place in relative privacy there were fewer 'rules' about how events should proceed. There was no doubt enormous variation in practices.

Largely through the pages of their journals – which combined the functions of networking, informing and educating, and as platforms for midwives' complaints and concerns – midwives were informed of unusual customs and beliefs surrounding birth, past and present, at home and abroad, at the same time being entertained and warned off.[68] They were also instructed at length on the code of hygiene which should govern their practices.[69] Through their own reports to the *Tijdschrift voor Praktische Verloskunde*

167

('Journal of Practical Midwifery'), midwives also joined in telling stories of outdated practices that they had encountered, as they intervened in births which had been mismanaged by incompetents, ejected unwanted helpers, tidied and cleaned up, got rid of the alcohol and the dirty bottles of oil used to ease the birth. There are also tales of great initiative, as midwives made mattresses from flannelette sheets stuffed with old newspapers, boiled rainwater, improvised baby clothes. It is difficult to assess the representativeness of these accounts, but many, like that of Mej. C.E. Roodenburg, described beliefs and ways of managing childbed similar to those which had aroused the horror of doctors writing on the subject, sharing not just the stories but the dismay of the doctors. But, taking this as a positive sign of progress, she had also heard neighbours criticize the old *baker*, who had not washed the newborn properly, 'and if it was not properly washed the first time, then you could never get it clean'. Roodenburg was apparently surprised by this comment, because cleanliness seemed to be in low regard otherwise, with the mothers left to 'stink and sweat' for nine days following birth.[70]

Writing in 1907 about her experiences on taking up midwifery practice, Mej. Schipper-Lens remarked that she had come across things 'that she had never heard of at the training school'.[71] She had tales of *verzien*, that breast-feeding during pregnancy would result in blindness in the foetus, while if the mother cried it would cause her child to be born with red eyes. But she was more concerned with the problems she encountered in persuading her clients to abandon practices associated with the 'old midwife'. She caused great consternation by not using the ever-present oil, which stood ready on the table (for as long as two weeks) to 'soften the parts', for waiting for the placenta to be delivered instead of tugging at it, and for washing the mothers after they had given birth. In one case, the husband – who seemed to have much say in such matters – forbade this: 'the whole thing must stay put, the more it stank, the quicker the woman would recover'.[72] The care of the child was still a sad affair, but in the last few years Schipper-Lens had seen some improvement, partly the result of parents reading popular books and newspaper articles. She had finally persuaded her mothers to abandon *brandewijn* for washing the new-born infant; she was now busy 'weaning' them off '*pap*', and persuading them to try at least to breast-feed, and, failing that, to combine breast- and bottle feeding.

168

By the 1930s, when a series of doctoral theses appeared on the subject of obstetric care in various regions of Holland,[73] it appears that many traditional practices were dying out, although the countryside still offered up considerable resistance. The authors were still being drawn into a world of 'folklore, sayings and practices', but more and more these were consigned to legend in contradiction to the brave new world of *consultatiebureaus* and school-trained midwives. Yet the picture was mixed. Hagenbeek, a doctor working in the province of Overijssel, reported in 1936 that care of the mother after birth was still shared by unschooled and schooled forces. The trained maternity nurse worked largely with doctors, while the midwife was left with the unqualified *baker*. In many cases, the midwife undertook the maternity nursing herself, to help out poor families and because she did not want the *baker* to come into contact with her clients. More women were also attending mothercraft courses and *consultatiebureaus*.[74] The province of Limburg, Starmans claimed, was busy catching up, improving standards and mortality rates, but there was a long way to go. These authors also pointed to the problems of competition between doctor and midwife which retarded progress; instead of working together the two groups continued to undermine each other.[75]

The impact of midwives is difficult to pin down, though in the pages of their journals we pick up on their keenness to reform childbirth practices. Many of the pupils entered the schools with high ideals. In Heerlen, training both lay and religious midwives, this was often reinforced by their Catholic faith. Midwives' ideas on how and under what conditions they should work seem to have coincided to a great extent with those of the school directors and other reformers. The rigorous admissions procedures ensured not only a willingness to learn and malleability, but also, to a certain degree, shared beliefs. The schools were closely involved in setting up *consultatiebureaus* and offered mothercraft courses, so the pupils were brought into immediate contact with the institutions promoting modern motherhood. Once qualified, some midwives helped set up clinics or more informal provisions offering antenatal care and advice on infant feeding, writing to the directors for advice on how to proceed and organize funding,[76] while others helped establish mothercraft courses.[77]

In one way at least the school system was too successful, even self-defeating. One great problem was persuading the pupils to work in the districts where their help was most needed. The work intended for the midwives was not only that of a missionary in the sense of reforming childbirth practices, but also in the sense of being sent out to poor, undeveloped regions, with a 'backward' culture.[78] It was a mission which demanded great sacrifice, something many midwives were not willing to make. Some had already sacrificed a good deal, struggling to be admitted to the schools and to pay the fees, working hard under the school regime. The letters sent to the directors by midwives in their practice-building years show their aim to be a good profitable practice. During training, the pupils lived in some comfort, with small bedrooms to themselves, pleasant dining halls, gardens and places to relax. They became used to delivering babies in pristine conditions, and both the complaints of the reformers and figures on childbirth attendance indicate that midwives did not take kindly to the idea of returning to the poorest areas to work, where conditions were appalling and rewards – financial or in terms of respect – few.

The purpose of the schools, particularly the Heerlen school, was to take pupils from targeted areas, with the expectation that they would return there once qualified. Preference was given to girls from North Brabant and Limburg, but in 1913–14 only four were admitted from these two provinces and five from other areas of the country.[79] Nor did girls from these districts necessarily return there after having glimpsed the 'good life'. In search of good practices and esteem, they spread out over the country. In 1920 one-quarter of the midwives working in North Brabant still lacked a school training.[80] In 1889 there was one midwife to every 10,204 inhabitants in North Brabant, compared with one for 5,643 in the country as a whole; by 1925 the gap had narrowed, but the discrepancy was still very apparent, with a ratio of 1:10,954 for North Brabant and 1:7,881 nationally.[81] In general midwives favoured setting up in the relatively wealthy towns to the west of the country.[82] The districts which most needed the services of midwives did not get them, despite the incentives offered by the local authorities in these deprived provinces in terms of large salaries, to compensate for the limited opportunities for private practice. Midwives' opting out meant that the aims of the government and school directors would long remain unfulfilled.

Some midwives had difficulties putting into practice what they had learnt and were simply not accepted in the areas where they worked. Letters to the Heerlen directors tell of problems in finding a place to practice, partly because of resistance to a Catholic midwife, but often because their methods did not fit, or because of an attachment to the old midwife and her way of doing things. Others, however, went on to have exemplary careers. Mevr. Offermans-Commans, a 1926 graduate of the Heerlen school, celebrated her 40th year in practice in 1951, having delivered some 6,000 babies, and raised six children of her own. Her eldest daughter was training to be a midwife.[83] Mevr. Ubaghs, was 'called' to midwifery, training between 1887 and 1889 at the Rotterdam state school. She returned to her birthplace in Limburg to practice, where she worked for half a century, delivering a total of 12,000 babies. The mothers she attended could not afford to pay her much, and, though the town council awarded her a subsidy of 50 guilders for her work amongst the poor, she never prospered. She helped the mothers out with milk and other necessities. Her work, she believed, was ample reward in itself.[84] Even girls like Theresia van Krieken who was described in the school reports as 'careless in carrying out orders', 'unable to recognize her own faults', and as having 'too much self-assurance', came good. She steadily built up a clientele in Helmond, before selling her practice to enter a convent, and work under her new name of Zr. Theresita in a colonial mission.[85]

Changes in childbirth practices early this century cannot simply be interpreted along gender lines.[86] Questions of status and the different social values of the reformers, midwives, traditional helpers and their clients produce a more complex picture.[87] By the 1920s and 1930s a greater variety of women were going into midwifery; many of the new intake of pupils felt less distanced socially from the school directors and their teachers and perhaps stronger feelings of superiority – of knowledge and status – over the women they delivered. Midwives came to share some of the opinions and much of the language of the doctors concerning childbirth practices. Neither midwives nor doctors sought out positive aspects of traditional beliefs or ways of proceeding in the birthing room.[88] In general, the school-trained midwives too appear to have concluded that *all* traditional practices were bad, and placed as little value as the doctors in separating out the more comforting and harmless aspects of custom and belief, and the supporting role of traditional female helpers. Though Dutch childbirth remained home-based using little medical intervention, it did not in this sense stay rooted in tradition.[89]

The midwife in many cases must have functioned as missionary and mediator, depending upon her character, background, and the circumstances of her practice. In reports to their journals midwives show a certain pride in getting the *baker* out of the house without offending the mother, and in demonstrating the value of new methods. Many apparently ran a gauntlet and, while fulfilling the requirements of the school, compromised in practice. The school directors strove to transform their pupils into well-trained midwives and well-adapted young ladies ready to go forth and reform childbirth and child-rearing practices. But like the West End shop assistants observed by Bernard Shaw, many midwives presumably became bilingual, able to speak the language of the schools and that of their clients.[90] The midwife and the reformer had much to gain from working together. For the reformer, the midwife was a necessary ally; there was little hope of changing practices, particularly in the countryside, without her. And for the midwife the early twentieth century was a time of mixed blessings. Adverse competition and poverty for some were balanced by financial rewards and flourishing practices for others. The midwives' work, abolishing superstition and bad practices, encouraging hygienic and modern methods, went hand in hand with an expansion of their role and increase in responsibility towards mothers and their infants.

ACKNOWLEDGEMENTS

I would like to thank Anne Marie Rafferty, Marijke Gijswijt-Hofstra, Hans de Waardt and Nanny Wiegman, and the participants at the Woudschoten conference on 'Healing, Magic and Belief' held in September 1994 for their comments, the Sociaal Historische Centrum in Maastricht for arranging the loan of the Heerlen material and the Gemeente Archief Delft for their hospitality. I am grateful to the Wellcome Trust for funding my project on 'Midwives in the Netherlands 1897–1941'.

NOTES

1 'Veertig jaar Katholieke moederschapszorg', *De Maasbode*, 16 May, 1953.
2 M.J. van Lieburg, 'De Rijkskweekschool voor Vroedvrouwen (1882–1926)', in E. Scholte, M.J. van Lieburg and R.O. Aalbersberg, *Rijkskweekschool voor Vroedvrouwen te Rotterdam*, Leidschendam, Ministerie van Volksgezondheid en Milieuhygiene, 1982, p. 64.

3 For obstetric attendance and midwife practice in the nineteenth century and the turn of the twentieth, see M.J. van Lieburg and H. Marland, 'Midwife regulation, education, and practice in the Netherlands during the nineteenth century', *Medical History*, 1989, vol. 33, pp. 296–317; H. Marland, 'The guardians of normal birth: the debate on the standard and status of the midwife in the Netherlands around 1900', in E. Abraham-van der Mark (ed.) *Successful Home Birth and Midwifery: The Dutch Model*, Westport, CT, Bergin & Garvey, 1993, pp. 21–44; F. van Gelder, 'Is dat nu typies vrouwenwerk? De maatschappelijke positie van vroedvrouwen', *Tijdschrift voor Vrouwenstudies*, 1982, vol. 3, pp. 5–33; J.J. Klinkert, *Verloskundigen en Artsen. Verleden en Heden van enkele Professionele Beroepen in de Gezondheidszorg*, Alphen a/d Rijn and Brussels, Stafleu, 1980.

4 In 1906 midwives were attending 59 per cent of deliveries, doctors 36 per cent. The remaining 5 per cent were delivered without any qualified obstetric assistance: C. van Tussenbroek, *De Ontwikkeling der Aseptische Verloskunde in Nederland*, Haarlem, De Erven F. Bohn, 1911, p. 183.

5 Van Lieburg and Marland, 'Midwife regulation', pp. 313–14; Abraham-van der Mark, 'Introduction to the Dutch system of home birth and midwifery', in Abraham-van der Mark (ed.) *Successful Home Birth*, pp. 1–18.

6 Obstetrics, meanwhile, remained a narrowly defined scientific subject, with focus on research on a modest scale. With few institutional facilities to support clinical work, obstetricians delivered only small numbers of women, primarily complicated cases. For the specialization of obstetrics, see A. Hiddinga, 'Dutch obstetric science: emergence, growth, and present situation', in Abraham-van der Mark (ed.) *Successful Home Birth*, pp. 45–76.

7 H. Marland, 'Questions of competence: the midwife debate in the Netherlands in the early twentieth century', *Medical History*, 1995, vol. 39, pp. 317–37. Levels of medical intervention are still low in the Netherlands, especially when compared with the United States. See the essays by P.E. Treffers, T. Tymstra and L.H. Lumey, in Abraham-van der Mark (ed.) *Successful Home Birth*.

8 Van Lieburg and Marland, 'Midwife regulation', pp. 300–1.

9 In 1920 569 patients were admitted: 336 obstetrical cases, 136 gynaecological cases, and 97 infants: Kweekschool voor Vroedvrouwen te Heerlen. 8e Jaarverslag, 1920, p. 34.

10 Historians have tended to steer away from analysis of the link between traditional childbirth practices and mortality rates, largely because of the difficulties of quantifying their impact. Loudon's monumental study of maternal mortality does, however, discuss questions of poor hygiene, poverty and the debate on 'primitive and civilized childbirth': I. Loudon, *Death in Childbirth: An International Study of Maternal Care and Maternal Mortality 1800–1950*, Oxford, Clarendon Press, 1992. Van Poppel has demonstrated the relationship between religious beliefs and practices and mortality levels, including infant deaths, in the

Netherlands: F. van Poppel, 'Religion and health: Catholicism and regional mortality differences in nineteenth-century Netherlands', *Social History of Medicine*, 1992, vol. 5, pp. 229–53.

11 North Brabant is often cited as the blackest of the obstetric blackspots: M. Pruijt, 'Van vroedvrouw tot verloskundige. De ontwikkelingen in het vroedvrouwenberoep in Nederland in de periode 1865–1940', doctoraal scriptie, Katholieke Hogeschool Tilburg, 1987; M. Pruijt, 'Roeien, baren en in de arbeid zijn. Vroedvrouwen in Noord-Brabant, 1880–1960', in M. Grever and A. van der Veen (eds) *Bij ons Moeder en ons Jet. Brabantse Vrouwen in de 19de en 20ste Eeuw*, 's-Hertogenbosch, Walburg, 1989, pp. 122–42; M. Pruijt, 'De verloskundige zorg in Noord-Brabant 1900–1940', *Sociale Wetenschappen*, 1988, vol. 31, pp. 175–93. For the background to Dutch infant welfare services, see H. Marland, 'The medicalization of motherhood: doctors and infant welfare in the Netherlands, 1901–1930', in V. Fildes, L. Marks and H. Marland (eds) *Women and Children First: International Maternal and Infant Welfare, 1870–1945*, London and New York, Routledge, 1992, pp. 74–96.

12 C. Vandenbroeke, F. van Poppel and A.M. van der Woude, 'De zuigelingen en kindersterfte in België en Nederland in seculair perspectief', *Tijdschrift voor Geschiedenis*, 1981, vol. 94, p. 481.

13 J.H. Starmans, *Verloskunde en Kindersterfte in Limburg. Folklore: Geschiedenis: Heden*, proefschrift, Universiteit van Amsterdam; Maastricht, Van Aelst, 1930, pp. 143–67.

14 C. Meuleman, *De Kweekschool voor Vroedvrouwen te Heerlen en de Kindersterfte in de Zuidelijke Provincien*, n. p., 1912.

15 Kweekschool voor Vroedvrouwen te Heerlen. 1e Jaarverslag, 1912–13, p. 9.

16 Statuten van de Vereeniging: 'De Kweekschool voor Vroedvrouwen te Heerlen', 1911, art. 3.

17 For this often explosive debate, see, for example, R.J.Th. Meurer, 'Vroedvrouw en zuigelingenzorg', *Nederlandsch Tijdschrift voor Geneeskunde* (hereafter *NTvG*), 1921, vol. 84:I, pp. 338–43.

18 Brief van één der Amsterdamse zuigelingenartsen aan de directeur van de GG & GD: dossier 3792, 1932. Quoted in J. Spoorenberg, 'De opvoeding van arbeidersvrouwen. Zuigelingenzorg in Amsterdam 1903–40', doctoraal scriptie, Universiteit van Amsterdam, 1981, p. 31.

19 Research into infant welfare provision in the Netherlands has focused on the infant welfare centres, *consultatiebureaus*. This is in part because most work has been carried out on towns, where these institutions were at their strongest. The place of the midwife in improving infant welfare has not been thoroughly explored. The midwife's own journal, the *Tijdschrift voor Praktische Verloskunde* (hereafter *TvPV*), in the first decades of the twentieth century shows how crucial this work was to the midwife. For a study of infant welfare work in Amsterdam based largely on the *consultatiebureaus*, see Spoorenberg, 'De opvoeding van arbeidersvrouwen', and for a more general account, N. Knapper, *Een Kwart Eeuw Zuigelingenzorg in Nederland*, Amsterdam, Scheltema & Holkema, 1935. For the relationship between the modern midwife and

hygienic practices, see the chapters by Løkke, Mottram and Loudon in this volume.

20 J.L.B. Gribling, *Het Vroedvrouwen-Vraagstuk in Noord-Brabant*, Breda, Diocesane Federatie, 'Het Wit-Gele Kruis', 1920, p. 7.

21 Ibid., pp. 2–5.

22 See H. Marland, '"A broad and pleasing field of activity"? The payments, posts and practices of Dutch midwives in the early twentieth century', in J. Woodward and R. Rütte (eds) *Coping with Sickness: Historical Aspects of Health Care in a European Perspective*, Sheffield, European Association for the History of Medicine and Health, 1995, pp. 67–91.

23 Catharine van Tussenbroek claimed that for the country as a whole some 5 per cent of women gave birth without qualified obstetric assistance in 1906. Some of these presumably were assisted by unqualified attendants, but others delivered without any help whatsoever. However, in some regions of the country figures for unattended deliveries were much higher. In Groningen the rate was almost 20 per cent and in North Brabant 13 per cent: Van Tussenbroek, *De Ontwikkeling der Aseptische Verloskunde*, pp. 183, 185.

24 Meuleman, *De Kweekschool*, p. 5.

25 Here, as with the writers I am quoting from, I will be using 'folk' and 'traditional' practices interchangeably. See, for a discussion of the terminology, F. Loux, 'Folk medicine', in W.F. Bynum and Roy Porter (eds) *Companion Encyclopedia of the History of Medicine*, London and New York, Routledge, 1993, pp. 661–75.

26 While a good deal of attention has been paid to role of the ceremony of childbirth in the early modern period, the continuing importance of ritual and women's knowledge and presence in the delivery room has been neglected for later centuries. For the early modern period, the work of Adrian Wilson has been very influential, including his article 'The ceremony of childbirth and its interpretation', in V. Fildes (ed.) *Women as Mothers in Pre-industrial England*, London and New York, Routledge, 1990, pp. 68–107. See also J. Gélis, *L'arbre et le fruit: la naissance dans l'Occident moderne (XVIe–XIXe siècle)*, Paris, Fayard, 1984.

27 The literature on the subject is enormous, but two of the most interesting examples are C. Bakker, *Volksgeneeskunde in Waterland. Een Vergelijkende Studie met de Geneeskunde der Grieken en Romeinen*, Amsterdam, H.J. Paris, 1928, who devotes a lengthy first chapter to pregnancy, birth and the lying-in period, and M.A. van Andel, *Volksgeneeskunst in Nederland*, proefschrift, Universiteit van Leiden, 1909. Andel was one of the most productive writers of this period on folklore and medicine.

28 Starmans, *Verloskunde en Kindersterfte in Limburg*, pp. 36–52.

29 Including several major studies, such as S. Sturkop, *Bijdrage tot de Kennis der Zwangerschapslusten*, proefschrift, Universiteit van Amsterdam; Amsterdam, Blikman & Sartorius, 1909. The role of maternal imagination has an enduring history. See H.W. Roodenburg, 'The maternal imagination. The fears of pregnant women in seventeenth-century Holland', *Journal of Social History*, 1988, vol. 21, pp. 701–16, and the

diary of Vrouw Schrader, a skilled and deeply religious midwife, who attributed many mishaps to the misbehaviour of mothers during pregnancy: H. Marland, M.J. van Lieburg and G.J. Kloosterman, '*Mother and Child were Saved*'. *The Memoirs (1693–1740) of the Frisian Midwife Catharina Schrader*, Amsterdam, Rodopi, 1987.

30 Starmans, *Verloskunde en Kindersterfte in Limburg*, p. 33.

31 R. van Daalen, 'Family change and continuity in the Netherlands: birth and childbed in text and art', in Abraham-van der Mark (ed.) *Successful Home Birth*, pp. 77–94. For the objects associated with birth, see Th.H. Lunsingh Scheurleer *et al.*, 'Enkele oude Nederlandse kraamgebruiken', *Antiek*, 1971, vol. 6, pp. 297–332.

32 Loux, 'Folk medicine', p. 663.

33 H.J. Ensink, *Moederschapszorg in het Markiezaat van Bergen op Zoom*, proefschrift, Universiteit van Amsterdam; Bergen op Zoom, Harte, 1940, pp. 47, 49.

34 Van Poppel, 'Religion and health'.

35 P.J.M. Aalberse, 'Kindergeboorten en kindersterfte', VI and VII, *Katholieke Sociaal Weekblad*, 1917, vol. 35, pp. 353–6, and vol. 37, pp. 373–7.

36 Ibid., VI, p. 354.

37 P. Meurkens, *Sociale Verandering in het Oude Kempenland: Demografie Economie en Cultuur van een Preindustriële Samenleving*, proefschrift, Katholieke Universiteit Nijmegen, 1984.

38 Van Poppel, 'Religion and health'. Methorst showed that the infant mortality rate for Catholics was 100 per 1,000 live births in the period 1907–10, compared with 70 for Protestants and 55 for Jews. Even in the post-war period Hoogendoorn noted that in Amsterdam and other large cities infant mortality was much higher amongst Catholics: H.W. Methorst, 'Geboorte-achteruitgang en zuigelingenbescherming', *NTvG*, 1916, vol. 60, pp. 1241–8; D. Hoogendoorn, *De Zuigelingensterfte in Nederland*, Assen, Van Gorcum, 1959.

39 Archief Vroedvrouwenschool Heerlen (AVH), 52. Correspondentie met bisschoppen in Nederland. Nota omtrent het aantal R.K. Vroedvrouwen dat in Nederland benoodigd is, nov., 1925.

40 H.R. Folmer, 'Volksgebruiken in Zeeland bij geboorte en kraambed', *NTvG*, 1927, vol. 70:IB, pp. 3112–18.

41 Ibid., pp. 3112–13.

42 Ibid., p. 3115.

43 Ibid., p. 3113.

44 Ibid., p. 3117.

45 J. van Galen and A. Mevis, 'Zuigelingenzorg in Oost-Brabant, 1918–1940', in N. Bakker *et al.* (eds) *Een Tipje van de Sluier. Vrouwengeschiedenis in Nederland*, vol. 2, Amsterdam, SUA, 1980, pp. 73–83.

46 P.A. Barentsen, 'Over de kindersterfte ten plattenlande van Oost-Noordbanbant', *NTvG*, 1922, vol. 66: IIA, pp. 610–22.

47 Ibid., p. 612.

48 Ibid., pp. 612–15.

49 See also P.A. Barentsen, *Het Oude Kempenland. Eene Proeve van Vergelijking van Organisme en Samenleving*, Groningen, P. Noordhoff, 1935.

50 F. Prochaska 'Body and soul: Bible nurses and the poor in Victorian London', *Historical Research*, 1987, vol. 60, pp. 336–48.
51 Archief Centrale Gezondheidsraad, 1902–20. Rapport 'Inlichtingen en Raadgevingen aan Vroedvrouwen', 4 maart 1905.
52 R.J.Th. Meurer, 'De beteekenis van de vroedvrouw', *Moederschapszorg*, 1930, vol. 6, p. 18.
53 Kweekschool voor Vroedvrouwen te Heerlen. 2e Jaarverslag, 1913–14, p. 5.
54 W.H. Posthumus-van der Goot and A. de Waal (eds) *Van Moeder op Dochter. De Maatschappelijke Positie van de Vrouw in Nederland vanaf de Franse Tijd*, Nijmegen, SUN, 1977, 1st pub. 1968, pp. 41–56, 161–7.
55 Vertelde Verleden, *Vroedvrouwen*, Amsterdam, Gilde, 1992, p. 7 (the collective memories of midwives in Amsterdam).
56 Ibid.
57 Ibid., p. 8.
58 M. Vicinus, *Independent Women: Work and Community for Single Women 1850–1920*, Chicago and London, University of Chicago Press, 1985, chapter 3, 'Reformed hospital nursing: discipline and cleanliness', pp. 85–120; N. Tomes, '"Little world of our own": the Pennsylvania Hospital Training School for Nurses, 1895–1907', in J.W. Leavitt (ed.) *Women and Health in America*, Madison, WI, University of Wisconsin Press, 1981, pp. 467–81.
59 Archief Afd. Volksgezondheid en Armenwezen, 1910–18. 442. Praeadvies over het Rapport van den Centralen Gezondheidsraad in Zake het Vroedvrouwenvraagstuk [1912].
60 AVH, 13. Samenvatting van het Verhandelde op de Vergardering van 3 oktober [Gezondheidsraad, 1922].
61 'Rapport der commissie in zake het vroedvrouwenvraagstuk hier te lande, benoemd door het hoofdbestuur der Nederlandsche Maatschappij tot Bevordering der Geneeskunst in samenwerking met het bestuur der Nederlandsche Gynaecologische Vereeniging', Feb., 1911: *NTvG*, 1911, vol. 55:I A, pp. 1117–19.
62 AVH, 187, 192. Geslaagde Vroedvrouwen, Cursus 1933–36, 1938–41.
63 *TvPV*, 1902, vol. 6, pp. 129–30.
64 AVH, 187. Geslaagde Vroedvrouwen, Cursus 1933–36: Johanna Maria Dijkstra.
65 Marland, '"A broad and pleasing field of activity"?'.
66 Archief Afd. Volksgezondheid en Armenwezen, 1910–18. 442. Centrale Gezondheidsraad. Ber. op 21 oct. 1911, no. 7955, 17 nov. 1911, no. 8605, Afd. V.A., Betr. Vroedvrouwvraagstuk, 14 juni, 1912, p. 8.
67 AVH, 181. Correspondentie en gelukstelegrammen.
68 For example, the lengthy series of articles by C.N. van de Poll, 'Het een en ander omtrent bijgeloof, volksgewoonten, enz. bij zwangerschap, baring en in het kraambed', *TvPV*, 1902–3, vol. 6, pp. 161–5, 186–90, 193–8, 209–14, 224–7, 245–8, 257–62, 273–7.
69 For example, M. Niemeijer, 'Iets over den werkkring van de vroedvrouw', *TvPV*, 1897, vol. 1, pp. 41–9.
70 C.E. Roodenburg, 'Eene bijdrage tot de medische volkenkunde', *TvPV*, 1901, vol. 5, pp. 138–9.

71 J. Schipper-Lens, 'Eenige volksbegrippen omtrent zwangerschap, baring, kraambed en zuigelingenverpleging', *TvPV*, 1907, vol. 10, pp. 379–83.
72 Ibid., pp. 380–1.
73 Starmans, *Verloskunde en Kindersterfte in Limburg*; P.E.G. van der Heijden, *De Zorg voor Moeder en Kind in Noord-Brabant*, proefschrift, Universiteit van Amsterdam, 1934; A.C. Drogendijk, *De Verloskundige Voorziening in Dordrecht van 1500 tot Heden*, proefschrift, Universiteit van Amsterdam; Amsterdam, H.J. Paris, 1935; J.H. Hagenbeek, *Het Moederschap in Overijssel. Een Onderzoek naar de Verloskundige en de Zuigelingenzorg in de Provincie Overijssel*, proefschrift, Universiteit van Amsterdam, Zwolle, H. Tulp, 1936.
74 Hogenbeek, Het Moederschap in Overijssel, pp. 130–3, 139–45.
75 See Marland, 'Questions of competence' and '"A broad and pleasing field of activity"?'
76 AVH, 187. Geslaagde Vroedvrouwen, Cursus 1933–36.
77 Pruijt, 'De verloskundige zorg in Noord-Brabant'.
78 The parallels between missionary work in the colonies and in the deprived southern provinces of the Netherlands was the subject of a paper, 'The missionary midwives: colonizing Dutch childbirth services at home and abroad, 1897–1930', presented at the Society for the Social History of Medicine's annual conference, 'Medicine and the Colonies', Oxford 20 July 1996.
79 Kweekschool voor Vroedvrouwen te Heerlen. 2e Jaarverslag, 1913–14, p. 5.
80 Pruijt, 'Roeien, baren en in de arbeid zijn', pp. 126, 129.
81 Centraal Bureau voor de Statistiek, 'Jaarcijfers voor Nederland, 1865–1935'. Figures from Pruijt, ibid., p. 126.
82 Marland, '"A broad and pleasing field of activity"?'
83 *Limburgsch Dagblad*, 24 Nov. 1950, 30 April 1951.
84 Ibid., 22 Feb. 1954.
85 AVH, 192. Geslaagde Vroedvrouwen, Cursus 1938–41: T.C. van Krieken.
86 As illustrated by Leap and Hunter, who have used oral history to good effect, to draw out lines of conflict between professional midwives and traditional handywomen: N. Leap and B. Hunter, *The Midwife's Tale: An Oral History from Handywoman to Professional Midwife*, London, Scarlet Press, 1993.
87 As Susan Pitt's analysis of discourses on childbirth practices in the interwar period shows, these cannot be understood solely in terms of male/female dichotomy: see the chapter by Pitt in this volume.
88 Only *verzien* was treated with respect by a few. Starmans wrote that two midwife respondents to his obstetric survey believed in *verzien*, a few had no opinion about it, while the majority thought it was nonsense. One doctor respondent found it not 'completely ridiculous', while Dr Meuleman of the Heerlen school declared that there might be something in a belief that had held sway through the centuries: Starmans, *Verloskunde en Kindersterfte in Limburg*, pp. 33–4.

89 See also the chapter by DeVries and Barroso in this volume.
90 B. Shaw, *Pygmalion: A Romance in Five Acts,* Penguin edn, 1941, play first produced in 1914, p. 10.

8

MIDWIVES AND THE QUALITY OF MATERNAL CARE

Irvine Loudon

If, in the second half of the nineteenth century, you had asked British medical practitioners what they thought of midwives, most would have said that they were dirty, ignorant, unskilful and dangerous. And if you had asked what should be done, most would have said that for practical reasons midwives could not be abolished, so they should be trained, examined, and registered. This would not only make them safer birth attendants for women too poor to pay a doctor; it would also enhance their other role, that of acting as the maternity nurse or 'monthly nurse'[1] for the middle classes who were delivered by general practitioners. Both the mother and the doctor needed skilled assistance before, during and especially after delivery.

Not all doctors were in favour of training. A substantial number of general practitioners opposed the compulsory training of midwives, fearing loss of business – a fear which became a reality for some after the Midwives Act of 1902. But the enlightened doctors of the 1880s and 1890s realized that Britain was way behind the Continent in the standard of its midwives. They recognized the necessity of formal training and reassured themselves that private patients would always pay for a doctor if they could, because doctors were more highly trained and able to deal with complications. That was the general opinion.

If you had asked the same questions of American obstetricians in the early decades of this century, you would have had a much more aggressive response. You would have been told that the midwife was typically old, ignorant and filthy, 'not far removed from the jungles of Africa, gin-fingering, guzzling . . . with her pockets full of snuff, her fingers full of dirt and her brains full of arrogance and

180

superstition; she was pestiferous and vicious' – and not least, 'un-American'.[2] To the American obstetrician the midwife was 'a relic of barbarism'[3] who must be abolished, except in areas of rural and urban poverty where women had no means of paying a physician. If European countries persisted in employing midwives on a large scale, it only showed how backward Europe was compared to America. Significantly, reports on maternal care in the United States often referred to deliveries by midwives as deliveries by 'non-medical personnel'.

In short, midwives had a pretty bad press in Britain and an appalling one in the United States. It was only in North-West Europe that a tradition existed of systems of maternal care in which midwives played a central and valued role. Thus it is not surprising to find that in the older histories of obstetrics published in the English-speaking world, midwives were largely ignored while page after page was devoted to famous obstetricians. It is only in the last twenty or so years that historians have started to examine in detail the lives, work, and social status of midwives, and the result has been a transformation of the history of childbirth. Thanks to these historians we now know a great deal about the social and economic history of the women who were described as midwives. One aspect, however, has received little attention. What was the quality of care provided by midwives? What were the effectiveness and efficiency of midwives compared with doctors? Were they, as so often assumed in the past, more dangerous as birth attendants than doctors? These are the questions I am going to attempt to answer in this chapter.

The process of answering these questions, however, is not without difficulties. First you must identify the women who were labelled as midwives. Clearly it cannot be assumed that they were a homogeneous group. You must specify the country and the period which is being investigated, and distinguish between trained and untrained midwives, monthly nurses and handywomen. And this leads to the question of what is meant by 'training'? Should the term 'trained midwife' be confined to those who were formally trained in the sense that they were first accepted as suitable (which implies at least a moderate standard of literacy and respectability) and were only allowed to apply for a licence after attending classes and passing an examination? Or should you also include midwives whose training consisted of an informal apprenticeship with an established midwife who was often their mother or some other member of the family? For the period with which we are concerned I will for the most part confine the term 'trained midwife' to those who had a formal training, and exclude those – however excellent they may have been – whose only training was an informal apprenticeship.

Next, we must define the criteria by which we measure the quality or effectiveness of maternal care. Today, the criteria would probably be perinatal mortality and morbidity, and almost certainly maternal satisfaction. In the Western world maternal mortality is of little use as a measure today simply because maternal deaths have become very rare. But in the period with which we are concerned when a successful delivery was one in which the mother survived, and with luck the baby as well, maternal mortality was not only the criterion of over-riding importance; for the historian it is the only criterion for which copious statistical evidence is available, so it is, of necessity, the yardstick we must use here.[4]

Much of this chapter is concerned with comparing maternal mortality rates for series of midwife deliveries and doctor deliveries. But there is a trap in such comparisons. There is rarely a problem if we are comparing the outcome of normal deliveries (defined as deliveries in which there were no life-threatening complications) by midwives and doctors. But suppose that a mother who arranged to be delivered by a midwife, was transferred in labour to hospital (or attended by a doctor at home) because of a serious complication. If the mother then died and her death was recorded as a hospital death or a death attributed to the doctor, the comparison might be invalid. In effect, the midwife would have to 'unload' her complicated deliveries onto the doctor called to the house, or the hospital. Thus her (the midwife's) mortality rates would be those of normal labours, the rates recorded by doctors and hospitals would be those of some normal and most if not all abnormal labours. For valid comparisons it was therefore essential that the outcome of all cases of midwife deliveries – that is all cases in which the patient booked a midwife for delivery – was accurately recorded and note was made of midwife cases in which a doctor was called or in which the patient was transferred to a hospital as an emergency admission in labour. Only then could the effectiveness of midwife deliveries be compared with that of doctors and hospitals. Such records were kept in only a few instances during the inter-war period in Britain and the United States, partly because obstetricians were often sensitive about being compared with midwives when the basis of comparison was rates of maternal mortality.

MIDWIVES VERSUS DOCTORS IN ENGLAND

We have a fair idea of the geographical distribution of deliveries between doctors and midwives in England during the second half of the nineteenth century.[5] What we do not have, however, is any information on maternal mortality rates in the country as a whole in terms of the birth attendant. Standard sources on maternal mortality such as national registers of causes of death are silent on the division of care between midwives and doctors; so one has to search for evidence in unlikely corners.

In the 1890s, the obstetrician Charles Cullingworth made an unexpected observation during the course of a lecture.[6] He had found to his surprise that the districts of London with the highest notification rates of maternal mortality were the middle-class areas:

> It will be observed that Westminster, Lambeth, Whitechapel, St George's-in-the-East, and Shoreditch, which might have been expected to appear high on the list, show a much smaller proportion of cases [of puerperal fever] than Hampstead and Islington, and even St James, Kensington and Chelsea.[7]

He was not in fact the first to have made such an observation. In the 1850s, the obstetrician John Roberton had noticed that maternal mortality was higher in the middle-class areas of Manchester than the working-class slums.[8] In 1887, a well-known London obstetrician remarked that deaths from puerperal fever were less common in working-class women than amongst the middle classes. He offered the explanation that the 'physical organs' of working-class women were 'in better working order, and are not subjugated and enfeebled by the excessive cultivation of the emotional and intellectual elements'. He concluded in true Victorian fashion that 'hard work and exercise are a preventative against the disease'.[9]

Later, in 1924, Dr Dudfield rediscovered the lower mortality rates in the working-class areas of London,[10] and Dr Fairbairn, who analysed rates of maternal mortality in Leeds between 1920 and 1929, found that while the maternal mortality rate for the city as a whole was 4.49/1,000 deliveries, it was 5.93 in the middle-class areas and 3.01 in the working-class areas. His explanation is worth quoting:

The midwife-employing class expect to deliver themselves, and that medical aid will only be required for unexpected and unlikely happenings. The woman who engages a doctor is an entirely different proposition, as she does so in the expectation that if things do not move quickly the artificial aid that is at hand will be immediately available.[11]

What was shown by these local studies was the phenomenon which I have called elsewhere the 'reverse social class connection'. With respect to most infectious diseases and also infant mortality during the period with which we are concerned, mortality rates were highest in the working classes and lowest in the upper classes; in maternal mortality it was the reverse.

The same phenomenon was shown in the 1930s when the maternal mortality rates according to social class in England and Wales as a whole were published by the Registrar General's office. The results can be seen in Table 8.1. These findings establish an important point. Although common sense suggests that women of the lower social classes were more likely to be badly nourished and anaemic, and therefore to have less resistance to the various causes of maternal mortality, social class was a much weaker determinant of mortality than the type of birth attendant. The

Table 8.1 England and Wales. Maternal mortality of married women according to social class, 1930–32

Cause of death	All married women	Class I & II professional and managerial	Class III skilled workers	Class IV semi-skilled	Class V unskilled
All causes	4.13	4.44	4.11	4.16	3.89
Total, excluding abortions	3.57	3.94	3.55	3.60	3.32
Puerperal sepsis	1.29	1.45	1.33	1.21	1.16
Puerperal haemorrhage	0.49	0.50	0.44	0.48	0.60
Toxaemia	0.79	0.81	0.81	0.84	0.68

Source: J.M. Munro Kerr, R.W. Johnstone and M.H. Phillips, *Historical Review of British Obstetrics and Gynaecology 1800–1950*, London, E. & S. Livingstone, 1954, table 9, chapter 29.
Note: Maternal mortality rate shown as maternal deaths per 1,000 births

higher mortality of women in social classes I and II was due to their being delivered by doctors, mostly general practitioners, who were much more likely to undertake repeated vaginal examinations and use instruments frequently in normal labours. Midwives who attended mostly social classes IV and V interfered much less.

There is another important point to note. General practitioners were much more likely than midwives to come into contact with non-maternity patients suffering from streptococcal disease and become carriers of the streptococcus. Unless they were scrupulous in antiseptic and aseptic procedures in midwifery (and most were not) they were much more likely than midwives to infect their midwifery patients. As one can see in Table 8.1, the largest differential in mortality was in puerperal fever rather than the other causes of maternal death.

The extremely low maternal mortality achieved by certain outpatient maternity charities in the nineteenth century (the Royal Maternity Charity was the outstanding example) – charities which undertook the delivery of the poorest of the poor in their own homes – can be explained along the same lines. The vast majority of deliveries were carried out by midwives who were trained and supervised by the honorary obstetricians attached to the charity. An added factor was the readiness with which the midwives could call instantly on skilled medical aid when complications arose.

But the most impressive results were those of the Queen's Institute nurse-midwives. Figure 8.1 shows the maternal mortality for England and Wales between 1905 and 1931, and the maternal mortality rate for deliveries undertaken by Queen's Institute nurse-midwives for the years between those dates for which records are available. It can be seen that the rates for the midwives were approximately half those for the country as a whole. Two points should be made about this. First, care was taken to ensure that the midwives' statistics covered all cases, including those in which a doctor was called in by the midwife or the patient was admitted to hospital as an emergency. Second, the numbers of cases delivered by these midwives was very large, rising steadily from 10,000 deliveries a year in 1908, to over 20,000 by 1915, over 50,000 in 1923, and over 60,000 a year by 1929. For both reasons the difference between the mortality in midwife deliveries and the national levels is highly significant. Much emphasis has been placed by historians (and also by pressure groups today) on the place of

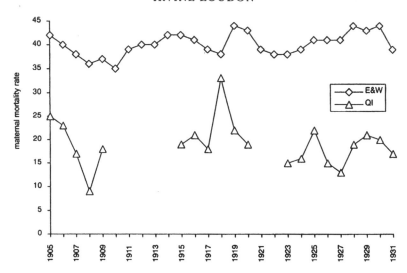

Figure 8.1 Maternal mortality 1905–31 in England and Wales compared with maternal mortality in certain years for deliveries undertaken by Queen's Institute nurse–midwives

Sources: J.M. Munro Kerr, *Maternal Mortality and Morbidity*, Edinburgh, E. and S. Livingstone, 1933, pp. 244–5, and Annual Reports of the Registrar General for England and Wales.

Note: Maternal mortality expressed as the number of maternal deaths per 10,000 births

delivery – on home deliveries versus hospital deliveries. The data we have considered suggest that it was not so much the place of delivery as the type of birth attendant which was crucial; for it seems clear that trained midwives were more effective as attendants at normal labours than doctors. There were some who realized this at the time. The Edinburgh obstetrician, James Young, who had undertaken intensive studies of the causes of maternal mortality, maintained, 'There are several strong advantages in a maternity service based on midwives'. It was less expensive, it helped eliminate the handywomen, and most of all it ensured that 90 per cent or more of normal deliveries were undertaken by a person who was expert in that aspect of midwifery, taking it out of the hands of doctors whose training 'has tended to a preoccupation with the abnormal and the morbid'.[12] Obstetricians and maternity hospitals were, of course, essential for cases in which serious complications arose; but in Britain between 1850 and 1950 the midwife was the safer birth attendant for normal deliveries.

MIDWIVES IN THE USA

In no country did the term 'midwife' cover such a wide range of women as in the USA in the first half of this century. At one end of the scale were a few highly trained midwives whose achievements, as we will see, were remarkable. At the other, were the untrained black midwives of the southern states, who continued to practise in large numbers up until the 1940s and 1950s. In the first forty years of this century the United States had the highest rate of maternal mortality in the Western world, and within the USA the states with the highest level of maternal mortality were those of the 'Deep South' where there was a close correlation between maternal mortality rates and the proportion of deliveries attended by black midwives.[13]

One investigator visited a remote farming area in a southern state where many black people lived in abject poverty in 'small tumble-down cabins or shacks'. Physicians often refused to attend a confinement because there was no guarantee that their fee would be paid. Out of 50 mothers who were interviewed, 26 were white. Of these, 10 were attended by a physician, 16 by a black midwife. All of the 24 black women were attended by black midwives, one of whom, unusually, was a black man.[14]

Table 8.2 provides an example of the division of maternal care between white and black mothers in South Carolina. It shows that the majority of white women were delivered by doctors, the majority of black by untrained black midwives. The maternal mortality of black mothers was much higher than that of white mothers. Table 8.2 also shows that amongst the black mothers delivered by mid-wives, there was an excess of deaths due to puerperal fever and haemorrhage. This is expected when the primary factor in the difference in maternal mortality was the type of birth attendant, for the untrained black midwives knew nothing of antisepsis, and it appears that they often treated post-partum haemorrhage by such measures as placing the woman over a bucket of hot ashes or putting an umbrella or a black hat over her face.[15] There are numerous similar stories of the dangerous customs practised by untrained black midwives of the southern states and there is little doubt they were not safe as birth attendants.[16]

Table 8.2 Maternal deaths by race and cause, South Carolina, 1934–35

	White population	Non-white population
Deliveries by		
Doctors	16,937	3,115
Midwives	2,291	17,593
Others	92	79
Total deliveries	19,320	20,787
Maternal deaths	128	215
Maternal mortality rate per 10,000 deliveries South Carolina 1934–35	66.3	103.4
Maternal mortality rate USA as a whole, 1930–34 (USA death registration area)	57.5	108.1
Deaths by cause as a percentage of total maternal deaths, South Carolina 1934–35		
Septic abortion	8.3	8.6
Full-term sepsis (puerperal fever)	14.8	19.5
Albuminuria and eclampsia	43.0	36.2
Haemorrhage	10.0	19.5

Source: South Carolina Medical Association, Committee on Maternal Welfare, Maternal Mortality in South Carolina, 1934–35 (1936), Supplement for 1940–41.

What could be achieved, however, was shown by the occasional training programmes established for black midwives in the southern states. In one instance at least, training black midwives led to a steep fall in the maternal mortality of the mothers they delivered. Indeed, in one example, training not only lowered mortality, but led to a turnaround: 'the districts in which the maternal death rates are lowest are those in which there are fewest physicians'.[17]

But the untrained midwife was not confined to the black midwives of the southern states. They were found in many remote rural areas throughout the country where the midwife was often a farmer's wife with a local reputation of being good at delivering babies. In a remote Midwest region in 1916 where the inhabitants were mostly of German descent:

Farmers' wives who have acquired more or less experience in such cases, attend most confinements. They may be called neighbourhood midwives, though all are unregistered . . . One of the women who attends all her neighbours as well as her numerous grandchildren had training as a midwife abroad . . . she and her husband were pioneers of this region forty years ago; they went into unbroken forest and cleared eighty acres. Eight of this woman's twelve children were born here; she often did not have a neighbour to attend her, but delivered herself, and lost little time from her hard work on the farm. A massive weather-beaten woman, she still, though old, works in the fields with the men, and can lift a huge kettle of potatoes to the stove as though it were a feather.[18]

This woman was unusual amongst 'neighbourhood midwives' in so far as she had been trained in Germany in her youth, but there were also many European-trained immigrant midwives in the cities who arrived with the mass emigration from Europe to the USA in the late nineteenth and early twentieth centuries, and theirs was an unhappy story.

Most immigrants with a profession, trade, or skill, could hope to find an opening in the USA. Many succeeded and thrived, but not the midwives for whom there was no tradition of female midwifery, no state or federal scheme to provide an occupational structure. They arrived to find themselves professionally isolated and despised. From force of circumstance they practised amongst the poor, and especially amongst their own people, but they were outsiders and they knew it. The immigrant midwives of New York and Chicago were vividly described in two memorable reports in the first decade of this century.[19] It was found that they had forgotten their training, lost their skills, and provided an appallingly low standard of maternal care. Many had turned to abortion as a means of making a living. What they lacked was support, supervision, and above all a sense of self-respect and pride in their occupation.[20]

We have no reliable statistics on the maternal mortality rate of deliveries by these immigrant midwives; but we do have important evidence from a remarkable experiment in New Jersey. In the first decade of this century, the immigrant midwives of Newark showed the same appalling habits and features as their counterparts in New York and Chicago. This was discovered by Dr Julius Levy, Director of Child Health in Newark, who promptly established a programme of education and persuasion (and the uniform and equipment) which transformed the standards of care and the sense of professional pride of these midwives.[21]

The result was amazing. Midwives achieved a much lower rate of maternal mortality than physicians in spite of the scales being loaded against them. As Levy explained,

> every puerperal death where it appears that a midwife was in attendance *at any time* [original italics] is charged to the midwife . . . even when it appears that the result was due to unnecessary interference or negligence on the part of the doctor.

Between 1916 and 1921 the maternal mortality rate for deliveries by physicians was 69 per 10,000 births. The rate for midwife deliveries was only 15.[22]

But the most impressive evidence of all comes from Kentucky where the Frontier Nursing Service was established in 1925. It was founded by a very remarkable woman, Mary Breckinridge, who came from the upper levels of southern society.[23] Initially she trained as a nurse, worked with the Children's Bureau, and in 1918 went to France to set up a child welfare scheme in the Aisne region which had been devastated by the war. While in Europe she learnt that whereas in the USA the occupations of nurse and midwife were kept apart, most British midwives were also trained nurses. From this she conceived the idea that the problem of maternal and child health in the remote mountainous areas of Kentucky might be solved by a service based on British style nurse–midwives.

After training in London as a midwife in 1923, Mary Breckinridge returned to Kentucky and built up a service based entirely on trained nurse–midwives most of whom either came from England, or were sent to England to be trained – Mary Breckinridge was very much an Anglophile. The nurse–midwives, who worked in pairs, were allocated to certain defined areas where they lived in cabins, and travelled by horseback to visit their patients. They provided full maternal care, and care of the child through its first few years. The nearest town – Lexington – was a slow and arduous day's journey on horseback. There were no roads in this remote mountainous area where the inhabitants were farmers of European stock who scraped a living from the land. Although there was a high level of ill-health amongst the women of this region, the achievements of the Service in terms of quality of care were just as remarkable as those achieved by Dr Julius Levy, as can be seen in Table 8.3.

These and other examples of high quality maternal care by *trained* midwives lead us to what seems to be an undeniable conclusion. It has been estimated that about 250,000 women in the

Table 8.3 The Frontier Nursing Service and the maternal mortality rate compared with certain other mortality rates

	Maternal mortality rate (per 10,000 births)
Frontier Nursing Service 1935–37	6.6*
Kentucky State (white population only) 1925–37	44–53
White women delivered in hospitals by physicians in the city of Lexington, Kentucky	80–90
USA 1925–37	
Total population	56–70
White population	51–63
Non-white population	90–120

Sources: N.S. Dye, 'Mary Breckinridge. The Frontier Nursing Service and the introduction of nurse-midwifery to the United States', *Bulletin of the History of Medicine*, 1983, vol. 57, p. 501; H.E. Browne and G. Isaacs, 'The Frontier Nursing Service: the primary care nurse in the community', *American Journal of Obstetrics and Gynecology*, 1976, vol. 121, pp. 14–17.
Note: * The mortality rate was based on 3,000 deliveries and two maternal deaths. For the period 1925–35 there were 12,000 deliveries with two indirect maternal deaths and nine direct maternals deaths giving a maternal mortality rate of 9.2 or, if the indirect maternal deaths are excluded, 7.5 per 10,000 births.

USA died of pregnancy-related causes in the 1920s. If the United States had developed a national system of maternal care based on home deliveries by trained midwives (such as those in Julius Levy's initiative in Newark and the Frontier Nursing Service in Kentucky), it is probable that the number of maternal deaths could have been reduced to around 50,000 and quite possibly to even less. It may be an extraordinary conclusion, but it is likely that at least 200,000 lives might have been saved by a maternity system based on trained midwives in the very country in which the midwife was branded as a relic of the barbaric past.

NORTH-WEST EUROPE

Henry Jellett, who once held the post of Master of the Rotunda Hospital in Dublin, wrote in 1929:

> Amongst 317,758 women confined under the care of the Queen Victoria Jubilee Institute, there were 106 deaths from sepsis, a rate of 0.33 per 1,000 births. The general rate for Holland during the same period (1921–27) was 0.77 per 1,000 live births; for Denmark, 0.55 per 1,000; for Norway, 0.71

per 1,000. In these countries the normal woman is attended by a midwife. On the other hand, the general septic rate for England and Wales for the same period was 1.46 per 1,000, for New Zealand 1.82, for Scotland 1.79, and for Australia, 1.70. In these countries, the normal woman is usually attended by a medical practitioner.[24]

Many obstetricians in Britain and the USA in the inter-war period were aware of the low rate of maternal mortality in the Netherlands, Denmark, Sweden and Norway (see Table 8.4). Those who took the trouble to visit these countries generally agreed with Jellett that the low rate was due to normal cases being delivered by a midwife rather than a doctor.

Dorothy Mendenhall, one of the workers at the Children's Bureau, visited Denmark and was deeply impressed by Danish midwives. It was, she claimed, a country where quackery was unknown, and regulations against untrained midwives were strictly enforced. 'The difficult thing for us [Americans] to realize', she said, 'is the position of trust and respect in which the midwife is held in Denmark'.[25] In 1926 George Kosmak, an influential American obstetrician, visited Sweden and was lyrical in his praise of the midwives: 'Bright, healthy looking, intelligent young women from

Table 8.4 Maternal mortality rates in various countries around 1920, and the usual attendants at normal births

Country	Maternal mortality rate	Usual attendant at normal births
Denmark (1920)	23.5	Midwives
The Netherlands (1920)	24.2	Midwives
Sweden (1918)	25.8	Midwives
Norway (1919)	29.7	Midwives
England and Wales (1920)	43.3	Midwives and doctors
Australia (1920)	50.1	Midwives and doctors
Ireland (1920)	55.3	Midwives and doctors
Scotland (1920)	61.5	Predominantly doctors
New Zealand (1920)	64.8	Predominantly doctors
France (1920)	66.4	Midwives and doctors
United States (1920)	79.9	Very predominantly doctors

Source: R.M. Woodbury, *Maternal Mortality*, Children's Bureau, US Dept. of Labor, Washington, DC, Publication No. 15, 1926.
Note: Rates are expressed as the number of maternal deaths per 10,000 births

whom our best classes of trained nurses would be recruited in this country'.[26]

Not everyone, however, was convinced that the low maternal mortality rates of North-West Europe were due to midwife deliveries. Some thought low mortality was due to the relative absence of industrialization and the cleanliness of these countries. Others believed that the difference was racial. The typical Dutch or Scandinavian mother, it was suggested, was more fitted for childbirth because she was stolid and uncomplaining, strongly built and probably had an unusually large pelvis. This myth was exploded by Woodbury in the United States. He found that when foreign-born Scandinavians settled in the USA and raised families, the maternal mortality rate of their womenfolk was as high as it was in other groups of white women. It was not racial differences, but the difference between maternal care in Scandinavia and the United States which determined the rate of maternal mortality.[27]

Is there any statistical evidence that the low maternal mortality of the countries of North-West Europe was due to the dominance of trained midwives? In fact, there is. One line of evidence which is concerned with maternal deaths from causes other than puerperal sepsis comes from Sweden. The other, which is concerned with deaths from sepsis, comes from the Netherlands.

In Sweden in the 1860s approximately 60 per cent of deliveries were undertaken at home by untrained 'traditional' birth attendants and about 37 per cent by trained midwives; only about 3 per cent were institutional deliveries. By the 1890s radical changes had occurred. Home deliveries by untrained midwives had fallen to about 18 per cent, but institutional deliveries had increased only slightly to about 5 per cent. Home deliveries by trained midwives, however, had increased to about 77 per cent. Figure 8.2 shows that in rural areas of Sweden during seven successive quinquennial periods from 1861–65 to 1892–94, as the percentage of deliveries by trained midwives increased, so there was a correspondingly steep fall in maternal mortality. Almost certainly the steep fall in maternal mortality in these rural areas was due to the increased proportion of deliveries by trained midwives.

The line of evidence from the Netherlands needs some introduction. Listerian antisepsis was introduced into obstetric practice in lying-in hospitals throughout the Western world in the 1880s.

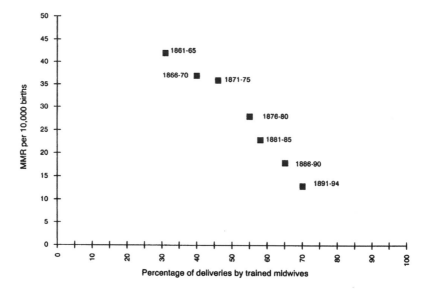

Figure 8.2 Sweden, rural areas, 1861–95. The correlation between the percentage of deliveries by trained midwives and the maternal mortality rate (MMR) due to maternal causes other than sepsis, for successive quinquennial periods

Source: L. Loudon, *Death in Childbirth: An International Study of Maternal Care and Maternal Mortality 1800–1950*, Oxford, Clarendon Press, 1992, Figure 24.3, p. 411. With acknowledgement to Ulf Högberg, *Maternal Mortality in Sweden*, Umeå University, Umeå 1985, p. III:5.

Previously, hospital maternal mortality rates in all countries, including Scandinavia and the Netherlands, had been horrific. The results of antisepsis in hospitals were dramatic. From the 1880s, the maternal mortality rates in lying-in hospitals fell to very low levels, but it has to be remembered that in all countries only a tiny proportion of total deliveries (usually less than 5 per cent) took place in hospitals. For antisepsis to be nationally effective it was essential that it was used – and used properly – in home deliveries; and in all countries there was a lag period of a few years before the lessons of antisepsis in hospitals were applied to home deliveries.

Figure 8.3 shows that apart from a peak in 1893 the general trend in mortality due to puerperal sepsis in London (and the same applied to England and Wales) was downwards from 1880 to 1910. At the time it was believed that this was due to the increasing use

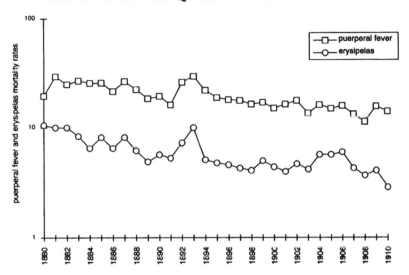

Figure 8.3 London, 1880–1910. Maternal mortality rate due to puerperal
fever and mortality due to erysipelas
Source: Annual Reports of the Registrar General for England and Wales.
Notes: Maternal deaths per 10,000 births. Erysipelas rates: annual deaths per 100,000
living. Logarithmic scale.

of antisepsis in home deliveries. But the use of antisepsis was not the
only possible explanation. The other possibility was a decline in the
virulence of the streptococcus (*Streptococcus pyogenes*) which caused
a very large majority of deaths from puerperal sepsis. The same
organism – indeed, the same strains of the streptococcus[28] – is the
cause of erysipelas. Figure 8.3 shows that deaths from erysipelas
declined at the same rate as maternal deaths from sepsis. Antisepsis
could have had no effect on deaths from erysipelas. Thus the decline
in puerperal sepsis mortality in London was probably due to a
decline in streptococcal virulence and not to the use of antisepsis.[29]

Now we should look at Figure 8.4 which shows the mortality from
puerperal sepsis in London and Amsterdam from 1880 to 1910.
Until the mid-1890s, mortality was virtually identical in the two
cities. Then they parted company. Mortality in Amsterdam fell to a
much lower level following a quite different path to maternal
mortality in London or the trend in deaths due to erysipelas.[30]
Something other than the decline in streptococcal virulence was
occurring.

195

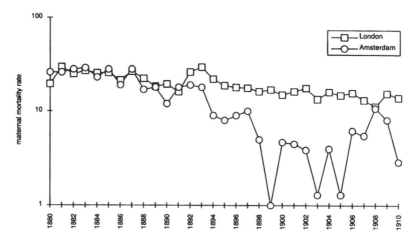

Figure 8.4 Maternal mortality rates due to puerperal fever, 1880–1910 in London and Amsterdam

Sources: Annual Reports of the Registrar General for England and Wales; Amsterdam Statistical Bulletin (Amsterdam Bureau of Statistics).

Notes: Logarithmic scale. Maternal mortality rate expressed as maternal deaths per 10,000 births.

I believe the explanation is simple. In London the large majority of deliveries between 1880 and 1910 were undertaken by untrained midwives and general practitioners of whom the majority either failed to use antisepsis at all, or only used it in such a perfunctory fashion that it was useless. In Amsterdam, where a majority of deliveries were undertaken by trained midwives, antisepsis was used properly by the 1890s and the midwives were supervised to ensure that their procedures were effective. It is difficult to think of any other explanation for the sudden difference after 1893 between London and Amsterdam shown in Figure 8.4.

CONCLUSION

When I undertook the research for my book *Death in Childbirth* on which much of this chapter is based, I found that I arrived at a conclusion I had not expected. Between 1850 and World War II, the lowest rates of maternal mortality were found in those countries, regions or areas in which maternity services were based largely or wholly on *trained* midwives. I found no exceptions, but it was also clear that the success of midwives was dependent not only on effective training, but also on being accepted and respected as professionals by the communities they served, and preferably by the medical profession as well.[31]

It was also important that wherever possible the midwife should be able to obtain skilled obstetric assistance rapidly when complications arose. But the unexpected finding was that even where such help was unavailable or available only with great difficulty (as in the Frontier Nursing Service) it was still possible for trained midwives to provide a maternity service with a very low rate of mortality compared with national rates before World War II.

Today rates of maternal mortality in Western countries have reached very low levels. But it has been estimated that at least half a million women still die every year of pregnancy-related causes. Ninety-nine per cent of these deaths, however, occur in developing countries where rates and causes of maternal mortality are very similar to those found in Western countries in the early nineteenth century. There is no other health statistic in which the disparity between developed and developing countries is so wide. It is always dangerous to extrapolate from the past to the present, but it may be that the findings presented in this chapter are relevant for the planning of maternity services in rural areas of the developing world in the 1990s.

NOTES

1 When a baby was expected in a middle-class family in the days before the middle classes resorted to hospitals or nursing homes, the role of the maternity nurse was to come and live in the house, and stay from the time of the delivery until approximately a month later. Her job was to provide general nursing care for the mother and infant, but not to deliver the baby: that was the job of the general practitioner or obstetrician. Many maternity nurses were midwives who regularly delivered babies of the lower classes, but they were often happy to undertake the task of 'monthly nurse' and forgo the delivery because it was well-paid – and the doctor was usually delighted to have a reliable midwife in the house to watch the patient and help him at the delivery. Not all monthly nurses, however, were midwives. A few were given a short training which did not include training in deliveries, and were certified as trained monthly nurses.

2 N. Devitt, 'The statistical case for the elimination of the midwife: fact versus prejudice, 1890–1935', *Women and Health*, 1979, vol. 4, p. 89.

3 J.B. DeLee, 'Progress towards ideal obstetrics', *American Journal of Obstetrics*, 1916, vol. 73, pp. 407–15.

4 Most mortality rates are measured as deaths per unit of population. Maternal mortality has sometimes been expressed as the number of women dying of maternal (or pregnancy-related) causes per 100,000 women aged 15-44, but this takes no account of the fertility rate. If women of childbearing age are having fewer children than they did formerly then it is obvious that they will be exposed to the risk of a maternal death less often. For this reason the maternal mortality rate (strictly speaking it is a *ratio* and not a rate) is defined as the number of maternal deaths per 1,000 or 10,000 births – or today 100,000 births. Until 1929 in England and Wales (and around the same time in most other countries) 'births' meant 'live births'; after 1929 'births' indicated 'total births': that is, live births + stillbirths.

5 On the whole, midwife deliveries predominated in the working-class areas of cities and in industrial towns, while doctor deliveries were predominant in suburbs and middle-class areas of towns and cities, and in most small market towns. In villages there was no general rule. See 'Report of the Infant Mortality Committee', *Transactions of the Obstetrical Society of London*, 1870, vol. 13, pp. 132–49, and 1871, vol. 14, pp. 388–403.

6 Charles James Cullingworth (1841–1908) began his career as a general practitioner in Manchester before becoming Professor of Obstetric Medicine at Owen's College in Manchester. In 1888 he moved to the post of Obstetric Physician at St Thomas's Hospital in London and remained there until his retirement.

7 C.J. Cullingworth, 'On the undiminished mortality from puerperal fever', *Transactions of the Obstetrical Society of London*, 1898, vol. 40, pp. 91–114.

8 J. Roberton, *Essays and Notes on the Physiology and Diseases of Women*, London, John Churchill, 1851.

9 R. Barnes, 'On the causes, internal and external, of puerperal fever', *British Medical Journal*, 1887, vol. ii, pp. 1036–42. The idea was current amongst Victorian doctors – and the belief persisted into the 1920s – that middle- and upper-class women in civilized countries (in contrast with women from 'savage tribes' such as 'the Esquimaux and the Hottentot') were so enfeebled by civilization and luxury that they were, by definition, a high-risk category needing active medical assistance at all their deliveries. See I. Loudon, *Death in Childbirth: An International Study of Maternal Care and Maternal Mortality 1800–1950*, Oxford, Clarendon Press, 1992, pp. 340–3.

10 R. Dudfield, 'A survey of the mortality due to childbearing in London from the seventeenth century', *Proceedings of the Royal Society of Medicine*, 1924, vol. 17, pp. 59–72.

11 J.S. Fairbairn, 'The medical and psychological aspects of gynaecology', *Lancet*, 1931, vol. ii, pp. 999–1004.

12 J. Young, 'Maternal mortality and maternal mortality rates', *American Journal of Obstetrics and Gynecology*, 1936, vol. 31, pp. 208–9.

13 See Loudon, *Death in Childbirth*, pp. 311–18, Figure 22.3, p. 367; Figure 22.4, p. 368; and Figure 22.5, p. 373. The states with the highest rates of maternal mortality were North and South Carolina, Florida, Mississippi, Alabama, Georgia, Delaware, and Louisiana.

14 Ibid., pp. 54–5.

15 Helen Dart, *Maternity and Child Care in Selected Rural Areas of Mississippi*, Children's Bureau, US Dept. of Labor, Washington, DC. Rural Child Welfare Series no 3. Children's Bureau Publication no. 88, Government Printing Office, 1921.

16 Ibid.

17 C.B. Crittenden and L. Skaggs, *Maternal Mortality in Kentucky: A Study of Puerperal Death, 1832–1939*, Kentucky State Department of Health, 1940.

18 Grace Meigs, 'Rural obstetrics', *Transactions of the American Association for the Study and Prevention of Infant Mortality*, 1916, vol. 7, pp. 46–61.

19 The investigations were carried out by a nurse, Elizabeth Crowell, and published as 'The midwives of New York', *Charities and Commons*, 1907, vol. 17; reprinted in J.B. Litoff, *The American Midwife Debate: A Sourcebook on its Modern Origins*, Westport, CT, Greenwood Press, 1986, pp. 36–49. Although one critic has suggested that I have placed too much emphasis on this one source (in Loudon, *Death in Childbirth*), I have yet to see any evidence that Elizabeth Crowell's findings were incorrect or in any way exaggerated.

20 See ibid.

21 J. Levy, 'The maternal and infant mortality in midwifery practice in Newark N.J.', *American Journal of Obstetrics*, 1918, vol. 77, pp. 41–53; and Devitt, 'The statistical case', pp. 81–96, 169–86.

22 The number of deliveries by physicians was 38,706, and the number of deliveries by midwives was 30,945. The difference in the maternal mortality rate was highly significant P< 0.001.

23 Mary Breckinridge, *Wide Neighbourhoods: The Story of the Frontier Nursing Service*, New York, 1952, repub. Lexington, KY, University of Kentucky Press, 1981; N.S. Dye, 'Mary Breckinridge. The Frontier Nursing Service and the introduction of nurse–midwifery to the United States', *Bulletin of the History of Medicine*, 1983, vol. 57, pp. 485–507, especially p. 501; H.E. Browne and G. Issacs, 'The Frontier Nursing Service: the primary care nurse in the community', *American Journal of Obstetrics and Gynecology*, 1976, vol. 121, pp. 14–17.

24 Henry Jellett, *The Causes and Prevention of Maternal Mortality*, London, J. & A. Churchill, 1929, pp. 13–14.

25 Dorothy Lee Mendenhall, *Midwifery in Denmark*, Children's Bureau, US Dept. of Labor, Washington, DC, 1929.

26 G.W. Kosmak, 'Results of supervised midwife practice in certain European countries', *Journal of the American Medical Association*, 1927, vol. 9, pp. 2009–12. See also the chapters by Romlid and Løkke in this volume.

27 Loudon, *Death in Childbirth*, Table 26.1, p. 448.

28 Ibid., app. 5, pp. 534–41.

29 The very poor standard of antisepsis in home deliveries in England and Wales during this period was attested to by numerous reports.

30 The wide variations in Amsterdam are an example of random variation due to small numbers. Amsterdam had a population of 564,000 in 1901 when London had a population of 4.5 million. This, combined with the lower mortality rate in Amsterdam, meant that this city had far fewer maternal deaths than London.

31 For midwives, doctors and antiseptic techniques in Manchester, see the chapter by Mottram in this volume.

9

THE END OF HOME BIRTHS IN THE GERMAN LANGUAGE ISLANDS OF NORTHERN ITALY

Christoph Brezinka

The German language islands of Northern Italy are small villages and hamlets stretching from the Italian–French border in the Aosta valley in the west to the Italian–Slovenian border in the east (see Figure 9.1). They were settled in the Middle Ages by immigrants from what is now Switzerland ('Walser'-language islands around the Monte Rosa)[1] and from what is now Austria and Bavaria (all the other language islands).[2] Only in the last village of the valley, isolated even by today's standards, could a separate language and a culture be maintained throughout the centuries.[3] Ancient customs, habits and traditions were abandoned less easily than in the Italian villages in the valley below and than in the areas where the original settlers of the language islands had migrated from. In childbirth too, home deliveries attended by a midwife who spoke the local language were still practised in the language islands when hospital birth had become commonplace elsewhere, but this custom too, eventually vanished. The aim of this study was to document the gradual fading of home deliveries attended by midwives in the language islands.

The twentieth century brought many changes: roads and electricity supplies were built to reach the mountain villages, mandatory schooling was introduced under Mussolini. Teachers and officials visited parents and told them not to speak their 'degenerate' German dialect with their children or they would fail in school. During World War I the population of entire villages (the villages of the Asiago plateau and Sappada in the Piave valley) were evacuated and resettled in Southern Italy because they were suspected of sympathizing with the Austrian enemy.[4] During World

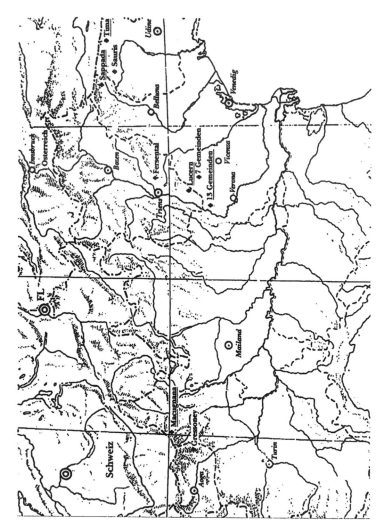

Figure 9.1 The German language islands at the southern boundary of the Alps
Note: All underlined places were visited

War II a large part of the population of the Trentino language islands (Val Fersina and Luserna) were resettled in Germany as part of the Hitler–Mussolini pact on the 'option' of the German-speaking population of South Tyrol.[5] Hitler made an arrangement with Mussolini in 1939 that would allow all ethnic Germans of Northern Italy to leave in order to be resettled in territories that the German army would still have to conquer in eastern Europe. Those that remained – thus 'opting' for Italy – would accept that their Christian names and surnames would be Italianized (turning Alois Bacher into Luigi Dal Rio), and that they henceforth would be loyal subjects of Italy and fascism.

Although the 'option' treaty between Rome and Berlin (Austria had lost statehood by then) had originally been intended only for the almost entirely German-speaking population of Bolzano province, the language islands of Trento province were included, and the dubious privileges of 'option' were extended to their inhabitants. More than half chose to leave for a country their ancestors had come from five hundred years ago. After a much-publicized start, this operation of ethnic cleansing stalled when resettlement in 'new' territories proved more difficult than had been anticipated and finally collapsed with Germany's defeat, adding the inhabitants of the language islands to the long lists of displaced persons of the post-war era. Although many of the original inhabitants returned after the forced resettlements of World Wars I and II, post-war modernization, tourism, and emigration to industrial centres in Italy and northern Europe, led to a rapid decrease in the younger population. Thus, only remnants and fragments of a formerly unique popular culture remain to be studied today. The German language islands have fascinated linguists and cultural historians for more than a century, resulting in a wide array of ethnographic publications, and, once recording devices became available, sound documents of the typical late-medieval German spoken there.

For ethnographers and linguists the language islands are a unique preserve because the use of language has not undergone the same changes as it has in present-day Germany, Austria and Switzerland. Linguistically and ethnographically the German language islands are the best-documented enclaves in Europe. Also customs, habits, myths and superstitions have lasted longer in the language islands than in the areas where the ancestors of the inhabitants of the language islands originally came from. For several years I visited the language islands regularly and listened to the tales of the inhabitants that they told in heavy German dialect interspersed with Italian words for all modern and technical terms. On learning that I was a gynaecologist I was told many stories about happy and unhappy births at the time when babies were still born at home. From these anecdotes it appeared that a very special 'birthing culture' had existed in the language islands until the 1960s. Linguistically and geographically the language islands had been a closed society, and memories from these times were quite vivid.[6]

This made me decide to embark upon a more systematic study and after making additional contacts through the Vienna-based 'Museum of the Language Islands' (*Sprachinselmuseum*) and the Walser Federation in Lucerne, Switzerland, I embarked upon a month-long tour of the language islands with a tape recorder in the summer of 1991. The language islands visited were (in keeping with the convention – official Italian name first, German dialect name second): Macugnaga/Makkanach in Novara province, Giazza/Lietzan, last of the formerly thriving 13 communities of the province of Verona, Luserna/Lüsern in Trento province, the villages of Val Fersina/Fersental in Trento province, Sappada/Pladen in Belluno province and Timau/Tischelwang in Udine province. In all these villages semi-structured interviews were conducted in German and Italian with retired midwives, school-teachers, organizers of local museums and cultural centres, and with the grandmothers who had witnessed the transition from home births to hospital births themselves.

GEOGRAPHY AND DEMOGRAPHY

There are great differences between the villages loosely summed up under the name 'language islands'. In the formerly proud and – under Venetian rule – autonomous and self-governing '13 communities' in the mountains north of Verona and Vicenza, only the hamlet of Giazza/Lietzan can still be nominally counted as a language island. There only a few old men still speak the German dialect that used to be known as '*cimbro*', with mythical connections to a German tribe in Roman times.[7] The death of the old language was hastened by a unique phenomenon: when in the 1950s and 1960s it became increasingly difficult for young men from the villages to find girls who would marry a farmer, a brisk trade in arranged marriages with girls from the southernmost regions of the

Italian peninsula began.[8] Nowadays a large number of the farmers' wives in this area are from the provinces south of Naples and they have brought their customs, dialect and culture with them.[9] On the other hand, German dialect is still the everyday language in Luserna/Lüsern, Sappada/Pladen and Florutz and Palai, two small villages in Val Fersina/Fersental. In Macugnaga/Makkanach hardly a person under the age of 70 still speaks the German dialect which is very similar to the '*Schwyzerdütsch*' spoken on the other side of the Monte Rosa in the Valais canton of Switzerland, where the Walser had migrated from. Here too, in the 1950s young men married Italian-speaking girls from the plains who had come to work in hotels as post-war tourism developed. Timau/Tischelwang lost a significant portion of its young population through emigration to Switzerland, once they had realized that they could quickly learn the Swiss dialect and be prized there for their bilingualism since they could also speak Italian.

A key aim of this study was to document the length of time it took for home births to be replaced by hospital births, concentrating on the changes taking place in the 1950s through to the 1970s. It was in Luserna/Lüsern that a German-speaking midwife, herself a native of the village, witnessed the end of home births, attending her last planned home delivery in 1973. Several other unplanned home deliveries would follow in the years to come, when snow-drifts blocked the road to the valley and to Trento hospital. In Sappada the last German-speaking native midwife died in 1938. In Macugnaga, Maria Zurbriggen, who was called 'the Zaseri'[10] died in 1916 at the age of 29. She had been a Swiss girl, who had trained as a midwife in Switzerland. She had eloped from her home town with her Italian lover, first to Asmara in Italian-occupied Eritrea in East Africa, and then to Macugnaga where her skills as a trained midwife who spoke the local dialect as well as Italian were greatly appreciated. Although she died more than seventy years ago, tales of her survive; she is a local legend. As one of the old women of Macugnaga, who had herself been brought into the world by 'the Zaseri' told me, it had been the last time 'one of us' had performed the duties of a midwife. In Val Fersina/Fersental, a midwife, who had graduated from the Innsbruck midwifery school in 1914 died in 1952. None of the sources in Giazza/Lietzan and Timau/Tischelwang could recall that there had ever been a girl from the village who went to midwifery school before going on to practise in her home community. When at the end of the nineteenth century midwifery ceased to be a matter of neighbours helping each other out and trained midwives were taken into local government service, these were invariably women from the plains between Venice, Verona and Milan, who were posted to the rural areas (see Table 9.1).[11]

PREGNANCY AND BIRTH IN PRE-HOSPITAL DAYS

I have tried to amalgamate statements from the interviews to give a coherent picture of the atmosphere surrounding home births in the language islands.

The bringer of children

In the 1960s children were told that their new brothers and sisters had been brought by the stork. This fable had been popular

Table 9.1 Midwives interviewed in the language islands and their places of training and work

Place/Name	Training	Experience
13 Communi – Bosco Chiesanuova, midwife V.B.	Trained at Verona Maternity Hospital 1958–60, worked in Negrar town hospital 2 years	Worked in Bosco Chiesanuova 1962–80 as an independent midwife, then until 1984 at the USL clinic, retired 1984
Sappada, midwife N.N	Trained in Venice Maternity Hospital probably 1928	In Sappada since 1932, retired 1965
Macugnaga, midwife L.B.	Trained in Milan 1952–54	Posted to Macugnaga in 1955, retired 1985
S. Orsola Val Fersina, midwife A.P.	Trained in Verona 1953–55, spent 5 years doing locums various villages	Started to work in village in 1958, retired 1980 with the introduction of USL clinics
Timau, midwife M.P.	Trained in Udine 1947–50	Worked as midwife 1950–63, then retired, and has since run the shop of husband's bakery
Luserna, midwife N.C.	Trained in Venice 1950–53	Village midwife from 1953–73

Note: USL = *Unitaria Sanitaria Locale*, out-patient clinics originally only in the areas of Germany and France where storks actually nested but spread to post-war Italy as the media found it a convenient symbol to advertise everything from nappies to baby food: it is a typical case of an imported myth. As in other areas of the Alps, the stork supplanted older myths and fables concerning the origin of children.[12] In Macugnaga/Makkanach it was the cuckoo who brought the children, in the 13 communities they were taken from the many caves typical of the region. In Sappada the midwife had to climb up one particular hill and peel them off a rock before bringing them to the parents, as in Timau/Tischelwang, where the children grew on a sheer cliff above the village. In Val Fersina it was 'old Orsola', the midwife who had practised from 1914 to 1952 who continued to bring them even after her death.

Pregnancy and labour

Once a woman was pregnant, there were a number of taboos and folk wisdoms to observe. For the Walsers of Macugnaga/Makkanach a strong pigmentation of the expectant mother's face was a sign that the infant would be a girl. Boys announced themselves by giving a characteristic shape to the maternal abdomen which was described as bulging upwards, as opposed to pointing forwards, which was typical for girls. In the 13 communities an object was carelessly dropped for the pregnant woman to pick up: if she took it up with the left hand, the child would be girl, with the right hand, a boy. A pregnant woman should not hang up laundry because this would cause the infant to be strangled with the umbilical cord.

A pregnant woman was not supposed to attend funerals or walk through a graveyard. When tourists started to arrive with their cameras, for reasons nobody can now recall, pregnant women were warned not to have their pictures taken (Macugnaga/Makkanach). The mother of one of my sources during one of her pregnancies had to hold the sheep fast while they were marked in the earlobes with the sign of the farm. The infant born subsequently lacked part of an earlobe. It was forbidden to scratch oneself during pregnancy or the infant born would have a birthmark where its mother had scratched. 'Mother of corn', ergot, was scraped from the ear of rye and chewed during the two weeks preceding the expected date of birth. In these two weeks, the woman would consume a spoonful of oil of linseed and oil of almonds every day.[13] These, and other injunctions protecting the pregnant woman from hard work, were not always observed, and the work had to be done anyway.[14] In all of the villages I heard anecdotes of babies born during work in the field or in the forest.

Once contractions had begun, the husband was sent to collect the midwife, in summer on horseback, in winter by sleigh. There was always a candle burning under the image of St Anthony of Padova, the all-purpose saint of the southern Alps. At one time, when the doctor was called to do a forceps delivery in Giazza/Lietzan, he asked for more light and one of the relatives present at the bedside simply put the St Anthony candle into his already gloved hand (midwife's anecdote, accompanied by fits of laughter after forty years). Birth took place in bed with the exception of Palai in Val Fersina/Fersental. Several sources there confirmed that birth would take place on the living room floor so as not to soil the blankets, Palai being the poorest of all the language islands.[15] The midwife from Macugnaga/Makkanach recounted how for some years the Southern Italian custom of putting the husband's hat on the woman's head to release the placenta had been followed.

The placenta was buried by the husband, in winter in the cellar, in the garden in the other seasons when there was no snow. The placenta had to be buried very deep so that dogs would not try to dig it out. Older women I interviewed voiced their disgust at the practice now commonplace in hospitals of disposing of placentas 'together with the dead bodies or to make cosmetics'. This aroused strong feelings: the placenta is 'something of us', and both in Macugnaga/Makkanach and Sappada/Pladen I was proudly shown the garden where at least half a dozen placentas had been buried. The Macugnaga/Makkanach midwife had her own reasons for favouring the practice: 'it was a good way to get rid of the husband and keep him busy for at least one hour so I could wash the baby and the woman'.

After birth the first substance a woman received was a glass of sweet Marsala wine (Macugnaga/Makkanach), 'pannada', a sort of pastry made from white bread and sugar (Val Fersina/Fersental, Sappada/Pladen) or broth (Luserna/Lüsern). In the following days, she was encouraged to avoid spicy foods and Sauerkraut, and eat spaghetti without sauce (Sappada/Pladen). On the third day she was served 'the most beautiful chicken from the pen' (Macugnaga/Makkanach). Baptism had to be performed quickly, and nobody should be allowed to see an unbaptized baby.[16] Even at the wedding ceremony the priest admonished every young couple to bring children for baptism at the latest within three days of their birth. All midwives learned at midwifery school that they should always carry a flask of holy water with them to be able to perform an emergency baptism if the new-born infant appeared likely to die. In Macugnaga/Makkanach infant boys received an amulet to prevent 'witches milk' (an evil spirit would suck the boy's breasts). The amulet was a tiny sword made of wood.

Reconsecration at the church door

All the women I interviewed had vivid recollections of the practice of readmission into the Church after birth. This took place three weeks to forty days after birth during which period the woman was not allowed into a church. It was believed that during this time span she again carried the original sin. At the end of this period, a formal and strictly ritualized process of reconsecration would be enacted in the parish church. The woman would be accompanied to the church – she must never be allowed to make this walk on her own as evil spirits could snatch her away, now that the protection her own baptism had afforded her had been weakened by giving birth. She had to wait at the door farthest from the altar. The priest would proceed to this door, lighting a candle, sprinkling the young mother with holy water and handing her part of his stole to lead her into the church.

The midwife of San Orsola/Eichleit in Val Fersina reported how she had gone to church for the reconsecration ceremony after the birth of her first child in 1962. She waited inside the church for mass to finish and when the priest noticed her he signalled her 'with very unfriendly gestures' to leave the church and wait outside. The ritually impure woman should not soil the holy space of the church. Reconsecration then took place at the church door. At precisely the same time that this woman was sent out of the church, the Second Vatican Council decided to drop the reconsecration rite and from then on it became customary for mothers to attend the baptism of their infants in church a few days after birth.

ROSA LENZI – THE LAST 'WILD MIDWIFE' OF TRENTINO

When midwifery schools were opened in Europe in the eighteenth and nineteenth centuries (Strasbourg in 1728 and Turin in 1732) a period of bitter conflict between the 'new' qualified midwives and the 'old' traditional midwives ensued.[17] Also in Trento province, until 1918 part of the Austrian province of Tyrol, this struggle is well documented in hundreds of complaints, court orders, injunctions and letters.[18] The last documents to deal with complaints against women practising midwifery without formal training date from the 1890s. It was all the more amazing to find in the summer of 1991 a woman who had practised midwifery until 1960 without ever having attended a school or having received a diploma. Her tools consisted of a pair of scissors that she sterilized over an open fire and a length of string with which to tie the umbilical cord.

Rosa Lenzi, born in 1897, had been apprenticed by her sister-in-law, Cecilia, who was also a self-taught midwife without formal training but who was the proud possessor of 'the book', apparently one of the textbooks used in the Innsbruck midwifery school before 1914. Shortly before her death in 1923, Cecilia had declared 'Rosa, I will give you the book', and from then on Rosa Lenzi took care of the few births that took place in the village. Even during World War II, when in the midst of the 'option' resettlement in Germany the German-speaking inhabitants of the valley were resettled first in Hallein near Salzburg and then in Budvar in occupied Czechoslovakia, she continued to act as birth attendant to her little community. When the 'optants' returned after 1945 she continued to work, under the tolerant eye of the general practitioner of the valley, who apparently had confidence in her obstetrical skills. By the time she stopped working in the early 1960s she did so for the same reasons as her qualified colleagues elsewhere. Births had been reduced to five a year, a road had been built where the Italian midwife from San Orsola could drive up with her Vespa and later her Fiat 500, and eventually the few remaining women went to the Trento hospital to give birth.

Her methods, particularly her peculiar blend of potent herbal medicines and superstition, could only have survived in the isolation of the language islands without massive intervention from the authorities:

Everything I did was with herbs and I usually mixed them into coffee or tea. We scratched the mother of corn off the rye and we put that into the coffee to speed up birth, then to give the woman strength during birth she received a mixture of coffee with herbs and ground muscat nuts. Moistened bandages with herbs inside them were put around her wrists, ankles and her forehead. The baby was born on the living room floor and immediately afterwards it was necessary to push the uterus really hard so the placenta would not crawl upwards towards the heart. When the infant looked squashed it was very important to bend it into shape before the cheese layer was washed off because only then could ears and nose still be straightened, cheeks smoothed and the eyes made beautiful. When the child had a birthmark the mother had to lick at it before it was washed for the first time. I never wanted any ugly children. Afterwards I gave the child a moistened cloth to suck as a pacifier. Inside I put a shredded apple for boys or camomile herbs for girls. The apple would give them a strong voice, camomile would make them beautiful. For eight days it was forbidden to visit the woman, any man except for the husband who came near the house had the '*covotten*' (heavy felt houseshoes) thrown at him.

A CHANGE OF VALUES AND ATTITUDES

In the old days it was almost a dishonour to go to hospital to have a baby.

(midwife Luserna/Lusern)

The last ones to stick with home births were the Mocheni [Italian term for the German-speaking inhabitants of Val Fersina/Fersental]. They had no insurance and they were the last ones to get roads built to their farms.

(midwife San Orsola/Eichleit in Val Fersina)

The change of attitudes expressed in these two statements took place in less than twenty years. The dishonour of giving birth in an institutional setting had a concrete background. In the early nineteenth century a 'maternity hospital and foundling home' was erected outside Trento city in order to offer an alternative to the frequent abandonment of unwanted new-borns outside churches and to infanticide that was rumoured to be widespread.[19] The founding charter of this institution declared its purpose bluntly as being 'for the deflowered and the fruits of their bodies'. A married woman had nothing to hide and thus no reason to give birth in a hospital.

Several factors contributed to the increase and gradual takeover

211

of hospital births after World War II. Until 1962 a pregnant woman could only be referred to hospital by a local doctor; midwives had no right to refer their patients. This was understood as part of the division of labour between the midwife and the doctor. Although they were independent practitioners, midwives were below the doctor in the local hierarchy. The doctor was formally responsible for all things medical in his area.

Yet all the midwives I interviewed had been given considerable freedom by their general practitioners; they were supposed to call him only when complications developed and he would decide whether a hospital birth was necessary. Transportation to hospitals was notoriously unsafe and unreliable. During an interview with the retired midwife from Macugnaga she pointed to a passing car, saying, 'There goes Vittorio with his family – when he was born he weighed only 1200 grams, they promised to send up an ambulance with a special incubator for premature babies, and we are still waiting for that ambulance.' Then she proceeded to tell the story of how, in the winter of 1961, she had transported a woman with a retained placenta on a toboggan down the steep foothills to the section of the road that motor vehicles could reach so that the placenta could be removed in hospital.

At the end of the 1950s hospital births and post-partum hospital care were gradually taken into the 'convention', Italy's complicated state health insurance system. The 'convention' had originally covered only the public sector and industrial workers. It gradually adapted and developed into a national insurance system which excluded only emigrants (Italians who worked, seasonally or all year round, in Germany, Belgium and other countries and who were expected to get insurance cover there), and farmers (who under Italian social security laws count as small businessmen, who were supposed to organize their own health insurance through farmers unions) from free access to hospital-based maternity care.

In 1962 Italy and Switzerland concluded a treaty on social security and health insurance. Until then, it had been customary for the wives of Italian 'guest-workers' in Switzerland to return home to be delivered free of charge by the village midwife rather than pay considerable sums to give birth in a Swiss hospital. The midwife of Timau/Tischelwang noticed a sharp decrease in the number of births she attended after this treaty came into force as the wives of emigrants no longer returned home to give birth. In addition, the newly constructed hospitals and modern maternity units in the fast-growing provincial towns of Domodossola, Trento, Tolmezzo, Auronzo and Negrar attracted more and more women. At the same time, young country doctors showed an increasing unwillingness to practise obstetrics, and, through lack of practice, were unable to assist, let alone supervise the midwife. In every midwife's tale there was a 'good old' country doctor who had respected her, who was himself skilful in obstetrics, and who unfortunately retired only to be replaced by a young man, who would tell women that hospital births were the safest. This went hand in hand with a shift in attitudes. The standard judgement of all the old midwives I interviewed was that modern young women were over-anxious, spoilt and demanding. There was also pressure in some families not to have the noise and dirt of birth at home but to make use of hospital facilities where everything, including the washing of sheets, was taken care of, just like in the stories of the glossy magazines. There was also a drastic reduction in the number of children each woman would have. The traditional Alpine family with at least half a dozen children had already begun to disappear before the introduction of oral contraceptives into Italy in 1968.

There was extensive road and bridge building to even the most remote villages after serious flooding in the summer of 1966. Increased mobility also brought more women to the hospitals as more village inhabitants came to own cars. Finally, there was a considerable loss of population through emigration to Germany and Switzerland and long-distance commuting to industrial centres in the Italian plains; consequently there were fewer births.

The transition from home birth to hospital birth took place as a continuous process without any clear dividing lines. The first women who went to hospital to give birth were the wives of the civil servants posted from Rome to the villages – the teachers, *carabinieri* (policemen) and *Guardia forestale* (state foresters). Not only did they have a positive attitude towards the town and towards medical progress, they also had easy access to hospital-based medical care under the 'convention'. This was different for the German-speaking farmers who knew that in town they would be regarded as a backward and uncouth minority, who were expected to pay for their hospital stays.

At this point the midwives played an important role as go-betweens and interpreters. Although the inhabitants of the language islands were mostly able to speak the local Italian dialect as well as their native language, they could not speak the 'proper'

Italian of the townspeople. The village midwife was usually the first woman to obtain a driving licence and her own car, usually a cheap Fiat 500, and it became customary for the midwife to drive her patients to hospital. Should birth occur on the way this was not considered a dramatic event as the woman could be assisted by the midwife. A number of children were born *en route* in the midwife's Fiat 500. Once inside the hospital, events depended on the relationship between the village midwife and the doctors and hospital midwives, but usually she was allowed to supervise the birth process up until delivery. She was an important link between the world of the hospital and the world of the farmers. This state of affairs lasted from 1960 to 1970.

In the interviews it seemed that the midwives regarded these years as the best time of their lives and not as the final phase in the dismantling of their professional independence. They were still attending births, they were driving to the outlying farms to do antenatal examinations and post-partum check-ups, and at least once a month they were taking a woman in labour into town. In hospitals they would meet friends and colleagues, they could attend their patient surrounded by all the new hospital equipment and with doctors in the background. When it became generally accepted that a woman went to hospital to give birth and when the means of transportation, both individual cars and flashy new ambulances (the pride of every village mayor), became widely available, the midwife's services were no longer needed, not even in the reduced role of chauffeur to the hospital that she had often quite willingly assumed. Sappada village council decided in 1965 not to replace the midwife who had retired that year. In the other villages midwives were reassigned to be aides in the new out-patient clinics (*Unitaria Sanitaria Locale, USL*) of the national health service that were established in small towns and villages. All the midwives I spoke to had soon opted for voluntary early retirement, since they could not, after all their years in independent practice, spend the rest of their working life 'adjusting the examination lamp for the *USL*-gynaecologist'.

Language had always been a sensitive issue in the language islands, creating a divide between 'us' and 'them'. Thus, professionals who could straddle that language divide were prized and respected – particularly when their profession dealt with such intimate matters as women's bodies and childbirth. Bilingual midwives were obviously preferred to those who would insist on

Italian being spoken all the time. The midwife in Sappada/Pladen who worked until 1965 was a 'strong and tough woman with whom you had to speak in Italian'. The Macugnaga/Makkanach midwife who practised from 1916 to 1956 became 'angry when we spoke German during birth'. In Luserna/Lüsern tri-lingual obstetrics was practised – in German, in the rural Trentino Italian dialect and in 'proper' Italian, depending on the family where the birth was taking place. In Timau/Tischelwang it was customary to speak German during birth, although the midwife who came from an all-Italian neighbouring village could barely understand it, but at least she would tolerate that practice. The situation was similar in Val Fersina where the midwife from San Orsola also served two German-speaking villages.

CONCLUSION

As in the rest of Europe, with the exception of the Netherlands, home births ended in Italy in the post-war years of economic growth. Home births were part of a lifestyle that was readily left behind, the cosy atmosphere of folklore, magic and straightforward pragmatism surrounding birth in the rural farmhouse was part of a heritage most country people were only too eager to forget. It is no coincidence that those that ranked lowest in the city- and progress-oriented society, the poor farmers from the language islands with their strange language and habits, were those that relied longest on home births.

Now that their language and lifestyle have almost totally disappeared, and with Italy discovering its own social history, proposals have been made to give the language islands special protected status and to organize language classes in the German dialect.[20] In some places a bizarre glorification of what little remains has taken place – with grandiose bilingual road signs, shop inscriptions and menus in hotels in Gothic stage-German. As late as the 1960s this would have been punishable as pan-Germanism. Now, it is usually the outward sign of the inward decay and death of the language.

Should one regret the slow fading away of the German language islands of Northern Italy at a time when, only a few hundred miles eastward, in former Yugoslavia, thousands of similar language islands are 'ethnically cleansed' and destroyed with tens of thousands of deaths and refugees? At least with respect to the

German language islands of Northern Italy there is the consolation that they are linguistically and ethnographically the best-documented enclaves in Europe. They also provide historians with a fascinating case study of the survival of traditional birthing practices and customs, and their eventual crumbling when confronted with the forces of modernization. As modernization won out, the midwife abandoned her role as attendant at home births, first cooperating and participating in the shift to the hospital, but finally being forced out of practice.

NOTES

1 L. Imesch, *Geschichte der Walser*, Brig, Rottenverlag, 1977.
2 B. Wurzer, *Die Deutschen Sprachinseln in Oberitalien*, Bozen, Athesia, 1983.
3 G. Tassoni, 'Il ciclo dell'uomo e dell'anno d'una minoranza etnica: i Cimbri veronesi', *Cimbri-Tzimbar*, 1989, vol. 1, pp. 21–66.
4 T. Liber, U. Leitempergher and A. Kolzlovic, 'I Kaiserjaeger su'll altipiano dei sette communi', in G. Rossato (ed.) *1914–1918 La Grande Guerra sugli altipiani. Novale di Valdagno*, Vicenza, Fotoedizioni Gino Rossato, 1988, pp. 307–13.
5 B. Erhard and H. Seyr, *Option-Heimat-Opzioni, eine Geschichte Südtirols, una storia del'Alto Adige*, Bozen, Tiroler Geschichtsverein, 1989. See also J. Reidmann, 'Der "Tiroler Langestrauertag" am 10. Oktober im jährlichen Gedenken an die Annexion Suedtirols durch Italien', in F.H. Riedl, C. Pan, M. Cescutti and R. Gismann (eds) *Tirol im 20. Jahrhundert*, Bozen, Athesia, 1989, pp. 191–202.
6 See also C.A. Lucas, R.M. O'Shea, M.A. Zielezny, J.L. Freudenheim and J.F. Wild, 'Rural medicine and the closed society. Pregnancy outcomes among Amish and non-Amish women', *New York State Journal of Medicine*, 1991, vol. 91, pp. 49–52.
7 C. Nordera, *Taucias Gareida – la rivista dei Cimbri – die Zeitschrift der Zimbern: 'il puach un zimbarn'*, Giazza-Verona, Taucias Gareida, 1989.
8 C. Malacchini, *Uomini in Cerca di Moglie (I matrimoni interregionali combinati, il ruolo della donna, interviste e statistiche, i problemi del celibato forzato e della vedovanza sui Monti Lessini)*, Giazza-Verona, Taucias Gareida, 1986.
9 M. de Manzoni, '"Donne e buoi dei paesi tuoi" – ma se in paese non ci sono?', *L'Arena di Verona*, 13 June, 1985, p. 12.
10 'Zaseri' is the name of a specific place in the valley where the midwife lived – colloquially people were not referred to by their written last names but by the farm where they resided.
11 C. Pancino, *Il Bambino e l'Acqua Sporca – Storia dell' assistenza al parto dalle mammane alle ostetriche (secoli XVI–XIX)*, Milano, Franco Angeli/Storia, 1984.
12 R. Beitl, 'Kinderherkunft und Kinderbringer', in *Der Kinderbaum, Brauchtum und Glauben um Mutter und Kind*, Berlin, G. Grotesche

Verlagsbuchhandlung, 1942, pp. 41–56; H. Prasch, 'Kinderherkunft und Kinderbringer in Tirol', in O. Dapunt (ed.) *Fruchtbarkeit und Geburt in Tirol*, Oberschleißheim bei München, Nourypharma, 1987, pp. 25–34.

13 See, for 'suspicious practices' surrounding childbirth, the chapter by Marland in this volume.

14 I. Schneider, 'Zur Interdependenz von Volksfrömmigkeit, Volksglauben und Kirchenbrauch bei Geburt, Taufe und Aussegnung in Tirol', in Dapunt (ed.) *Fruchtbarkeit und Geburt in Tirol*, pp. 43–68.

15 G. Sellan, 'Costituzione della famiglia mòchena e della proprietà fondiaria nel tempo', in *La Valle de Fersina e le Isole Linguistiche di Origine Tedesca nel Trentino*, S. Michele All'Adige, Museo dei Usi e Costumi della Gente Trentina, 1978, pp. 259–82.

16 J. Frankenstein, 'Über die Nottaufe in Vergangenheit und Gegenwart', in Dapunt (ed.) *Fruchtbarkeit und Geburt in Tirol*, pp. 85–90.

17 Pancino, *Il Bambino e l'Acqua Sporca*; U. Hakemeyer and G. Keding, 'Zum Aufbau der Hebammenschulen in Deutschland im 18. und frühen 19.Jahrhundert', in *Zur Geschichte der Gynäkologie und Geburtshilfe in Deutschland*, Berlin-Heidelberg, Springer-Verlag, 1986, pp. 63–88; G. Panseri, 'La nascita della polizia medica', in *Storia d'Italia*, Annali 3, Torino, Einaudi, 1980, pp. 155–96.

18 E. Renzetti and R. Taiani, 'Ein Handwerk gerät unter Kontrolle: Hebammen im Trentino im 18. und 19.Jahrhundert', in Dapunt (ed.) *Fruchtbarkeit und Geburt in Tirol*, pp. 109–22.

19 J. Anderle, 'Maternità illegittima ed esposizione infantile nel Trentino dell'800: il triplice istituto delle Laste', *Studi Trentini di Scienze Storiche*, 1981, vol. LX:2, pp. 129–93.

20 A. Langer, 'Le Minoranze Linguistiche del Trentino e la Normativa Europea', in *Vie di Pace – Frieden schließen Berichte aus Europa*, Bozen/Bolzano, Edizione Arcobaleno, 1992, pp. 78–88.

10

MIDWIFERY AND MEDICINE

Gendered knowledge in the practice of delivery

Susan Pitt

The history of childbirth from the eighteenth to the twentieth centuries is often seen as one of the gradual encroachment of medical men into what was once an entirely female preserve. Jean Donnison, in her book *Midwives and Medical Men* charts the 'decline of the midwife' and the 'ascendancy of men' through the eighteenth and nineteenth centuries.[1] This process culminated in the 1902 Midwives Act which ensured the continued existence of midwives, but at the cost of putting them in a 'uniquely disadvantaged position among the professions'.[2] The Central Midwives Board was established by the Act to control entry into the profession through training and examination, both monitored to a large extent by doctors. As the twentieth century progressed, the autonomy of the midwife was further eroded as the place of birth moved from home to hospital. In 1927 only 15 per cent of births occurred in institutions. By 1946 this figure had reached 54 per cent,[3] and by 1980 it was a massive 98.6 per cent.[4] According to Dingwall *et al.*, this had transformed the midwife into a maternity nurse; she had become 'an extension of the doctor rather than an alternative practitioner' in her own right.[5] By the end of the 1970s the accepted view was that no labour could be regarded as normal until it was complete,[6] thus undermining the role of the midwife, the guardian of normal labour.[7] It is tempting to assume that the practice of delivery had become entirely controlled by men. Men had assumed a powerful influence over the training of midwives and also over their working practices, which now took place almost exclusively in hospital.

However, there are two important problems with this thesis. First, although the theory of childbirth had come to be strongly controlled by medical ideas, the practice may have been very different. Once trained, both midwives and doctors improvised to a certain extent in the way they put the canon of knowledge they had acquired into practice.[8] In doing so they may have incorporated ideas and practices from diverse sources. Second, and as a result of the above, no simple correlation can be assumed between the doctor/midwife divide and the gender of their practice. This chapter is intended to demonstrate that if medicine and midwifery are considered as discourses,[9] then a more subtle analysis of the ways in which those discourses were gendered can be reached. This analysis is based on oral history material from research into maternity provision in the Swansea area between the end of the Second World War and the mid-1970s.

It is fundamental to the argument to challenge any claim to neutrality or objectivity on the part of medicine or midwifery. They are imbued with culturally constructed meanings. By a kind of metaphorical resonance they incorporate into themselves the values and assumptions of the society in which they operate, and their own values in turn help to shape that society. Since history began, science and medicine have been important influences in the cultural construction of meanings associated with maleness and femaleness. Ludmilla Jordanova has argued that further to this construction of gender meanings, medicine has served to sanction those meanings, to make them seem natural and eternal, and has therefore contributed to their stability.[10]

Following Ludmilla Jordanova again, it will be argued here that 'our entire philosophical set describes natural and social phenomena in terms of oppositional characteristics' such as male/female, nature/culture, body/mind.[11] This does not imply that these structured oppositions are necessary or permanent fixtures in the way the human mind works. On the contrary, these dichotomies can be seen as operating in historically specific ways. The male/female dichotomy does seem to be an enduring one (although its meaning has been written and rewritten over the centuries), but the mind/body opposition can be clearly linked to the Enlightenment and the influence of figures such as Descartes on subsequent Western thought. As Ludmilla Jordanova points out, 'each polarity has its own history but it also develops related meanings to other dichotomies'.[12] Not only is there a dialectical relationship between the two halves of the pair, but their meanings are enhanced by metaphorical association with the other pairs. In this way particular

219

characteristics come to be regarded as male or female at a given historically specific and socially specific moment. Thus, in modern Western thought 'mind' is associated with maleness and 'body' with femaleness, and they are attributed value accordingly. There is no sense in which these male and female characteristics are pinned down to the biological sex of any particular person which means that the interactions between them, and the way those interactions change over time, are extremely complex.

In an attempt to apply these ideas to the study of gender in the practice of delivery, the discourses of the professionals interviewed have been analysed in terms of the oppositional concepts utilized and those oppositions have been related to gender. This analysis has revealed the following associations:

medical discourse	midwifery discourse
male	female
clinical beings	social beings
avoidance of risk	acceptance of risk
clock time	nature's time
control, intervention	letting-be, allowing
goals	process
seeing, examining, detached	listening, feeling, attached
discursive knowledge	embodied knowledge[13]

These discourses of medicine and midwifery should not be conceptualized as two solid and separate categories, but rather as networks which overlap with each other and with other discourses in wider society. Neither should they be seen as historically static – each newly trained practitioner learns to operate within a particular discourse, but at the same time has the chance to change it through their actions. The analysis of such discourses through oral history is fraught with difficulties because the intention is to try to reveal the gendered associations operating within these discourses in their own historical moment, rather than to impose modern conceptions of male and female characteristics onto the past. Oral testimony necessarily exists in the present and it would be impossible to completely disentangle recent influences from those of the period under discussion. What is presented here is a kind of 'snapshot' impression derived from interviews with a group of practitioners who were all working in the immediate post-war period, rather than an attempt to chart the historical process of change in these discourses.[14]

This analysis is based on interviews conducted with the following five professionals:

- Mrs Lilla Morgan, a district midwife who qualified in the 1930s and worked for thirty-one years in the Townhill area of Swansea before retiring in 1968.
- Mrs Glenys Thomas, another district midwife who qualified in 1949.
- Sister Gerty Morgan, who was born in Swansea but went away to London for her training and early working life during the 1930s and the war years. She returned to take charge of the new maternity unit at Morriston Hospital in 1947, and worked there until she retired in the late 1960s.
- Mr John Davies, a consultant obstetrician and gynaecologist who qualified in 1949.
- Dr David Smith, a general practitioner who qualified in 1950.[15]

This is just a sample of the nineteen interviews carried out with professionals gathered by the snowball technique – one contact put me in touch with others, who then put me in touch with further people. Although this was not a 'scientific' approach, in a small town such as Swansea this technique did enable me to meet a reasonable cross-section of the professionals who were working in the area at the relevant time. Interviews were conducted in the homes of the interviewees and were taped and subsequently transcribed. A single interview of one and a half to two hours was used for each person as it was felt that one-off interviews would elicit more immediate and candid responses. The questions asked followed a broadly similar framework for each, covering their training, work, and detailed points about the practices they employed in the antenatal, intra-natal and postnatal periods.[16] These five practitioners were chosen to include both doctors and midwives who worked in the hospital as well as the community, so as to allow comparison between the professions and between different working environments. While it cannot be claimed that this was a 'representative' sample or that the views expressed were necessarily typical of practitioners working in this period, this kind of study does allow insights into these people's working lives as *they* remember them and make sense of them. The aim is not to produce an 'objective' account, but to allow expression to notions which have a reality of their own.

First of all, the way in which doctors and midwives perceived the pregnant woman will be considered. Was she a social being, part of a community with a life that extended forwards into the future and back into the past from the point of her birth experience? Or was she a clinical being, isolated from her normal social circumstances, a case? The midwives interviewed all situated themselves very definitely within the community. As Mrs Lilla Morgan said, 'I bought a house on Townhill Road by the college. Semi-detached. I was there, I was up on the hill for thirty-one years doing my midwifery.'[17] She described how women would come to her door when they knew they were pregnant. 'They didn't worry about whether it was a clinic day or no. If you was having your dinner it didn't matter, they had to come in and tell us their troubles.'[18] Mrs Glenys Thomas complained of the way in which the areas she had to cover were extended more and more, as fewer births took place at home. She felt that she became over-worked towards the end of her working life, but she may also have been regretting the loss of that sense of being part of the community. Even Sister Morgan, despite working in what Ann Oakley has called the socially sterile environment of the hospital,[19] still felt that community sense very strongly. She had read in the paper of the death of a local man, and she recalled how:

> they gave names of the family left, his wife, his daughter. I delivered the wife of the daughter [*sic*]. And then the daughter's name was there, and I delivered her. And I thought 'Well goodness me. All those people, I delivered those'. The grandmother you see, the grandmother, the mother and the daughter.[20]

For Mr John Davies there was a much more clearly defined distinction between his work, which was in the hospital, and his leisure time in the community beyond. Dr David Smith's position as a GP seems to have been an intermediate one. He commented on the benefits of attending home confinements:

> looking after the babies was – a real start of family doctoring, wasn't it? You know, you got to know the patients and – there's a bond formed between you and a definite rapport with a pregnant woman, and especially when she's had the baby, and hopefully everything went okay, and thank goodness nearly always it did, and you had a rapport, and it's a good way of doing general practice.[21]

Dr Smith situated himself within the community, but at the same time there appeared to be some kind of barrier between him and his patients which separated him to some extent from them. John Berger and Jean Mohr's observations of a rural general practice in the 1960s suggested that the GP was allotted the part of 'gentleman' even though the GP himself did his best to modify that role.[22] This difference in the position of doctor and midwife may be in part the result of the doctor's association with illness. According to Berger and Mohr, 'The doctor in order to recognize the illness fully . . . must first recognize the patient as a person: but for the patient . . . the doctor's recognition of his illness is a help because it separates and depersonalizes that illness'.[23] This need for separation and depersonalization might be carried over into the doctor's role in childbirth, whereas the midwife is associated only with childbirth in which there is need for neither.

There are other ways in which midwives revealed a notion of the patient as a social being. Mrs Glenys Thomas talked of her concerns about the lack of 'respect' within the nursing profession today; 'with patients, you know, you'd call them by their Christian names, even older people they call them by their Christian names'.[24] It seems that what is really concerning her here is the way in which hospital patients are placed outside of normal social taboos. The marks of social respect which are normally given to older people are neglected in a situation where the patient is just another clinical being. Sister Morgan talked of her horror at the idea that a deformed baby she had delivered could have been put in a glass jar in a pathology museum. No matter how bad the deformity, this was still a human being and should be treated appropriately.[25] In contrast to this, Mr John Davies made the following comment when talking about his work as a house officer: 'There were thirty obstetric beds, and thirty gynaecology beds, and you were responsible for the lot'.[26] Faced with such a work-load there was little chance to think of the patients as individuals in a community. This depersonalization can also be seen in Dr David Smith's descriptions of his own responsibilities as a junior hospital doctor: 'So our responsibility was there for the antenatals, and the postnatals too'.[27] It is significant that this was in reference to hospital practice; in general practice this may have been less marked.

This view of the patient has further implications for the avoidance or acceptance of risk, but in a way which is the reverse of what one might at first expect. The view of the patient as a clinical being results in the statistical outcomes of delivery becoming paramount, so that risks to the life of the mother or the baby should be avoided at all costs. 'Death itself becomes almost an accident – a failure of technique.'[28] Mr John Davies made this clear when he talked about the thought processes involved in assessing a patient: 'I mean is the baby in danger? Is the mother in danger?'[29] In contrast to this the midwives seemed much more inclined to express what Wendy Savage has called the 'fundamental anxiety about birth'.[30] As Mrs Lilla Morgan said, 'It is a worry. They don't know how it's going to go, do they?'[31] Both Sister Morgan and Dr David Smith admitted to experiencing fear along with many other emotions whilst attending women in childbirth. The awareness of the patient as a social being made them aware of the danger, but also that this danger was part of life, and was therefore to be incorporated into their practice rather than denied.

In considering the perception of time, a distinction emerged in the interviews between a reliance on clock time and on nature's time. Mr John Davies and his fellow consultants developed a uniform labour ward policy which covered all aspects of the management of labour, including 'how long it should be allowed to go on'. He stated that, 'the principal policy was that they should be delivered within twelve hours. If this involved interference, rupturing membranes, stimulating them, yes. They shouldn't be allowed to go on longer than that.'[32] This can be contrasted to Sister Morgan's attitude: 'I mean when labour starts normally, well the time is due, and it's time for the baby to come.' And again, 'I never hurried the placenta. I'd give it its own time.'[33] This difference in approach can be related to the difference between wanting to be in control, to actively intervene in the process of delivery, and the desire to let things be, to wait for them to take their course. Sister Morgan expressed a dislike of technical intervention in delivery such as artificial induction, whereas for Mr John Davies these kinds of intervention were the only 'real' events of delivery; the doctor's role was to deal with the abnormalities of labour. When talking of Fairwood Hospital, where only normal deliveries took place, he said, 'You couldn't do much there, you could put a pair of forceps on but you couldn't do anything else.'[34] Dr David Smith described his life as a junior doctor as being at the 'sharp end', but he also expressed a grave mistrust of technology in childbirth. He also took an intermediate position when he talked of 'waiting' for the placenta to be delivered, but gave away his impatience by adding 'sometimes you'd just massage the tummy a little bit'.[35]

A picture is emerging of the male practice of delivery in which the patient was seen as a clinical being, divorced from her social circumstances, who required active intervention to see her through to the goal of a live baby and live mother. This contrasts with the female practice in which both practitioner and patient were social beings working through a process which formed part of their lives within a community. So far the hospital consultant appears archetypically male in this, and the midwife archetypically female, whether she worked in the district or in the hospital, but the general practitioner seems to draw on both male and female discourses in his practice of delivery.

This analysis can be taken further by looking at how these different practitioners interacted with the female body in their practice of delivery. Midwives placed great emphasis on hearing and feeling in an attached way in their examination of the body. Mrs Lilla Morgan talked of diagnosing pregnancy by being able to feel the uterus and by listening to the foetal heart through a foetal stethoscope, which involves leaning over with your ear up close to the woman's abdomen. In the days before electronic monitoring of the foetal heart this was the only way of knowing how the baby was coping with the stress of delivery, and Sister Morgan was very certain of which method she thought more appropriate. After she had retired she had read of a case in the paper where a baby had been stillborn, despite the mother protesting that there was something wrong. She said, 'Now if they'd taken her off that machine and used the stethoscope, like we always did, they would have detected something there'.[36] The electronic monitoring is somehow detached, objective, and therefore not reliable. Of course doctors examined their patients too, but very often in childbirth this involved measuring, seeing, being detached. The dilatation of the cervix was measured in centimetres rather than in terms of the number of fingers that could be felt to fit into the gap, the monitors and scans were observed from a distance and the information recorded on charts. It is interesting to note that even Mr John Davies expressed concern at over-reliance on the resulting 'partograms'; it is as if their apparent objectivity rendered them dangerous because practitioners tended to believe the chart rather than their own assessment of the situation.[37] Yet he did not argue against their use altogether. This suggests that there were male and female roles which could be performed by practitioners of either sex; normal delivery was the female province while the male role was to intervene when the female process failed. This view enabled a single practitioner to incorporate elements from both medical and midwifery discourses into his or her practice depending on whether the particular situation required male or female forms of assistance.

The last of these dichotomies is a fundamental one; that between discursive knowledge and embodied knowledge. While talking of their training, both Mr John Davies and Dr David Smith made constant reference to learning from books, whilst for the midwives it was more of an apprenticeship, learning by example. Yet both doctors made it clear that the training that they had received as medical students had not really prepared them for their subsequent work on the wards. As Dr David Smith put it, 'I think you are very naive, and very gauche when you qualify.'[38] According to Mr John Davies, they learnt from the midwives even after they had qualified as doctors: 'They'd watch you, they'd prompt you, because they were experienced and we weren't . . . . You didn't quarrel with the sister, you got on very well. If you did quarrel, you didn't learn very much.'[39] So it seems that although the theoretical ideas were controlled by medical men, it was the midwives who controlled the practical learning of the art of delivery.

It became clear to me during these interviews that the midwives sometimes found it difficult to express the nature of their practice verbally, and often resorted to gesturing with their bodies in an attempt to communicate. In response to the question 'What position did you prefer to deliver women in?', Dr David Smith replied 'On the back, in the lithotomy position',[40] while Mr John Davies said 'We delivered them, if they were anaesthetised, in the lithotomy position, it was easy. If they were conscious, do them on their sides'.[41] Both were able to sum up in a few words what they did. This can be contrasted with the midwives who seemed to be literally struggling for words. As Sister Morgan put it:

> Well usually, actually, you know, when they reached the, the second stage, it was easier for the mother to sort of lay down on the dorsal. But for delivery I like to turn them on the lateral position.
> [Why is that?]
> Well you have more control on them,[42] I found. And on the lateral you can deliver on your own, you know you wouldn't need anyone to, that's how I used to find it. I used to find it much easier, just put your arm around the leg . . .
> [To support the top leg?]
> You know, bring her right to the edge of the bed, that's how

I used to – and you could, I don't know, guide it better. You had this hand on the head, and this hand sort of on the perineum, on the chin . . . . Oh, I'd love to deliver another baby.[43]

All through this conversation she was moving parts of her own body to try and demonstrate how she did it. This is not just the result of midwives being in some way less eloquent than doctors, they all found no difficulty in expressing other aspects of their work. It seems that there is a whole sphere of meaning and knowledge which is not expressed in language at all, but in bodily mnemonics.[44] This raises the whole issue of how to approach a history of midwifery. Oral history has been claimed by feminists as a way of avoiding some of the problems of more traditional sources, yet it is still logo-centric.[45] How can a discipline which is so centred on discursive phenomena ever do justice to a form of knowledge which is expressed through the body?

The notion of an embodied knowledge throws some light on one of the key areas of dispute between women and their attendants in childbirth; the knowledge that women have of the functioning of their own bodies. The midwives interviewed demonstrated a belief in women's self-knowledge. Sister Morgan expressed this most clearly when she was talking about artificial induction of labour: 'Well the mothers know the dates, and we should go by the mother's instinct. They, they know. How, I don't know, I've never been a mother so I wouldn't know, but they know'.[46] Dr David Smith quoted his own wife talking about the introduction of over-the-counter pregnancy tests: 'Well, this is daft. As if they couldn't tell if they were pregnant without them'.[47] His approval of this comment suggests that he too gave value to women's own knowledge of their bodies. This contrasts with Ann Oakley's description of how the use of ultrasound scans from the 1970s onwards was seen by some hospital consultants as a way of introducing a mother to her unborn child.[48] Ludmilla Jordanova has pointed out how medicine more generally has given the visual sense priority over other ways of knowing the body.[49] The male, visual, discursive knowledge is given higher status than the female, felt, embodied knowledge, thus marginalizing the role of both midwife and mother.

So, to approach some kind of conclusion, it seems that there are two separate discourses operating in childbirth in the period from the end of the Second World War until the mid-1970s; the discourse of medicine, which is male, and the discourse of midwifery, which is female. This is not to say that in practice either doctors or midwives drew exclusively on one discourse in their practice of delivery. On the contrary, it has been demonstrated that any one practitioner may have practised in both male and female ways, depending on the situation. This means that arguments about the 'male takeover' of childbirth need to be framed very carefully in terms of the gender of practice, rather than the biological sex of the practitioner.

While the midwives interviewed here seem to have been entirely female in their practice, this would not always have been the case. As more and more births occurred in hospital, and midwives had fewer opportunities to learn and practise the female discourse, they increasingly adopted methods which can be seen as belonging to the male discourse. Thus, midwives were implicated in the practices of routine episiotomy, regular vaginal examinations and convenience inductions which are commonly associated with increasing male intervention in childbirth. The point is that such practices are no less male in their significance by virtue of having been carried out by a practitioner who is biologically female. The common assumption is that because both midwives and mothers are biologically female, they necessarily share a common interest which has been undermined by the intervention of men. Yet, the Association for Improvements in the Maternity Services found itself protesting as much about the way pregnant women were dealt with by midwives, as about their treatment by doctors.[50] As long as the focus remains on sex rather than gender, this apparent paradox will not be resolved.

What has been outlined here is a frozen image of the characteristics of the discourses of childbirth in the post-war period – an image which is necessarily blurred because of its prolonged time exposure. Tess Cosslett has also highlighted this difficulty in finding 'pure' expressions of the discourses of childbirth, because of the way in which they exist as overlapping networks within wider society.[51] Yet it is this very blurring which allows historical change to occur, and which allows for human agency in that process. By emphasizing the fluid nature of gendered discourses in childbirth it is possible to move away from models which assume women to be simply the victims of the ascendant power of men. Instead there is a constant process of negotiation going on between all the parties concerned. This is why the definition of what constitutes a 'normal' birth could change so radically during the course of the twentieth century, without there being any single point of disruption or revolution.

This fluidity also provides us with possibilities for the future. Instead of simply pushing all biological males to the sidelines in an attempt to recapture childbirth for women, it becomes possible to consider the gendered meanings of the practices of childbirth. Professionals of both sexes need to consider how their practices set up particular relationships of power with the pregnant woman, and to think of new ways to gender their practice of delivery.

ACKNOWLEDGEMENTS

I am grateful to Ludmilla Jordanova and to Anne Borsay for their comments on an earlier draft of this chapter, and to all the midwives and doctors who were so willing to help with the project.

NOTES

1 J. Donnison, *Midwives and Medical Men: A History of Inter-Professional Rivalries and Women's Rights*, London, Heinemann, 1977, pp. 21, 42.
2 Ibid., p. 174.
3 E. Peretz, 'A maternity service for England and Wales: local authority maternity care in the inter-war period in Oxfordshire and Tottenham', in J. Garcia, R. Kilpatrick and M. Richards (eds) *The Politics of Maternity Care: Services for Childbearing Women in Twentieth Century Britain*, Oxford, Oxford University Press, 1990, p. 34.
4 R. Dingwall, A. M. Rafferty and C. Webster, *An Introduction to the Social History of Nursing*, London, Routledge, 1988, p. 170.
5 Ibid., p. 171.
6 S. Robinson, 'Maintaining the independence of the midwifery profession: a continuing struggle', in Garcia *et al.* (eds) *The Politics of Maternity Care*, p. 78.
7 The term 'normal' is a slippery one. Throughout the period of increasing hospitalization in the twentieth century the midwife was consistently seen as the proper attendant in 'normal' labours. This was established by the 1902 Midwives Act and was repeatedly confirmed, particularly by the World Health Organization's definition of the role of the midwife in 1966. The definition of what constituted normality was, however, increasingly constrained and the role of the midwife redefined accordingly. In the inter-war years both twin and breech births were considered normal and were attended by a midwife on her own responsibility, yet by the 1970s such births had become the responsibility of doctors. For details of what constituted normality at various times, see J. Towler and J. Bramall, *Midwives in History and Society*,

London, Croom Helm, 1986, pp. 181, 217, 233, 253, 259. For analysis of the significance of this redefinition, see W. Arney, *Power and the Profession of Obstetrics*, Chicago and London, University of Chicago Press, 1982, pp. 7–9.

8 According to S. Robinson, midwives retained a great deal of control over their working practices through to the end of the 1950s, still being the most senior person present in three-quarters of all confinements. It was the 1960s and 1970s which saw increasing medical control over the practices of midwives, even when doctors were not actually present at the time of delivery: Robinson, 'Maintaining the independence of the midwifery profession', p. 74.

9 The term 'discourses' is intended in the sense used by Foucault to mean systems for producing authoritative statements: C. Tilley, 'Michel Foucault: towards an archaeology of archaeology', in C. Tilley (ed.) *Reading Material Culture*, Oxford, Blackwell, 1990, pp. 281–347.

10 L. Jordanova, *Sexual Visions: Images of Gender in Science and Medicine between the Eighteenth and Twentieth Centuries*, London, Harvester Wheatsheaf, 1989, p. 5.

11 Ibid., p. 21.

12 L. Jordanova, 'Natural facts: a historical perspective on science and sexuality', in C. P. MacCormack and M. Strathern (eds) *Nature, Culture and Gender*, Cambridge, Cambridge University Press, 1980, p. 43.

13 I have struggled to find appropriate terms here. By 'discursive knowledge' I mean the kind of knowledge which can be expressed in words to contrast it to 'embodied knowledge' which, whilst not 'unthinking', is expressed through the body, in action rather than words. Anthony Giddens has made an analogous distinction between 'discursive consciousness' and 'practical consciousness' in *The Constitution of Society: Outline of the Theory of Structuration*, Cambridge, Polity Press, 1984, p. xxiii. I am not arguing that embodied knowledge cannot be regarded as a discursive practice; indeed, I would hope that it could be analysed in this way, as in Ricoeur's discussion of 'meaningful action as a text': H. Moore, 'Paul Ricoeur: action, meaning and text', in Tilley (ed.) *Reading Material Culture*, pp. 85–120.

14 Further research has revealed a tendency for the discourse of midwifery to be displaced by the discourse of medicine over time, so that by the 1970s there was relatively little to choose between their practices.

15 The names of Mrs Glenys Thomas, Mr John Davies and Dr David Smith are false and their biographical details have been kept to a minimum to maintain their anonymity. Both Mrs Lilla Morgan and Sister Gerty Morgan were happy to be identified.

16 For a fuller discussion of this work, see my PhD thesis 'Midwifery and medicine: discourses in childbirth, c.1945–1974', University of Wales, Lampeter, 1996.

17 Mrs L. Morgan, interviewed by S. Pitt on 3 June 1992.

18 Ibid.

19 A. Oakley, *The Captured Womb: A History of the Medical Care of Pregnant Women*, Oxford, Blackwell, 1984.

20 Sister G. Morgan, interviewed by S. Pitt on 13 Oct. 1992.

21 Dr D. Smith, interviewed by S. Pitt on 5 Nov. 1992.
22 J. Berger and J. Mohr, *A Fortunate Man*, Cambridge, Granta Books, 1989, p. 89.
23 Ibid., p. 74.
24 Mrs G. Thomas, interviewed by S. Pitt on 15 June 1992.
25 Sister G. Morgan, comments made after tape-recorder was switched off following interview with S. Pitt on 13 Oct. 1992.
26 Smith, interview.
27 Dr D. Smith, interviewed by S. Pitt on 5 Nov. 1992.
28 B. Ehrenreich and J. Ehrenreich, 'Medicine and social control', in J. Ehrenreich (ed.) *The Cultural Crisis of Modern Medicine*, New York and London, Monthly Review Press, 1978, p. 53.
29 Davies, interview.
30 R. Kilpatrick, 'Interview with Wendy Savage: "How obstetrics might change"', in Garcia *et al.* (eds) *The Politics of Maternity Care*, p. 336.
31 L. Morgan, interview.
32 Davies, interview.
33 G. Morgan, interview.
34 Davies, interview.
35 Smith, interview.
36 G. Morgan, interview.
37 Davies, interview.
38 Smith, interview.
39 Davies, interview.
40 Smith, interview.
41 Davies, interview.
42 The use of the word 'control' here has caused some comment. When heard in the context of the whole interview the sense is one of practical controlling of the woman's leg and the emerging head rather than one of 'having control over' the woman in a more general sense.
43 G. Morgan, interview.
44 P. Connerton, *How Societies Remember*, Cambridge, Cambridge University Press, 1989, p. 102.
45 My own motives for using oral history were strongly influenced by my feminism.
46 G. Morgan, interview.
47 Smith, interview.
48 Oakley, *The Captured Womb*, p. 185.
49 Jordanova, *Sexual Visions*, p. 91.
50 The Association for Improvements in the Maternity Services was founded in 1960 having originally been called the Society for the Prevention of Cruelty to Pregnant Women. This point was made by the current Chairwoman of the Association at a seminar 'From shellshock to natural childbirth', held at the Wellcome Institute on 18 March 1992.
51 T. Cosslett, *Women Writing Childbirth: Modern Discourses of Motherhood*, Manchester, Manchester University Press, 1994, p. 6.

11

THE CONTROLLING POWER OF CHILDBIRTH IN BRITAIN

Jan Williams

The preference for unnatural childbirth practices, which seems to be spreading across the world, despite countermovements to tune into the natural process, has led birth, in many places, to be a major psychological disaster zone, in which almost everything is done the exact opposite way from how it would happen if allowed to.

(R.D. Laing, 1983)[1]

Why is this? Who controls childbirth? It would appear that 'control' is the key word. Initially, I intended to examine the question of why so many couples report disappointment in their birth experiences. I considered the 'them' and 'they' of the antenatal clinic and labour ward of whom parents often speak vehemently. Already in the back of my mind was the power inherent in the medical profession and particularly so in obstetrics, where the health of the foetus may be used as a very persuasive weapon when noncompliance by the mother is met. Another factor I had considered was the domination of obstetrics by male doctors using extensive technology. Both appear to contribute to the diminishing role of the midwife. However, on closer examination of the situation it has become evident that it is not as simple as a battle between the sexes, or the omnipotent nature of medicine, although these still remain important. The medical professionals themselves are enmeshed within a web of power which seems all-pervasive, radiating out from the core of the hospital and involving each of the participants in its force. It would appear that women today have many more options in childbirth than ever before, but in reality these options exist only within the confines of a very tightly controlled situation.

It is my intention to explore the characteristics of this situation. I will consider the meaning of 'natural' and then show how childbirth in Britain today has become a medical event, occurring almost exclusively in hospital and resembling, according to Angela Phillips, 'treatment for a life-threatening illness'.[2] Some of the ways in which mothers and their partners have attempted to regain control of their own experiences, principally by attending 'natural' childbirth classes will be discussed. As a theoretical base I will be using selected works of Michel Foucault[3] on the mechanisms of power, focusing particularly on knowledge, observation and surveillance, and William Arney[4] has provided a comprehensive and persuasive outline of obstetric power. To illustrate certain points I will quote, using pseudonyms, from some of the experiences of women who have attended the classes I have facilitated as an antenatal teacher with the National Childbirth Trust.[5]

Power is a highly complex notion and comes in many forms. Foucault states in the first of his volumes on the history of sexuality: 'Power . . . the multiplicity of force relations immanent in the sphere in which they operate and which constitute their own organisation . . . power is everywhere'.[6] He stresses that it is the understanding of the mechanisms of power that is important and suggests looking at its effects by focusing on opposition struggles at the periphery and then tracing inwards. This helps to move away from the single concept of domination towards a notion of the circulating network of power existing at different levels and in different forms throughout society. In trying to regain control of childbirth, women have access to certain forms of power but are also simultaneously influenced by it. The same is true for the obstetrician and midwife. It is not as simple as the 'them and us', or of individual frames of reference shaping behaviour. As the case examples will illustrate, there are competing discourses both between lay and professional groups and between health professionals themselves. Each has their own set of power relations; strategies are developed and hegemonies formed to deal with situations which exist as a result of constant power struggles and confrontations. The midwife is as much victim of these as the woman she is assisting in delivery.

'Natural childbirth' is an ambiguous term as childbirth practices are enmeshed within cultural forms and can be seen to shift over time. Raymond Williams states that 'Nature is perhaps the most complex word in the language.'[7] He devotes five pages to a discussion of its origins, shifting meanings and difficulties. It is a, word which has been found to be problematic within the childbirth movements too. The National Childbirth Trust goes to great lengths to point out that the 'N' of the abbreviated title does NOT stand for 'Natural' as it did in 1956 when the trust was originally formed. In 1961 'Natural' became 'National'. This change was effected partly in response to pressure from doctors who were 'offended'[8] by the original wording. However, within the context of contemporary Western society, I understand Laing's use of 'unnatural' to refer to those interventions by medical personnel which assist the body in giving birth. As will be seen, these interventions are often premature, and may lead to a cascade of further interventions which, in retrospect, may be viewed as unnecessary.[9] Instead of helping the body when difficulties do arise, a 'natural' response from carers, the same carers anticipate problems, attempt to prevent them and in so doing engage in practices which may create physical and psychological dangers for both mother and baby.

Traditionally, childbirth in Britain was considered to be the province of women. A body of knowledge was built up and birth occurred at home with female supporters in attendance. There was little systematic or formal instruction taking place, but skills were often passed down, sometimes through families from mother to daughter, under a form of apprenticeship. Control of childbirth was mostly informal and almost invisible, operating through a system of cooperative mutual aid. Men were only marginally involved or were excluded. The transformation of midwifery from the control of women themselves with the midwife, meaning 'with-woman', to domination by obstetricians, from the Latin *obstare* meaning 'to stand before', is both rich and fascinating and is well documented elsewhere.[10] Brief reference to such accounts will only be made in order to show how the gender and practice divisions between midwife and obstetrician have arisen.

Male midwives emerged in the sixteenth century and made surgical intervention their speciality. They were called to assist with labours which had become obstructed. Their use of surgical techniques for difficult labours helped to establish the precedent for midwives dealing with 'normal' deliveries and obstetricians with 'abnormal' ones. Attempts at achieving a common understanding of what constitutes 'normal' reveal enormous complexities in defining this state.[11] Indeed, the division was highly ambiguous and it was the midwife who usually decided which labour crossed the boundary so 'abnormal' births were her province too. Often the midwife made decisions on an intuitive basis derived from experiential learning.

In the eighteenth century some formal instruction began for both sexes. The surgeon, William Smellie, for example, held separate classes for men and women, teaching them different things, and thus increasing the segregation of roles. The new scientific knowledge and increased experience, combined with the development of obstetric forceps, provided the theory on which the female midwives' definition of 'normal' could be challenged. The profession of obstetrics was, and is, based upon the pathological potential of pregnancy and childbirth. In order to secure a position of dominance, obstetricians needed to gain control over the 'residual normalcy'[12] of childbirth by exploiting this pathological potential. This was the beginnings of prophylactic treatment in childbirth, the 'as if' or 'in case' syndrome, the ability to view childbirth as 'normal' only in retrospect.

Foucault[13] describes the power of the medical gaze; it was no longer the look of any observer but that of a 'doctor endowed with the power of decision and intervention'. This medical gaze was a very useful tool, used to establish discipline over the delivering woman. Discipline was felt necessary if control over the situation was to be achieved and obstetrics was to fully become a science. Labour was divided up into temporal stages, allowing the opportunity for each section to be managed independently from the other and within its own set of governing rules.

Early in the twentieth century it was realized that the condition of the mother during pregnancy as well as labour had considerable implications for the survival potential of the new-born. For the first time the poor and working classes became a focus for obstetric attention other than for teaching purposes. The potential to improve the health and well-being of individuals through the organization of social power was enormously increased with the formation of the National Health Service in 1948. In addition, scientific developments created a new form of obstetric control which transformed discursive practice. The medical gaze became modified by the 'normalizing gaze'. The ability to extensively monitor both the mother and the foetus represents a change in the deployment of obstetric power, a new mode of social control over childbirth. Oakley refers to this as a 'covert form of social control' and notes that in certain languages the term is 'ante-natal control'.[14]

Pregnancy is seen as a process. All factors which could affect the physiological process are analysed and the 'normal' trajectory mapped out, allowing for some deviations from the central course. Each pregnant woman can be continually observed, her progress and that of the foetus monitored, and the results compared against the 'norm'. Deviations from the 'norm' can then be managed to bring them back within limits. Clinical experience is used to augment this. This method of surveillance and control is at the heart of contemporary British obstetric practice. Foucault used the Benthamite concept of the panopticon, an architectural device used in prisons to ensure the threat of constant visibility,[15] to describe the new form of social control under which subjects were separated, individualized, and subjected to constant scrutiny. By analogy, the pregnant woman is seen, tested, monitored, and continually observed using the latest technological equipment, and any deviations in her progress are investigated. Technologies are offered to 'normalize' her, to obtain the healthiest possible mother and baby. Monitoring, surveillance and normalization operate as part of a structure of control, which is independent of the agents of control. The woman herself is involved in assessing foetal movements and the 'they' and 'them' to whom newly delivered parents so often refer, are caught up in the pervasive web of power themselves.

Knowledge is fundamental to this situation. The inextricable link between knowledge and power is explained by Foucault, who suggests that they operate in a mutually generative fashion, working to strengthen each other. The more that is known of the physiology of pregnancy and birth, and the greater the advances in technology to further this knowledge, the greater the power to which childbirth is subjected. And the greater the control, the more can be found out. The ability to monitor the foetus itself has resulted in a shifting of focus from the mother to the baby and appears to justify a wider range of interventions which are themselves not without danger: witness the past uses of X-ray and currently of chorionic villus sampling.

Between the formation of the NHS and the Winterton Report of 1992,[16] a series of reports by obstetricians, midwives and independent bodies have recommended hospital delivery for all, ignoring studies which look at official stillbirth figures and favour the safety of home delivery over hospital birth at all levels of predicted risk.[17] This is because of the 'in case' syndrome. If the equipment is there, it will be too readily used and a cascade of interventions with their accompanying complications may begin. However, statistics comparing home and hospital delivery are just a fraction of the information recorded and utilized to map the depth, extent and success of maternity services. Computerized central monitoring maintains and compares international, national, regional, and local results. The entire space of maternity services is controlled. This involves both clients and workers. This information may assist lay groups such as Community Health Councils to question practice, and it may also result in improvements in service for the consumer, an example of the effect of the countervailing power relations between different discourses.

Entering into hospital and becoming a patient is a very vivid experience. Poor communication, lack of information and the use of medical jargon all work to exclude the patient from medical discourse. Medical language, heavily bound with knowledge, is very powerful and can operate in a strongly excluding fashion. Uttered by experts, it needs to be decoded. The ability to do this is not only severely restricted by a lack of that specialized knowledge but also by the anxiety which is created by the very situation. It is one of the strands within the overall web of power through which the doctor is able to sustain superiority over the patient, using the power of medical discourse over everyday speech. The patient position is one of subordination and loss of autonomy. On entering hospital the client is interpellated into a specific subject position.[18] The initial move may be as subtle as changing from day dress to hospital night wear. The patient is formed by being constructed as the subject of an institutional ideology with a number of components. The patient is dependent on the hospital staff. The patient is told what to do, and must not step out of line for fear of being victimized and not being granted 'favours'. The layout of the ward ensures there is no privacy. A strict time structure is imposed which also regulates the intake of food and drink. Movements around the hospital are restricted. Individuality is lost.

I would suggest that in admission to hospital for childbirth the 'patient position' is intensified. There is pleasure for the doctor to be gained from the medical position of dominance. Foucault discusses 'a sensualization of power and gain of pleasure' in the doctor–patient relationship.[19] The intimacy of obstetrics accentuates this. The woman is exposed, in all senses of the word, to the hospital staff around her. She listens intently for anything said about her baby and tries to deny her own personal feelings. As Ruth said, 'After having a baby I haven't got any inhibitions left'. Interestingly, in many maternity units the control for opening and closing blinds on the windows in doors is on the OUTSIDE.

Yet, birth is not a disorder, the woman is not ill, but still she is interpellated into the position of patient. The anxieties are not only for her own healthy body and what is about to happen to it, but for her unborn child and its safety. Women are already discursively positioned by superstition, old wives' tales, romantic, idealized versions of birth, and also by sound antenatal education, gained both formally and informally. Frequently this is dismissed or overruled by medical personnel, as the quoted experiences will illustrate. The woman may be exposed not only to the competing discourses of the midwife and the obstetrician, but also to those of the anaesthetist and of the paediatrician. It is common practice for all the parties involved to be discussing 'the case' within the woman's hearing but not in terms which she can comprehend. Medical jargon can be powerfully excluding. A *fait accompli* may then be presented of what 'we feel to be best for your baby'. This puts the woman into a very vulnerable position at a time when she may be least able to cope.

Induction is a prime example of the conflicting discourses of expectant mother, client, obstetrician, and midwife, and of the negotiation which occurs between them. The condition of both mother and baby are progressively monitored to assess the optimum time for delivery. If 'nature' does not act accordingly and labour begin spontaneously, pressure may be exerted on the woman to allow the doctor to commence the process. When induction fails, a full range of medical interventions are put into action, which may lead ultimately to caesarean section. There is much debate within the obstetric profession itself as to what constitutes the indications for induction and the woman is the prey of both this and her own knowledge.[20] Often she will be put under pressure at an antenatal appointment which she will be attending alone.

Ellen was lying partially clothed on the couch. The male obstetrician was accompanied by a student (Clive) who, without full explanation, had just attempted a vaginal examination. The midwife was clearing away the equipment. The conversation ran:

Doctor: 'My colleague's just going to examine you, relax your knees.'

Ellen: 'Ouch, that hurts.'

Doctor: 'It's time this baby made an appearance. Let's hope Clive here has got things going for you.'

Ellen: 'But I was only due on Monday.' (three days ago)

Doctor: 'We don't like to leave them in when they're ready, all sorts of things can happen after term, the placenta can stop functioning, the baby's head gets hard as the bones start to ossify. It all makes the birth much more difficult.'

Ellen: 'Oh, I see. Well, I'd like to discuss it with my husband. We wanted everything to be natural.'

Doctor: 'If nature doesn't work we have to help it. Your husband's opinion won't alter my decision. It's your baby but I strongly advise you to come in and let us induce you. You can go home and get your things and come back in tomorrow. That should give you time to have a chat with your husband and, you never know, Clive might have done the trick. Nurse here will make arrangements for you.'[21]

When the doctor and the medical student had left, the midwife informed Ellen that she did not have to come in. She could go home and have a kiss and cuddle with her husband and see if that worked, but it would be best to explain to Sister first so that a cardiotocograph (foetal heart trace) could be arranged just to make sure the baby was all right.

In this short and apparently typical encounter, Ellen's control was taken away by her physical positioning, by the examination, and by ignoring her protestations. She was told what would be happening, her attempts at discussion were blocked, and there was total disregard for her anxiety and need for support as she heard and magnified the doubts of her ability to manage the birth herself. She was exposed to the power of medical discourse by both the doctor and the midwife. The midwife initially appeared to contradict the doctor, which was confusing, and then applied her own pressure, implying all might not be well and suggesting a test which Ellen did not recognize and was too upset to ask about. It would appear that both the midwife and the doctor were reacting to the power which they are under to keep Ellen's pregnancy within 'normal' boundaries. They used their own professional positions of power to keep Ellen in subordination. Power is extending in all directions to form an entangling web of constraining force. Childbirth is a rule-governed activity, within which the discourses of 'normality/abnormality' dominate, and those of the health professionals are all competing.

Women are caught up within these struggles, but often with positive outcomes. Rose had been pushing for nearly an hour and the baby was making slow progress but both appeared to be coping well. The unit she was in worked under the rule of notifying the doctor, with a view to forceps, if pushing went on over the hour. The midwife suggested to Rose that they say the second stage had only been going for thirty minutes to give her some extra time. Rose was glad to agree. This type of 'juggling' with the rules is commonly reported in birth experiences.

Conflicting discourses which can cause problems for the woman are those of the midwife and the nurse. The majority of midwives are trained nurses and it would appear that some find it extremely difficult to tolerate a woman experiencing pain and refusing analgesia. This can result in immense pressure on the woman to do something which she had previously decided she did not want to do. Women often have an image of how their birth will be. This image is shaped by their culture, discussions, experiences, and the relationship between the woman and her partner. Women who know what they want, when they get to the hospital often find themselves unable to ask for it. They take up the patient position and are frightened to question practice. After the birth of her daughter following a long and painful labour in which she had an intravenous infusion of drugs to stimulate contractions, Liza said, 'I had fallen into the trap of accepting the treatment because I was their patient . . . I wanted them all to go away and leave me alone but I couldn't say any of this . . . I felt dreadful . . . I didn't enjoy the birth at all'.

It is widely believed that women have never had greater choice in their delivery. The issuing of birth plans by the hospital perpetuates this illusion. Women are invited to document the kind of birth they would like – who they want to be present, what sort of pain relief they envisage having, the position they hope to adopt for delivery, and so on. These are discussed with the midwife and the obstetrician too if there is anything which contravenes normal protocol. A degree of adaptation is possible to allow for accommodation rather than confrontation with women's wishes. The eradication of routine enemas and shaving of the pubic area are examples of this. However, in reality, free choice does not exist. Birth plans may be seen as a public relations exercise in medical hegemony. Monitoring opens both pregnancy and labour up to view. The modern obstetric disaster is not the stillborn baby, but the baby who escapes the system and is born without medical attention. This is what makes news in the tabloid press.

Foucault describes the examination as a 'normalising gaze, a surveillance that makes it possible to qualify, to classify and to punish ... the examination is highly ritualised'.[22] Labour ward protocols have been devised, partograms are adhered to, and deviance from the norm results in disciplining. Discipline extends to both the health workers and the parents. There is the question of professional accountability and what corresponds to safe practice, how much individual clinical judgement is permissible in the management of birth. Punishment of the woman can be extremely subtle. If it is felt the client is not complying with the medical staff, the partner may be asked to leave, emotional support is removed, and the atmosphere made tense as the midwife overtly displays her displeasure, and commonly emotional blackmail is used as fears for the baby are expressed. The role of the midwife fluctuates from controller to negotiator to advocate. The position is not a fixed one.

Women entering the labour ward of most hospitals in Britain today join a technological routine. It is assumed that they will agree to the foetal heart being monitored for half an hour initially; the equipment is there and so it is used. This is the first indication of an interventionist policy for labour although everything appears to be normal; the 'as if' syndrome comes into operation. It must be recognized that some women do find this use of technology reassuring and actively seek its use, but false positives can occur in electronic monitoring with problems in interpretation which may lead to unnecessary interventions. There is a fine line between foetal stress and distress.

Olive had had a very straightforward pregnancy, had gone into labour spontaneously and was coping well on arrival at the hospital. The initial foetal heart trace showed some lack of variation which could have been an indication that something was wrong, but could also mean that the baby was sleeping. The possibility of a problem could not be ignored. The midwife suggested to Olive that all might not be well. This naturally created anxiety. She suggested that the baby might be distressed and have moved its bowels. She said she needed to check for this by breaking Olive's waters to see if they

241

were meconium-stained. In breaking the waters an internal electrode could be fitted onto the baby's head to monitor it more accurately. Faced with all this Olive felt powerless and agreed to whatever the midwife felt was necessary for the safety of her baby. Once broken, the waters were clear, there were no signs of distress. The foetal heart trace began to show variation but the midwife suggested leaving it in position just to be sure. Olive was now confined to bed with a wire from the baby strapped to her leg. The wire was connected to a machine which was inches away. Following the artificial rupturing of the membranes the contractions increased abruptly in both concentration and intensity. The midwife suggested something for pain and Olive, who had hoped to cope by moving around, breathing through her contractions and being supported and encouraged by her partner Phil, agreed. She decided only to take 'gas and oxygen' which she knew would not harm the baby but it distanced her considerably from events. Olive and Phil had a healthy baby, born with no signs of distress, and for that Olive was grateful, but she felt she had become a passive participant in her baby's birth, the details of which she had to rely on Phil to tell her. It was not the birth she had looked forward to. Technology had introduced a suspicion that proved to be false but had set a cascade of interventions into progress.

The woman is not the only victim. Monitoring can restrict medical choice too. Janice wanted the opportunity to deliver her breech baby without intervention. Her consultant favoured caesarean section but was prepared to take a risk and allow a trial of labour, but under epidural and with the use of forceps. Janice obtained a second opinion and delivered a healthy baby in a private clinic without any medical intervention. Both Olive and Janice's deliveries show that the obstetrician and the midwife are entangled in the web of power. Monitoring observes not only the women and their births, but the actions of the midwife and obstetrician too. The case of Wendy Savage further illustrates this.

It would appear that two issues were implicated in 'the Savage enquiry', that of professional conduct and that of gender.[23] Mrs Savage was then working as a senior lecturer in obstetrics and gynaecology at Mile End Hospital in East London. A series of tensions and (under surface) differences between herself and her senior male colleagues culminated in her suspension and an enquiry into her competence. The enquiry centred around five cases where Mrs Savage had used her own clinical judgement in allowing the women under her care to transgress the rigid boundaries of labour normally adhered to. She strongly believed in each labour being treated individually with the woman involved. The enquiry exonerated Mrs Savage but she was kept from clinical practice for fifteen months. During this time the public support from mothers and individual health professionals who recognized and supported Mrs Savage's courage in resisting the normalizing regimes of contemporary childbirth was tremendous.

Conflicting discourses within the profession of obstetrics itself also support Mrs Savage's main argument. Research in Cambridge has shown that feelings of satisfaction, involvement and personal control in their birth experiences can lead to fewer clinical problems for women.[24] The dichotomy between a mother-centred birthing experience and a scientifically governed birth illustrates the dynamic nature of knowledge. Knowledge is not static, disputes within discourses generate new knowledge. Extra-discursive events obviously affect this tool. Many hospital delivery rooms are now comfortably furnished with the facility to dim lights and play music and have pools for water births, but electronic advances allow complete supervision.

During the classes I teach the process of labour is discussed and rituals for coping are practised. The woman is encouraged to trust in her own body to give birth in its own unique way, yet it is the ability to maintain control in labour which is actually being taught. Among the group there is a mutual sharing of fears and anxieties and of hopes. Arney suggests this involves more opening to the normalizing gaze, 'that by using natural childbirth techniques a woman submits to a panoptic regime of control'.[25] By entering into the confessional mode of interaction, the woman opens herself to even greater visibility and the need is created to convert all feelings into discourse. In this way behaviour can be known and measured against the 'norm' and so be controlled and managed. Support in labour becomes constant visibility, be it from the midwife or from the woman's labour partner. Whilst the woman may feel that she has control of her situation rather than the midwives and doctors, in reality that control is all part of the panopticon machine in which she is merely playing a more active part. She is bound not only by the circulating strands of obstetric power but also by peer pressure to comply to the strict rules of the group. This pressure to conform can be a major cause of disappointment when events force deviations from the planned experience, casting the woman outside of the norms of the group.

In all counter-discourses to the main obstetric discourse, women are attempting to gain control for themselves but are caught in two ways. First, they are subject to the law; it is illegal to give birth without a midwife present. Second, alternative childbirth practices are always within, and hence subject to, the obstetrically controlled space which radiates out from the hospital. Both obstetric and midwifery discourses are able to exert their own powers over counter-discourses which is evident in relation to home birth. Home birth is an obvious attempt by parents and community midwives to keep control, but despite figures on stillbirths showing it is safer for 'low risk' mothers to deliver out of hospital and the recommendations of the Winterton Report of 1992, it is very difficult in many areas to obtain a home birth. Independent midwifery services are thriving but the financial cost is often prohibitive. Every woman has an absolute legal right to have a home delivery. The pressure is such, however, that very few women succeed in withstanding the emotional punishment they often experience on making such a request. The suggestion invariably is that the woman will be putting her baby's life at risk and must take that responsibility, powerful medical discourse placing the woman in a position of subordination similar to that of the patient. It will be interesting to observe the effect of new government health strategies on this situation. Individual responsibility and choice are promoted, but, because of financial constraint or a lack of services, that choice is, in effect, not there. Changes in the organization of health care, with the centralization of services and smaller maternity units being closed, mean that women are having to travel longer distances to give birth in hospital.

Ria wanted her second baby to be born at home. Her general practitioner belonged to a group practice. She was willing to supervise Ria's care, but the GPs who might have had to deputize for her, were not. Ria wrote a letter requesting a domiciliary midwife and was provided with a community midwife who took over her care for the remainder of her pregnancy. Ria delivered a second son safely at home. She had had the type of birth she wanted and was entitled to, but she needed to be very secure in her own discourse to refuse to take up the 'patient position'. Interestingly her GP juggled with the rules and agreed to be called if Ria needed sutures afterwards but was unable to take responsibility for the actual birth because of the dispute within her own discourse. The autonomy of both the midwife and the mother is greatly increased in a home birth, but of course the midwife is still working within the rules of her profession and thus both are subject to panoptic control.

Male domination and medical omnipotence are important contributors to the control of childbirth but the issues are far more complex. Childbirth is enmeshed in a web of power. The baby, the woman, her partner, the midwife, and the obstetrician are all involved. Power and knowledge are linked together in a mutually generative way which has resulted in the routine medicalization of pregnancy and birth under the strict control of monitoring and surveillance via the panoptic machine. Within this control the individual discourses of the medical professionals compete with that of the woman and with each other. In so doing, they exert their own powers over the woman. The resistance of the counter-discourses of alternatives in childbirth all work within the rule of a background of obstetrical expertise and safety. They are within the power network radiating out from the hospital and are subject to the powers of the individual discourses. All this operates to the detriment of the woman's psychological experience.

It appears that the woman is allowed choice in her care and mode of delivery, but this is an illusion. It is an illusion which heightens disappointment when medical intervention actively takes control of her labour under the operation of the 'as if' syndrome which treats every labour as pathological. Mrs Savage's philosophy of involving the woman, judging each labour individually and assisting only when something is known to be wrong, is still governed by panoptic control but the authoritarian power of the discourses within it are less; control is less rigid. The woman is an active participant in her own birth experience; if help is needed, she does not feel so disappointed or cheated, 'she has been allowed to have a go'.

NOTES

1 R.D. Laing, cited by E. Noble, *Childbirth with Insight*, Boston, Houghton Mifflin, 1983, p. xiv.
2 A. Phillips and J. Rakusen, *The New Ourbodies, Ourselves*, London, Penguin, 1989, p. 613; see also chapters 18–19, pp. 340–401.
3 Particularly M. Foucault, *The History of Sexuality* (1976), London, Vintage Books edn, 1990; M. Foucault, *Discipline and Punish* (1975), Harmondsworth, Peregrine Books, 1979; M. Foucault, *The Birth of the*

Clinic (1963), London, Tavistock, 1973. See also C. Jones and R. Porter (eds) *Reasoning Foucault: Power, Medicine and the Body*, London, Routledge, 1990.

4 W. Arney, *Power and the Profession of Obstetrics*, Chicago and London, University of Chicago Press, 1982.

5 Particular examples taken from birth reports written by women who attended birth preparation classes facilitated by me between 1988 and 1991.

6 Foucault, *History of Sexuality*, p. 92.

7 R. Williams, *Keywords*, London, Collins, 1976, pp. 219–24.

8 P. Briance, 'The birth of the NCT', *New Generation*, 1990, vol. 9, p. 5.

9 For a comprehensive discussion of interventions, see S. Inch, *Birthrights*, London, Green Print, 1989.

10 See Arney, Power and the Profession of Obstetrics, p. 21; A. Oakley, 'Wisewoman and medicine man: changes in the management of childbirth', in J. Mitchell and A. Oakley (eds) *The Rights and Wrongs of Women*, Harmondsworth, Penguin, 1976, pp. 19–58; A. Witz, *Professions and Patriarchy*, London and New York, Routledge, 1992, pp. 104–27; A. Wilson, *The Making of Man-Midwifery: Childbirth in England, 1660–1770*, London, UCL Press, 1995.

11 Discussed in H. Marland, 'Smooth, speedy, painless and still midwife delivered? The Dutch midwife and childbirth technology in the early twentieth century', forthcoming in L. Conrad and A. Hardy (eds) *Women in Modern Medicine*, Amsterdam, Rodopi, 1997, see also Witz, *Professions and Patriarchy*, chapter 4.

12 Arney, *Power and the Profession of Obstetrics*, p. 51.

13 Foucault, *Birth of the Clinic*, p. 89.

14 A. Oakley, *The Captured Womb*, Oxford, Basil Blackwell, 1984, p. 252. See also Foucault's discussion of pastoral power in H. Dreyfus and P. Rabinow, *Michel Foucault Beyond Structuralism and Hermeneutics*, Brighton, Harvester Press, 1982.

15 Foucault, *Discipline and Punish*, pp. 200–2.

16 A committee set up under Mr Nicholas Winterton to conduct an inquiry into the quality of services available to women during pregnancy and childbirth. Recommendations were made for improving maternity services by marrying the needs and desires of women and families with views of professionals on how the services should be provided: Health Committee, Second Report, Maternity Services, 1992, vol. 1, London, HMSO.

17 See M. Tew, *Safer Childbirth? A Critical History of Maternity Care*, London, Chapman and Hall, 1990, pp. 231–89.

18 Using the terminology of the French philosopher Louis Althusser who believes that following the acquisition of language, one is hailed by differing ideologies and will recognize oneself in the position which is offered. This position is accepted and one is interpellated into a particular subjectivity. See Althusser, 'Ideology and the State', in *Lenin, Philosophy and other Essays*, London, NLB, 1971.

19 Foucault, *History of Sexuality*. See also L. Jordonova, *Sexual Visions: Images of Gender in Science and Medicine between the Eighteenth and Twentieth Centuries*, New York and London, Harvester Wheatsheaf, 1989, p. 150, who cites surgeon Hugh Dudley describing the sensual fascination and power of surgery.
20 Inch, *Birthrights*, pp. 56–78.
21 The use of dialogue as an example is drawn from A. Oakley, *Women Confined Towards a Sociology of Childbirth*, Oxford, Martin Robson, 1980. See Chapter 1 for discussion of the medicalization of antenatal care.
22 Foucault, *Discipline and Punish*, p. 184.
23 W. Savage, *A Savage Enquiry*, London, Virago Press, 1986.
24 S. Rose, 'A proper trust – your life in their hands', BBC MCXCI.
25 Arney, *Power and the Profession of Obstetrics*, p. 230.

12

MIDWIVES AMONG
THE MACHINES

Re-creating midwifery in the late twentieth century

Raymond G. DeVries and Rebeca Barroso

It was a strange sight, even by the standards of a large American hospital. Here, among the world's most advanced obstetric technology – electronic monitors, infusers, ultrasound devices and well-appointed surgical suites – a woman was giving birth on the floor.

The labouring woman was Hmong, a recent immigrant from Laos. She arrived at the hospital by ambulance, sent by her relatives who claimed she was not in labour, just 'overdue'. Neither she nor her partner spoke English. While the nurse–midwife was reviewing her scant prenatal records, she quietly left her bed and began squatting on the floor. As she squatted, her waters broke. The attending nurse–midwife hurriedly placed some 'sterile' linen under the woman and joined her in a squatting position. Within minutes, a healthy baby boy slipped into the hands of the midwife.

The odd image of a squatting woman giving birth surrounded by the gleaming, modern equipment of an American maternity ward is an apt metaphor for midwifery's problematic relationship with technology. Can midwifery, with its low-technology, non-interventive tradition, find a place in an environment where competence is equated with the use of the latest, high-technology devices? In deciding how to respond to the new technologies of birth, midwives face a troublesome dilemma: if they adopt the instruments of modern medicine, they risk sacrificing their distinctive tradition; if they cling to their tradition, they are marginalized as anachronistic, quaint, or perhaps, dangerous practitioners.

The importance of machines to modern obstetrics is illustrated in the conclusion of this story, as told by the nurse–midwife:

I handed the baby to the nurses as soon as I clamped and cut the cord. I had no safe place to put him while I helped the mother move from the slippery floor. For the next five to ten minutes I was busy finishing the birth of the placenta and checking on blood loss. It seemed just a few minutes before the nurse brought the baby back, dried and wrapped in a warm blanket. When it was all over, I felt good that I attended this birth in a way that respected the culture of the mother. A few hours later when I was doing the required paperwork, I was shocked to see a note in the baby's records: '10 cc clear gastric fluid per aspiration'. They had taken this perfectly healthy, vigorous baby and [using suction] emptied his stomach!

Because there was no medical indication for this procedure, the midwife concluded that the nurses felt an overwhelming, but irrational, need 'to use the equipment'. Low-technology midwifery had to be baptized by high-technology medicine.[1]

THE RE-CREATION OF HEALTH CARE PROFESSIONS

The dilemma of 'midwives among the machines', is, in fact, a special case of a problem faced by all health care professions. As the world around them changes, health care professions must adapt, they must 're-create' themselves.

The sources of change in health care practice are varied. The need for professional 're-creation' is often the result of change coming from within the profession itself. As a profession develops new technology and new techniques, practitioners must adjust, changing routines and discarding old theories, making room for the latest professional knowledge. Who now, for example, purges and bleeds their patients?

But change in technique is not the only source of change originating within the profession. Decisions regarding the organization of a profession also bring about change. Professions consciously re-create themselves when they develop new educational programmes, create new areas of specialization, or reallocate tasks among occupational groups. These same decisions can also set in motion processes with unintended, sometimes negative, consequences for that self-same profession. Starr offers an eloquent description of this, showing how the professional autonomy secured by American physicians early in this century eventually (and ironically) lead to the 'corporatization' of health care, forcing doctors to adjust to a new, corporately controlled environment.[2]

Less obvious, but no less important sources of professional re-creation are changes in society and culture. Included among the many influences exerted on medicine by society are changes in the economy and in the political environment, the reorganization of health care financing, and demographic shifts such as baby booms, ageing populations, and increased urbanization. Health care systems must also adjust to shifts in cultural ideas about gender, family, work, science, and religion. Notice, for example, the way health care changed in response to new cultural conceptions of gender: the gender balance in medical occupations has been altered, there is a new concern with the treatment of women as patients, and medical research has been re-focused to include women.

A new, or re-created, medical practice is best seen as the result of a combination of factors. The increasing popularity of walk-in medical clinics in the United States offers a case in point. 'Immediate-care centers' are franchised and intended for quick-stop care for minor problems, earning them the name 'Doc-in-the-boxes' (a pun on the name of a well-known 'drive-through' restaurant, 'Jack-in-the-box'). Their appearance and rapid proliferation can be attributed to: the corporatization of health care (a corporate strategy to increase profit), changing residential patterns (large suburban tracts offer an ideal 'market' for these clinics), and the desire of physicians for more reasonable work hours deriving from new attitudes about work and family.[3]

All health care professions are influenced by these changes, but not all are equally free to re-create themselves. Some, more than others, must labour in an environment where their 'social capital' is limited. A profession's history and consequent cultural authority determine the freedom it has to shape its place in the medical marketplace. Professions with greater prestige, greater income, and greater power are more free to influence political, organizational, and cultural processes. Professions like nursing, established as an adjunct to the profession of physicians, find their position controlled by those with more 'social capital'.[4] Professions closely connected to a tradition, like midwifery and homoeopathy, find their ability to adjust and re-create themselves limited by that tradition.

In the following pages, we examine the ways in which midwifery has chosen, and is choosing, to re-create itself. We begin by recasting the history of midwifery as a continuing effort of midwives to re-create the profession in light of its tradition, its position *vis-à-vis* physicians, and developments in society. Next we look at the strategies of re-creation used by midwives on both organizational and individual levels. In order to highlight the socially situated nature of professional re-creation, we use data from both the United States and the Netherlands. We conclude by reviewing the factors that impede the midwives' task of re-creating themselves, focusing on the idea of 'risk' and its place in the medical division of labour.

RE-CREATING MIDWIFERY

The history of midwifery in the United States and the Netherlands has been told by many.[5] These histories, like the earlier chapters in this anthology, are a rich source of information about the evolving relationships among health occupations. The details of midwifery's history vary by location and time period, but in each chronicle we find midwives re-creating themselves, or being re-created by others, as the conditions around them, and in their profession, changed.

Reviewing these histories, we find certain events common to the re-creation of midwifery in all industrializing societies: the development of the machinery of obstetrics – from forceps to the most recent techniques of prenatal testing – the rise of hospitals, an increasing faith in science, and changing demographic patterns.

Nearly all histories of midwives assert that midwifery forceps gave a technological edge to male birth attendants. The initial response of midwives was to denounce the new technology, to assert the superiority of the 'hands-off' tradition of midwifery. Elizabeth Nihell, an eighteenth-century English midwife, equated the tools used to assist at birth with military weapons: 'those instruments, those weapons of death, would one not imagine that the art of midwifery was an art *militaire*?'.[6] Those sympathetic to midwifery's tradition of a patient and natural approach to birth, point out that forceps ushered in a new, 'meddlesome midwifery'.

But not all midwives were content to re-create themselves as an alternative to interventionist obstetrics. Marland points out that a significant number of midwives in the Netherlands sought the right to use forceps. She cites an address delivered in 1910, signed by

251

over three hundred Dutch midwives, that claimed the use of forceps and the right to suture were 'vital to the well-being of their *occupation* and their clients' (emphasis added).[7]

Although midwives failed to gain access to tools of modern obstetrics, their attempts to bring the technology of medicine to the tradition of midwifery must be seen as a prudent strategy to preserve and extend their profession. The centralization of care (and 'scientific' technology) in hospitals and increasing public faith in science threatened to eliminate independent midwifery. Physicians, competitors of midwives, easily capitalized on new public attitudes to paint midwives as old-fashioned, unscientific, and dangerous.[8]

In the United States, midwifery suffered further as a result of two important demographic changes: declining immigration and decreasing family size. Reduced numbers of new immigrants diminished the social contexts that supported the traditions and customs brought from the 'old country'. Immigrants wanted to become 'American' and the 'American' thing to do was to use a hospital for birth with a physician in attendance. For immigrant families with many children the desire for a hospital birth was often limited by the ability to pay, but as families became smaller, hospital confinement became a luxury most could afford. Lacking an effective organization, American midwives could not respond to changing preferences of clients.

During the latter half of the twentieth century, midwifery has faced increasing pressure to change, to accommodate to the new obstetrics. The social and political position of midwives offered little room to re-create their profession in a way that would extend, or even preserve, their independence. They did not have the resources – in terms of political influence, public confidence in their 'scientific' competence, or support from hospitals and other medical organizations – to compete with obstetrics. Given these limited resources, midwives in most industrializing nations were forced to re-create themselves as assistants to obstetric specialists. In the United States this meant creating an alliance with the established (though subordinate) profession of nursing and seeking work in medically under-served areas. In many European nations midwives became 'extensions' of doctors, the so-called 'lengthened arm' of obstetricians. As the term implies, midwives found legitimacy by working under the direct supervision of another profession, subordinating their tradition to the ever 'new',

promising, modern approach of medicine. Even in the Netherlands, where an autonomous profession of midwifery survived, the
political and cultural power of midwives was no match for that of
doctors. Elements of Dutch culture and the Dutch medical system
supported the tradition of midwifery, but without the protection of
influential gynaecologists/obstetricians, it is likely that Dutch midwifery would look much like midwifery in other industrialized
nations.[9]

The 'assimilationist' strategy of re-creation chosen by midwives
threatened to extinguish the separate tradition of midwifery. In
effect, midwives were exchanging their own tradition for the tradition of medicine or nursing. But the 1960s created a detour on
the path to extinction. Societal and cultural change in the form of
the feminist movement and a new and vigorous questioning of
technology gave midwives the opportunity to emphasize their
distinct tradition, to re-create themselves as separate from medicine.

In the light of this new cultural atmosphere midwives could
renew their identity as a 'low-tech, high-touch', women-centred
occupation. The very image that had weakened the profession
earlier in the century now gave them a niche in the medical
marketplace. Midwives found further support for their profession
during the 1980s and 1990s as governments and health care
organizations sought to control the costs of medical care. In this
environment midwives asserted themselves as more 'cost-effective',
extending their appeal beyond new cultural ideas about women
and technology to economic concerns of policy-makers and health
care administrators.

STRATEGIES OF RE-CREATION

The changed cultural attitudes of the 1960s and the economic
realities of the 1980s and 1990s allowed midwives to maintain a
foothold in modern medical systems. But the future of the profession remains unclear. To the extent that it promises to manage risk
and to reduce pain, the machinery of modern obstetrics has wide
appeal. Midwives face the difficult task of finding a way of re-
creating midwifery that preserves the distinctiveness of the profession while remaining up-to-date in obstetric techniques.

The strategies used by midwives to respond to this unmanageable
situation fall into two categories: first, *organizational strategies*, efforts
taken by, or on behalf of, midwife organizations, efforts to preserve

a place for the profession in the medical marketplace, and, second, *individual strategies*, efforts by individual midwives to establish and protect the distinct practice of midwifery. These strategies of re-creation, be they organizational or individual, are influenced by social context, a fact that becomes clear in the contrast between the situations of midwives in the Netherlands and the United States.

ORGANIZATIONAL STRATEGIES: RE-CREATING THE PROFESSION OF MIDWIFERY

The United States

Midwives in the United States, quite commonly used at the turn of the century, were pressed nearly to extinction in the years between the two World Wars. Factors mentioned above – increasing faith in science and medicine, changed patterns of immigration and de-creasing family size – reduced the popularity of midwifery, as did the 'midwife debates' that took place in the second and third decades of the century. These 'debates' were not, in fact, debates at all. They are better described as diatribes by physicians against midwives. Capitalizing on new attitudes, midwives were portrayed as untrained, incompetent and dangerous, the cause of high infant and maternal mortality.[10]

If, in the face of these conditions, the practice of midwifery was to survive in the United States, an organizational strategy was needed. It was not enough for individual midwives to practise the tradition of midwifery, as many 'granny-midwives' in the southern part of the country were doing,[11] the profession needed to find a way to secure a place for that practice in the changing medical system. The strategy chosen was to ally with the established profession of nursing, adding midwifery training (often secured in England) to certification in nursing. Through the work of Mary Breckenridge and the Frontier Nursing Service in Kentucky, and later the Maternity Center Association in New York City (with its own training programme), midwifery claimed a legitimate place in American medicine. In 1955, nurse–midwives took a further step to defend the interests of their profession by establishing the American College of Nurse–Midwifery (ACNM, now the American College of Nurse–*Midwives*).

Two of the most important tasks of the ACNM were the creation of a nationally recognized programme of certification and obtaining licensure in all states and jurisdictions. The 'recognized place' of midwifery remained limited, however, with the newly (re-)created profession serving poor women on the rural and urban fringes of society.[12] Table 12.1 shows that up through the 1970s midwifery played an increasingly limited role in maternity care. The flame of midwifery was not completely extinguished in the United States, but by 1970 midwives were attending less than one half of one per cent of births there, and the percentage of births outside of medical settings fell to less than one.

Table 12.1 Distribution of live births by place of delivery and attendant, United States, 1940–92 (percentages)

Year	Place of delivery Hospital	Not in hospital*	Physician	Attendant Midwife	Other
1940	55.8	44.2	90.8	8.7	0.6
1945	78.8	21.1	93.5	6.1	0.3
1950	88.0	12.0	95.1	4.5	0.4
1955	94.4	5.6	96.9	2.9	0.3
1960	96.6	3.4	97.8	2.0	0.2
1965	97.4	2.6	98.3	1.5	0.3
1970	99.4	0.6	99.5	0.4	0.1
1975	99.1	0.9	98.8	0.9	0.3
1980	99.0	1.0	97.4	1.7	0.8
1985	99.0	1.0	96.7	2.7	0.6
1990	98.9	1.1	95.3	3.9	0.8
1991	98.9	1.1	94.8	4.4	0.8
1992	98.9	1.1	94.5	4.9	0.6

Sources: US Department of Health and Human Services, *Vital Statistics of the United States, Vol. 1 – Natality*, Hyattsville, MD, US Department of Health and Human Services, 1993; National Center for Health Statistics, 'Advance report of final natality statistics, 1990', *Monthly Vital Statistics Report*, 1993, vol. 41, no. 9, supplement; National Center for Health Statistics, 'Advance report of final natality statistics, 1991', *Monthly Vital Statistics Report*, 1993, vol. 42, no. 3, supplement; National Center for Health Statistics, 'Advance report of final natality statistics, 1992', *Monthly Vital Statistics Report*, 1994, vol. 43, no. 5, supplement.
Note: * Includes free-standing birth centers

How did American midwifery respond to the social and cultural changes of the 1960s? This opportunity to re-create and reaffirm midwifery as separate from the tradition of medicine led to a curious bifurcation of midwifery in the United States. The tenor of the times was a natural source of support for midwifery, but many would-be clients and supporters of midwifery saw nurse–midwifery as a 'sell-out', too much a part of the 'system'. Thus was born an

American version of the direct-entry midwife: variously called the lay midwife, the empirical midwife, or, most recently, the traditional midwife.

The rhetoric of traditional midwifery, as suggested by the name itself, stressed the need to re-create midwifery in its *true* image, forswearing any connection with 'medicine'. Traditional midwives saw themselves as being a genuine response to a new generation of clients with a healthy distrust of technology and believed that hospital-based nurse–midwives 'co-opted' women, promising a midwife birth but doing regular obstetrics.[13] To avoid being co-opted themselves, traditional midwives rejected formal training in favour of apprenticeship and self-education. Textbooks written by physicians were acceptable, but the medical socialization that attended training programmes for nurses, midwives, and physicians was to be avoided. Traditional midwives continue to favour home birth, herbal remedies, and simple, non-medical solutions to problems of labour. As might be expected, the training and competence of these women was (and remains) uneven.

Traditional midwifery flourished among the 1960s and 1970s counter-culture. In keeping with the counter-cultural spirit of 'do your own thing', hierarchical organization, legal regulations, and alliances with existing medical organizations were avoided. Lacking any formal organization, it is difficult to speak of an 'organizational strategy' of traditional midwives of the 1960s and early 1970s. In resisting the 'medical establishment', some traditional midwives did ally themselves with an odd collection of marginal health practices from reflexology, to aromatherapy and iridology, thus keeping them at the margins of mainstream health care. On the other hand, it is possible to see these midwives as part of a larger consumer-based 'alternative birth movement' in the United States that is often given credit for the creation of alternative birth settings inside and outside of hospitals.[14]

Increasing resistance from physicians, in the form of legal actions and unwillingness to provide medical back-up, caused traditional midwives to begin organizing in the hope of gaining legal recognition. In the late 1970s, several state associations of traditional midwives were created, many of which approached state legislatures with licensing legislation. These attempts to gain legitimacy through licensing were largely unsuccessful and today the laws governing the practices of traditional midwives remain a hodgepodge of difficult-to-interpret rules and regulations.[15] In most states traditional midwives remain outside the existing medical system, with no access to hospitals and strained relationships with physicians and nurse–midwives.

Repeated failures of state organizations to gain licensure and increased prosecution of non-nurse–midwives for violation of medical practice acts, led to the creation, in 1982, of a new, national organization, the Midwives' Alliance of North America (MANA). The founders of MANA saw it not just as an organization of traditional midwives, but as an opportunity to promote the profession by connecting with other, more established midwives. Membership was open to all midwives, be they nurse–midwives or traditional midwives, and efforts were made to connect with midwife organizations in other countries and with the International Confederation of Midwives (ICM). Seeing the need for a publicly recognized 'standard of care', and in keeping with the non-medical approach of traditional midwifery, MANA created, in 1989, a certification programme for non-nurses, the North American Registry of Midwives (NARM). According to MANA, 'the test serves as a tool to determine whether entry level knowledge has been achieved, and it assists in fostering reciprocity between local jurisdictions'.[16]

Because they had re-created midwifery in two different ways, it proved difficult for MANA and ACNM to work together. Each claimed to represent the true tradition of midwifery in the United States.[17] But by the early 1990s, the organizations saw the need to join forces and formed the 'Interorganizational Workgroup' (IWG). The IWG produced, in 1993, a statement on 'Midwifery Certification in the United States' that allows for the certification of two types of midwives: the 'Certified Midwife' and the 'Certified Nurse–Midwife'.[18]

The dialogue between nurse and traditional midwives has also increased as a result of the movement of many traditional midwives into nurse–midwifery in the 1980s and 1990s. One of the more important reasons for a traditional midwife to become a nurse–midwife is the desire for a steady and reasonable income. In the early 1990s, the average annual income of a nurse–midwife was $55,000, while for most traditional midwives it was nearly impossible to earn a living.[19] In the words of one traditional midwife, 'my work is an expensive hobby'.

For their part, nurse–midwives used the favourable cultural climate of the 1960s and 1970s to expand their position, locating themselves between the extremes of obstetrician-controlled, high-technology birth and 'do-it-yourself', no-technology home birth. Seeking to claim this middle ground, they simultaneously emphasized the tradition of midwifery 'with woman' and their connection with the latest and best hospital technology. Note the language used by one nurse–midwife to describe her profession: 'a certified nurse–midwife . . . is a specialist with obstetrical nursing experience and graduate training in midwifery . . . she [also] has the attitudes and approaches of the age-old profession . . . that . . . women today are seeking'.[20] During the 1970s, nurse–midwives expanded their training programmes, seeking cultural credibility by locating them in university settings, associating with schools of medicine or schools of nursing.[21]

In an effort to increase the supply, and hence the visibility, of nurse–midwifery, the profession is experimenting with new methods of education. The best known of these programmes is the Community-Based Nurse–Midwifery Education Program (CNEP) run by the organization that pioneered nurse–midwifery, the Frontier Nursing Service. CNEP students spend a short period at the facility in Kentucky, finishing their training via self-directed study, regular communication with professors via a computer network, and a residency with a nurse–midwife service in their home community.

A different sort of organizational strategy for the re-creation of midwifery is the establishment of new institutions for the management of birth. The 'free-standing birth center' (FSBC) is particularly suited to the autonomous practice of midwifery. Such centres are structurally and administratively separate from hospitals, equipped for management of low-risk births. Staffed, in most cases, by nurse–midwives, FSBCs have arrangements for 'back-up' with local hospitals. By separating their sphere from the sphere of specialist physicians, midwives are given more latitude for practice. As explained by one nurse–midwife:

> The birth center nurse–midwife is constantly reminded that, while the birth center is a place for the practice of *midwifery*, the hospital is the place for the practice of *medicine*. In the birth center the whole system is designed to nurture the practice of midwifery. In the hospital, medical practice is the norm, midwifery is 'different' and thus much more of a struggle . . . It is simply easier to practice midwifery in a birth center.[22]

Physicians are not especially supportive of FSBCs, but, because they reduce costs, they are increasingly popular with health insurance companies.[23] Convinced that the future of midwifery lies in the creation of new settings for birth controlled by nurse–midwives, a CNEP instructor requires all students to develop a detailed plan for the creation of a free-standing birth center in their communities.

Faced with the extinction of their profession, the organizational strategies of re-creation used by American midwives have included: (1) alliance with an existing profession; (2) the creation of programmes to train and certify the competency of midwives; (3) the establishment of organizations to represent the interest of midwives; and (4) the creation of new forms of delivering maternity care. We will consider the wisdom and success of these strategies after reviewing the situation in the Netherlands. However, at this point we can note modest gains for American midwives at the organizational level. Referring back to Table 12.1, we see that the changes that began in the 1960s, on a cultural and social level and among midwives, resulted in a small but steady increase in their share of maternity care after 1970.[24]

The Netherlands

The situation of midwives in the Netherlands is unique in the world. Dutch midwives and the maternity care system of which they are a fundamental part are often held up as a model for other countries.[25] The two features of the Dutch system that attract most attention are the high percentage of home births and the autonomous status of midwives. Midwives are part of the primary care system of the Netherlands, the so-called 'first line'. As such, they have the authority to decide which women can remain in the first line – giving birth at home or having a 'polyclinic', short-stay hospital birth – and which must see a specialist. This is quite the opposite of the situation typical in other countries, where specialists make the decision about the appropriate level of care.

The historical conditions that produced the existing system in the Netherlands are well described by Van Lieburg and Marland.[26] Hingstman[27] suggests there are four 'pillars' on which the Dutch maternity care system rests:

1 The 'protected' position of the midwife, whose profession was defined and protected in the 1865 'Act on the Practice of

Medicine', and who was given 'primacy' – healthy mothers are only reimbursed for midwife care – in the health insurance law.

2 A generally accepted screening system for high-risk pregnancies, standardized criteria that define as clearly as possible the conditions requiring referral to a specialist.

3 A well-organized maternity home care system, that allows continuity of care in home births.

4 The socio-cultural environment in the Netherlands that regards pregnancy and childbirth as normal physiological processes.

In comparison to midwives in the United States it would seem that Dutch midwives have no pressing need to re-create their profession. Table 12.2 shows that, while there has been a substantial decline in home birth, midwives are providing for a stable and large proportion of the nation's births. None the less, in the face of shifting social and cultural conditions midwives in the Netherlands are concerned to preserve their position. The organizational strategies used by Dutch midwives include efforts to become more 'scientific', actively supporting features of the culture and the health care

Table 12.2 Distribution of live births by place of delivery and attendant, the Netherlands, 1940–92 (percentages)

Year	Place of delivery		Attendant*	
	Hospital**	Home	Physician	Midwife
1940	n/a	n/a	51.3	47.7
1945	n/a	n/a	62.8	36.1
1950	n/a	n/a	58.1	41.1
1955	23.9	76.1	58.5	40.9
1960	27.4	72.6	63.0	36.6
1965	31.5	68.5	64.2	35.3
1970	46.7	57.3	62.7	36.7
1975	55.6	44.4	59.9	38.6
1980	64.6	35.4	59.7	39.4
1985	63.4	36.6	57.8	41.7
1990	67.9	32.1	53.9	44.1
1992	68.5	31.5	53.1	45.8

Sources: Centraal Bureau voor de Statistiek, *1899–1989: Negentig Jaren Statistiek in Tijdreeksen*, 's-Gravenhage, CBS Publikaties, 1989; Centraal Bureau voor-de Statistiek, *Geborenen Naar Aard Verloskundige Hulp en Plaats van Geboorte*, Voorburg, CBS, 1990, 1992.
Notes: n/a: not available
* Excludes births with shared responsibility and cases where attendant is unknown
** Includes, starting in 1970, 'polyclinic' (i.e. short-stay) hospital births

system favourable to midwifery, seeking reforms that will protect the profession, and finding new ways of delivering care.

Although home birth remains popular in the Netherlands, more clients are choosing to give birth in the 'polyclinic'. Polyclinic births are short-stay hospital births attended by midwives or general practitioners. They are favoured by parents who wish to have '*alles bij de hand*' (everything, that is, medical equipment, on hand). Midwives supervise the majority of these births, but the trend is troubling because it reflects a growing faith in obstetric technology, and because in the polyclinic not only do midwives feel less free to exercise their profession, but there is a higher rate of transfer to specialist care.[28] On an organizational level, midwives have responded to this trend in two ways: first, to become more 'scientific', that is, to pattern themselves after 'scientific' medical professions, and, second, to reinvigorate public confidence in home birth.

Recognizing the power of science in modern society, midwives face the challenge of becoming more 'scientific' without necessarily becoming more technological. One strategy to accomplish this is to distinguish 'physiological' (normal) birth from 'pathological' birth. Thus separated, midwives can use scientific methods to study normal pregnancy and birth and claim jurisdiction as experts in physiological birth. Science is used to assess technology itself, examining its appropriate and inappropriate uses. In an effort to expand the 'scientific' competence of midwives, a fourth year was added to the education of midwives entering their training schools in 1993, a significant portion of which is dedicated to training in scientific research methods.

Carefully conducted, scientific studies not only enhance the image of a profession, but yield information useful to the promotion of the profession. Recognizing this, the Dutch Organization of Midwives (*Nederlandse Organisatie van Verloskundigen*, NOV) encourages its members to co-operate in studies of the quality of care. This co-operation was rewarded by favourable results in a recent comparative study of polyclinic and home birth. The study concluded that home birth was at least as safe as polyclinic birth for first-time mothers, and safer for women who already had one child.[29] This study became the centrepiece of a public campaign to encourage home birth, entitled '*een goede keuze bevalt beter*' – a play on words, meaning both 'a good choice births better' and 'a good choice brings a more pleasing result'. The campaign, sponsored by the NOV with the support of the Dutch government, was intended to encourage more women to choose home birth by showing the rationality of this cultural ideal. According to the NOV, the goal of the campaign was to reach pregnant women, their partners, and other influential relatives, as well as midwives and other caregivers; information about the safety and desirability of home birth was given by means of brochures, press releases, a nationwide telephone information line, and visits to groups of midwives, nurses, and physicians.[30]

Because Dutch health care is organized differently from that in the United States,[31] midwives, through their national organization, have a voice in the creation of policy affecting their profession.[32] This voice has been used to protect the 'indications list' that defines the work terrain of midwives, to secure a reduction in the average number of births expected of each midwife – in the hope of reducing 'burn-out' and attrition of midwives – and to generate support for research projects promoting the practice of midwifery. The government, concerned with the costs of health care, is inclined to support midwives and home birth because research consistently demonstrates that they reduce costs while providing compatible, or better, outcomes than clinical births attended by physicians.[33]

But even Dutch midwives, with their favoured position and new orientation towards science, are handicapped by their tradition. This is most visible, of course, in questions related to the use of technology. The tradition of midwifery suggests the practice should avoid technology and promote the confidence of women in their ability to give birth without assistance from machines. But Dutch midwives are also a medical profession, with the freedom to use certain medical procedures.[34] Questions naturally arise: why not promote more polyclinic births? After all, centralizing care means less travel, greater ease in attending births, more assistance from nurses and support staff. Why not use ultrasonography routinely? Sending women elsewhere for a sonogramme increases the chance that they will stay under the care of specialists and makes the profession appear 'old-fashioned'.[35] The consequent debates over whether new technology should or should not be employed weaken the image of the profession in the eyes of a public convinced of the value of technology. By way of contrast, the more eclectic and experimental tradition of physicians allows them to 'own' new technology. They may discuss its appropriate and inappropriate uses, but they never suggest that technology itself is undesirable.

Like their American counterparts, midwives in the Netherlands are also experimenting with new methods of delivering care. The best-known effort in this regard is the 'Geboortecentrum' (birth centre) in Amsterdam. It is not a centre where birth occurs – midwives already have a great deal of autonomy in home births and polyclinic births – it is rather a centre that collects all the various services related to pregnancy and birth under one roof: a prenatal clinic, pregnancy and post-partum courses, a bureau to arrange post-partum care, once-a-week consultations with an obstetrician, a shop with articles for pregnancy and birth, and a clinic for care of the new-born. The idea is to strengthen the position of the midwife, putting her in control of various services associated with birth, keeping women in the 'first line'. Here, too, the tradition of midwifery becomes an obstacle, with some midwives complaining that this type of centre results in the improper commercialization of the profession.[36]

WHAT WORKS, WHAT DOES NOT

We can now review the organizational strategies used by midwives to adapt their profession to changing circumstances. Do these strategies re-create the profession in a way that insures its existence and preserves its identity?

The comparison of Dutch and American midwifery reveals a striking difference in the strength of the voice midwives have in policy-making. Like midwives in the United States, Dutch midwives must compete against the prestige and power of physicians, but in the Netherlands midwives have a legitimate place in the govern-ment bureaucracy that controls health care, allowing them to influence decisions about the place of midwifery in the health care system. The structure of Dutch health care – with direct govern-ment control of health care costs by the *Ziekenfondsraad* ('Sick funds council') and the *Centraal Orgaan Tarieven Gezondheidszorg* ('Central committee for health care tariffs') – protects and promotes mid-wifery. Midwives have a seat on the *Ziekenfondsraad* and are regarded by the government as safe and economical. The American health care system allows midwives little influence in the creation of policy. Health policy in the United States is shaped through lobbying efforts of professional groups and medical organizations. Compared to physicians, American midwives have a very small, poorly funded lobby, and hence little ability to protect their position.

Some strategies work to guarantee a place for the profession, but threaten to alter the profession so radically that it remains distinct in name only. The affiliation with nursing in the United States is an example of this. The uncritical acceptance of medical technology will bring similar results. A number of Dutch midwives are resisting the trend towards polyclinic births for this reason. They claim that polyclinic births are not merely 'transplanted' home births, but are the first step in a technological transformation of the profession.[37]

Some strategies are essential for the profession but their ability to transform and extend midwifery is constrained by context. Included here are decisions to create midwife organizations. These organizations are necessary to give midwifery a voice, but the strength of that voice is dependent on social and cultural situation. In the United States, the presence of two (more or less) competing organizations hindered the effective re-creation of midwifery.

The decision of traditional midwives in the United States to avoid official organization and to identify with a variety of marginal health practices dissipated professional strength. This radical strategy was seen as a corrective to the medicalization of nurse–midwifery, but it allowed established medical professions to discredit both traditional and nurse–midwifery as dangerous and strange.

Most promising are strategies that strengthen the structural position of midwives and work to create supporting cultural ideas. The 'birth center' idea, in its manifestation in the United States and in the Netherlands, is a strategy of this sort. It gives the profession more autonomy while making it attractive to policy-makers and clients. As more clients use these services, cultural ideas are transformed in a way that favours the profession. In both countries midwives have created national organizations to promote birth centres, the National Association of Childbirth Centers in the United States, and the *Vereniging Geboortecentrum Nederland* ('Association of Dutch birth centres') in the Netherlands.

As important as these organizational strategies are, they form only a part of the re-creation of midwifery. It is the everyday practices of midwives where the tradition is given life. Midwife organizations might preserve the profession, but the profession loses its meaning if the practices of midwives become indistinguishable from physicians. Thus we turn to strategies employed by midwives as individuals to find a way to practise midwifery among the machines of obstetrics.

INDIVIDUAL STRATEGIES: RE-CREATING THE PRACTICE OF MIDWIFERY

The United States

In the United States it is nurse–midwives who are called upon to find individual strategies for re-creating the profession. Traditional midwives, existing outside the mainstream medical system, are free to practise as they please. The organizational strategies of nurse–midwives have earned them a place in a 'medical' environment where they must find ways to remain midwives and not become 'physician extenders'. This is especially difficult when working in a hospital surrounded by medical technology, much of which appears to simplify the work of midwifery. For example, when a labour is proceeding slowly, the tradition of midwifery might suggest that a woman walk around or lie in a warm bath. But in a hospital this is difficult to arrange. It is much more efficient to administer a drug to speed labour.

Given this situation, midwives who wish to remain faithful to the tradition of midwifery must find ways to overcome the limitations of their surroundings including: a lack of knowledge, lack of access to proper equipment or facilities, and limits created by hospital policy.

As the machinery of obstetrics becomes more prevalent, new knowledge replaces old knowledge. For example, knowledge of how to deliver a breech birth vaginally is all but lost in the United States where a breech presentation is almost always an indication for caesarean section. The gradual obsolescence of the fetoscope is another example of lost knowledge. The 'doptone' which uses sonar technology to amplify sounds from the uterus, is a much easier way to find foetal heart tones and to allow them to be heard by the expectant parent(s). But some midwives argue that the fetoscope (or wooden 'tooter'), the traditional tool of the profession, is the better instrument. Without electronic amplification it is possible to find the point where the heart tones are the clearest and loudest, allowing the precise position of the child to be identified. Furthermore, the fetoscope brings the midwife much closer to the woman, allowing the caregiver to assess level of relaxation, skin tone, and overall condition. Midwives in training who wish to learn the proper use of the fetoscope find that their teachers have lost the ability to use one. The response is self-education or association with an 'old-fashioned' midwife, but midwives who gain this knowledge encounter a second problem: difficulty finding fetoscopes on hospital obstetric wards.[38]

Lack of equipment and facilities is a serious constraint on the continued practice of midwifery. A warm bath is a preferred way to promote relaxation and thus stimulate labour, but in many hospitals there are no bathtubs. A midwife reports similar problems with items needed to use traditional techniques for supporting and relaxing the perineum. In her hospital, all women having an epidural must give birth in a delivery room under sterile conditions, making it impossible to use poultices and oils to minimize perineal pain and prevent lacerations. The midwife's response is to improvise: using available sterile pads, doing a 'clean catch' of a lubricant into a sterile cup in order to allow it to be used in the sterile environment, looking for hot water in labour rooms.

Hospital policy is another constraint on the practice of midwifery. Many hospitals in the United States have a policy, set by their department of anaesthesia, prohibiting obstetric patients from receiving anything by mouth after admission. The rationale for the policy is the rare danger of aspiration with the use of general anaesthesia. Midwives, believing in the necessity of adequate hydration and nourishment, are forced to find a way around such policies. A simple solution used by some midwives is to deny admission to a labouring woman until she has had something to eat and drink.

These individual strategies are, in fact, strategies of subversion. As such, they show the power of medical technology. Because the task of reforming the structure of medicine and the culture that supports it is so overwhelming, the best midwives can do is to find ways to work within medical settings without compromising the ideas and values of their profession. In fact, many midwives find subversion too difficult or too costly (in terms of their relationships with colleagues) and hence they simply follow the medical protocols.[39] In the Netherlands, where the context is different, midwives are able to devise different strategies.

The Netherlands

Given their legitimate place in the 'first line' of Dutch health care, midwives have less need to subvert the system. Their position as 'gatekeepers' in the first line gives individual midwives the power to defend the practice of midwifery. When a woman first suspects or knows she is pregnant, her first visit is to the midwife or the general practitioner. A specialist cannot be seen except by referral from the first line. This gives midwives a great deal of power over the behaviour of specialists. Midwives tell of situations where a local gynaecologist is treating women poorly, or discouraging women, sent for consultations, from having a home birth. The response is to simply cease sending women to this specialist. Eventually, the specialist will call and ask what might be done to once again receive referrals. This strategy works best in areas where several hospitals exist and compete for clients; but even midwives in rural areas report travelling extra distances to avoid unwanted practices in a local hospital.

Dutch midwives do, however, feel an increasing need to subvert culture. As more women choose polyclinic births, seeking the safety of medical technology, midwives are becoming more active in promoting home birth. Not just organizationally, as discussed above, but also in individual practices midwives seek to encourage women to remain at home for birth. Many midwives will ask women choosing a polyclinic birth to explain their choice. In so doing midwives are protecting (and promoting) a cultural value that says home birth is the preferred choice, and all other choices must be explained.[40] Women who persist in their desire for a polyclinic birth are advised that when contractions start they can choose to remain at home; when labour begins some midwives will visit the home, reminding the woman and her partner that it is possible to simply stay at home.

But why encourage home birth? Is it not possible to practise midwifery in a Dutch hospital? It is true that Dutch midwives exercise a great deal of autonomy in the hospital, but many midwives believe that the peaceful, familiar setting of the home is one of the tools of traditional midwifery. In the hospital you cannot tell an over-wrought partner to go and make some coffee, in the hospital the labouring woman feels less at ease, less in control, she is not free to walk about. And, as in the American situation, as simple a thing as a bathtub is often unavailable.

CONCLUSION: MIDWIVES, MACHINES, AND THE 'RISKS' OF BIRTH

Not all efforts to re-create midwifery are equally successful. Our review of the situation of midwives in the Netherlands and in the United States makes it clear that the structural position of midwifery affects the possibilities for re-creation. Individual strategies of re-creation can be little more than subversive or marginal if the profession has not secured a legitimate and autonomous place in the health care system. Midwives interested in preserving a place for a distinctive profession, one that is not simply the 'lengthened arm' of physicians, must work towards gaining structural legitimacy. And in order to gain this legitimate place, there must be an effort to re-create and reinforce cultural ideas that support midwives. Thus, free-standing birth centers will not gain great success in the United States unless women (re)gain trust in their ability to give birth without the assistance of the technology of obstetrics.

Thus we are brought back to the image of midwives among the machines. The response of midwives to the machines of obstetrics, from forceps to ultrasonography, has been uncertain. For good reason. If midwives shun obstetric technology they seem out of date. In an exposé of nurse–midwives in public hospitals in New York City, midwives at one hospital were faulted for having a caesarean section rate of 12.9 per cent, far below the city average of 23.1 per cent.[41] In a technological culture it is unthinkable not to use the latest technology; this is one reason many midwives in the Netherlands were anxious to bring ultrasonography into their practices. But if midwives adopt obstetric technology, they set in motion a process that changes their profession so drastically that it becomes subsumed by, or indistinguishable from, obstetrics.[42]

Why do the machines of obstetrics have this effect on midwifery? It is because these machines expand the notion of risk and increase uncertainty. Ultrasonography and other means of prenatal diagnosis turn every pregnancy into a risky pregnancy, supporting the idea of many American obstetricians that 'a pregnancy is low risk only in hindsight'. Because the technology is available, women are forced to make a choice: should it be used or not? Their choice is often influenced by their placement in a 'risk group', thus, normal pregnancy ceases to exist and uncertainty over the outcome of pregnancy grows. The wealth of information produced by the technology of obstetrics also increases uncertainty.[43] Electronic

268

foetal monitors, for example, produce an unending stream of data, all of which is subject to different interpretations, each leading to a different clinical decision.[44] Increasing risk and uncertainty mean one of two things for a midwife: either she, as an expert in normal birth, is no longer needed, or she must become more technological. What is to be done with the midwife? The question itself suggests the subordinate, passive position of her profession, a position controlled by cultural and social factors. It is true that midwives have little control over societal and cultural forces: support and resistance often come unbidden. But a profession that understands the way these forces work is better equipped to work with them, to influence them, to turn the question around: what should the *midwife* do?

ACKNOWLEDGEMENTS

This research was supported in part by the Fogarty Center of the National Institutes of Health, USA (grant number F06-TWO1954), the Catherina Schrader Stichting and the Netherlandese Organisatie von Verloskundigen.

NOTES

1 Field notes; R. Davis-Floyd, *Birth as an American Rite of Passage*, Berkeley, University of California Press, 1992, provides an in-depth analysis of ritual uses of technology in modern obstetrics.
2 P. Starr, *The Social Transformation of American Medicine*, New York, Basic Books, 1982.
3 See E.F. Merritt, 'Family and the medical profession: conflicting claims', *Journal of the American Medical Association*, 1993, vol. 270, pp. 1606ff.
4 See, for example, C. Davies, *Gender and the Professional Predicament of Nursing*, Buckingham, Open University Press, 1995.
5 See, for example, F. Kobrin, 'The American midwife controversy: a crisis of professionalization', *Bulletin of the History of Medicine*, 1966, vol. 40, pp. 350–63; J. Donnison, *Midwives and Medical Men: A History of Inter-Professional Rivalries and Women's Rights*, London, Heinemann, 1977; J. Litoff, *American Midwives: 1860 to the Present*, Westport, CT, Greenwood Press, 1978; J. Litoff, *The American Midwife Debate*, Westport, CT, Greenwood Press, 1986; W. Arney, *Power and the Profession of Obstetrics*, Chicago, University of Chicago Press, 1982; J. Leavitt, *Brought to Bed: Childbearing in America, 1750–1950*, New York, Oxford University Press, 1986; M.J. van Lieburg and H. Marland, 'Midwife regulation, education, and practice in the Netherlands during the nineteenth century',

Medical History, 1989, vol. 33, pp. 296–317; I. Loudon, *Death in Childbirth: An International Study of Maternal Care and Maternal Mortality 1800–1950*, Oxford, Clarendon Press, 1992; H. van der Borg, *Vroedvrouwen: Beeld and Beroep*, Wageningen, Wageningen Academic Press, 1992; H. Marland (trans. and ed.) *'Mother and Child Were Saved': The Memoirs (1693–1740) of the Frisian Midwife Catharina Schrader*, Amsterdam, Rodopi, 1987; H. Marland (ed.), *The Art of Midwifery: Early Modern Midwives in Europe*, London, Routledge, 1993.

6   Quoted in J. Aveling, *English Midwives, Their History and Prospects*, 1872, repr. 1977, New York, AMS Press, pp. 122–3.

7   H. Marland, 'Questions of competence: the midwife debate in the Netherlands in the early twentieth century', *Medical History*, 1995, vol. 39, pp. 317–37, on p. 328.

8   See Kobrin, 'American midwife controversy', and R. Wertz and D. Wertz, *Lying In: A History of Childbirth in America* (expanded edn), New York, Free Press, 1989.

9   See J. Klomp, *De Jaren Zestig: De vroedvrouwen Bijna Verdwenen, Leve de Vroedvrouw*, Bilthoven, Catharina Schrader Stitching, 1994.

10   See N. Devitt, 'How doctors conspired to eliminate the midwife even though the scientific data support midwifery', in D. Stewart and L. Stewart (eds) *Compulsory Hospitalization: Freedom of Choice in Childbirth?*, Marble Hill, MO, NAPSAC, 1979, pp. 345–70. See also Wertz and Wertz, *Lying In*, and Litoff, *The American Midwife Debate*.

11   For more on 'granny-midwives', see O.L. Logan, *Motherwit: An Alabama Midwife's Story*, New York, Plume, 1989.

12   See P. Langton, 'Competing occupational ideologies, identities, and the practice of nurse–midwifery', *Current Research in Occupations and Professions*, 1991, vol. 6, pp. 149–77.

13   See R. DeVries, 'The alternative birth center: option or cooptation?', *Women and Health*, 1980, vol. 5, pp. 47–60.

14   See J. Mathews and K. Zadak, 'The alternative birth movement in the United States: history and current status', *Women and Health*, 1991, vol. 17, pp. 39–56.

15   See I. Butter and B. Kay, 'State laws and the practice of lay midwifery', *American Journal of Public Health*, 1988, vol. 78, pp. 1161–9; R. DeVries, *Regulating Birth: Midwives, Medicine and the Law*, Philadelphia, Temple University Press, 1985. See also P. Tjaden, 'Midwifery in Colorado: a case study in the politics of professionalization', *Qualitative Sociology*, 1978, vol. 10, pp. 29–45, and G. Giacoia, 'Lay Midwives in Oklahoma', *Journal of the Oklahoma State Medical Association*, 1991, vol. 84, pp. 160–2.

16   From 'The North American Registry of Midwives', Newton, KS, MANA, n.d.

17   See J. Rooks, 'The context of nurse–midwifery in the 1980s: our relationships with medicine, nursing, lay–midwives, consumers and health care economists', *Journal of Nurse–Midwifery*, 1983, vol. 28, pp. 3–8.

18   See Women's Institute for Childbearing Policy (WICP), *Childbearing Policy Within a National Health Program: An Evolving Consensus for New Directions*, Boston, WICP, 1994, and Langton, 'Competing occupational ideologies'.

19 D. Korte, 'Midwives on trial', *Mothering*, 1995, vol. 76, pp. 52–63.
20 B. Brennan and J. Heilman, *The Complete Book of Midwifery*, New York, Dutton, 1977, p. xi.
21 See K. Whitfill and H. Varney Burst, 'ACNM-Accredited Nurse–Midwifery Education Programs', *Journal of Nurse–Midwifery*, 1993, vol. 38, pp. 216–27.
22 S. Stapleton, 'The pleasures and perils of hospital privileges for birth center nurse-midwives', *NACC News*, March/April 1995, pp. 6–7 (emphasis in original).
23 See Mathews and Zadak, 'The alternative birth movement', and E. Annandale, 'Dimensions of patient control in a free-standing birth center', *Social Science and Medicine*, 1987, vol. 25, pp. 1235–48.
24 See also E. DeClercq, 'The transformation of American midwifery: 1975 to 1988', *American Journal of Public Health*, 1992, vol. 82, pp. 680–4.
25 See, for example, M. Mehl Madrona and L. Mehl Madrona, 'The future of midwifery in the United States', *NAPSAC News*, 1993, vol. 18, pp. 1–32, and G. Chamberlain and N. Patel (eds) *The Future of Maternity Services*, London, RCOG Press, 1994.
26 Van Lieburg and Marland, 'Midwife regulation, education, and practice'; Marland, 'Questions of competence'.
27 L. Hingstman, 'Primary care obstetrics and perinatal health in the Netherlands', *Journal of Nurse–Midwifery*, 1994, vol. 39, pp. 379–86.
28 T. Wiegers and G. Berghs, 'Bevallen ... thuis of poliklinisch?', *Tijdschrift voor Verloskundigen*, 1994, vol. 19, pp. 266–76.
29 Ibid.
30 The proceedings of the conference are summarized by M. Amelink and C. van Leent, 'Een goede keuze bevalt beter', *Tijdschrift voor Verloskundigen*, 1994, vol. 19, pp. 343–6.
31 A complete description of the Dutch health care system cannot be given here. For more information see L. Graig, *Health of Nations* (2nd edn), Washington, DC, Congressional Quarterly, 1993, pp. 115–28.
32 For a description of the relationship between Dutch midwives and the government, see E. Van Teilingen and L. van der Hulst, 'Midwifery in the Netherlands: more than a semi-profession?', in T. Johnson, G. Larkin and M. Saks (eds) *Health Professions and the State in Europe*, London, Routledge, 1995, pp. 179–86.
33 A study by G. Berghs and E. Spanjaards, *De Normale Zwangerschap: Bevalling and Beleid*, Nijmegen, University of Nijmegen, 1988, has been important in this regard. No differences were found in the outcomes of births to low-risk women under the care of midwives, general practitioners and specialists, *except* that those under specialist care had more interventions.
34 The Dutch government classifies midwifery as a 'medical' occupation, separating it from 'paramedical' occupations such as physical therapy and exercise therapy.
35 See C. van Leent, 'Pret-echo', *Tijdschrift voor Verloskundigen*, 1992, vol. 17, pp. 405–6, and J. Wladimiroff, 'Prenatale diagnostiek van aangeboren afwijkingen met behulp van echoscopie', *Tijdschrift voor Verloskundigen*, 1993, vol. 18, pp. 357–60.

36 See E. de Miranda, 'Het geboortecentrum in Amsterdam', *Tijdschrift voor Verloskundigen*, 1992, vol. 17, pp. 393–4; B. Smulders, 'Twee jaar Geboortecentrum Amsterdam: een discussiestuk', *Tijdschrift voor Verloskundigen*, 1994, vol. 19, pp. 81–6.

37 See, for example, A. Schoon, 'De "keuzevrijheid" voor de plaats van de bevalling', *Tijdschrift voor Verloskundigen*, 1995, vol. 20, pp. 182–7.

38 An article by R. Barroso and R. DeVries, 'Fetoscope use among nurse-midwives', is in preparation.

39 See Stapleton, 'The pleasures and perils'.

40 In the United States women requesting a home birth must explain their decision since the default choice is hospital birth.

41 D. Baquet and J. Fritsch, 'New York's public hospitals fail and babies are the victims', *New York Times*, 1995, vol. 144, 5, 6, 7 March, pp. 1ff. See also N. Kraus, 'Mismanaged journalism: responsible reporting in peril at the *New York Times*', *Journal of Nurse-Midwifery*, 1995, vol. 40, pp. 304–12.

42 A. Jacobson, 'Are we losing the art of midwifery?', *Journal of Nurse-Midwifery*, 1993, vol. 38, pp. 168–9.

43 See M. Sandelowski, 'Toward a theory of technology dependency', *Nursing Outlook*, 1993, vol. 41, pp. 36–42.

44 See A. Grant, 'Monitoring the fetus during labour', in I. Chalmers, M. Enkin and M. Keirse (eds) *Effective Care in Pregnancy and Childbirth*, vol. 2, Oxford, Oxford University Press, 1989, pp. 846–82.

INDEX

The following abbreviations have been used in this index:
IMU: International Midwives Union
MI: Midwives' Institute

Printed in the United Kingdom by
Lightning Source UK Ltd., Milton Keynes
137999UK00003B/3/A